Enforcing the Law

Bureaucracies, Public Administration, and Public Policy

Kenneth J. Meier
Series Editor

Enforcing the Law

The Case of the Clean Water Acts

Susan Hunter and
Richard W. Waterman

M.E. Sharpe
Armonk, New York
London, England

Library of Congress Cataloging-in-Publication Data

Hunter, Susan, 1947–
Enforcing the law : the case of the Clean Water Acts / by
Susan Hunter and Richard W. Waterman; with
contributions by Amelia Rouse and Robert Wright.
p.   cm.
Includes bibliographical references and index.
ISBN 1-56324-682-1 (alk. paper) — ISBN 1-56324-683-X (pbk. : alk. paper)
1. Offenses against the environment—United States.
2. Law enforcement—United States.   3. Water—Pollution—Law and
legislation—United States. I. Waterman, Richard W.   II. Title.
HV6403.H86   1996
364.1'42—dc20   96-3676
CIP
Printed in the United States of America

The paper used in this publication meets the minimum requirements of
American National Standard for Information Sciences—
Permanence of Paper for Printed Library Materials,
ANSI Z 39.48-1984.

∞

BM (c)   10   9   8   7   6   5   4   3   2   1
BM (p)   10   9   8   7   6   5   4   3   2   1

Contents

List of Tables and Figures

Tables

Figures

Acknowledgments

It was probably inevitable that two people named Hunter and Waterman would write a book on environmental politics. In this task, however, we had much help. First, we thank all of the usual suspects, that is, our families and friends, who put up with listening to us talk about this project over the last eight years. In the case of Susan and her husband George, we must also thank their dogs, who provided us with no useful methodological suggestions, but were always there, ready to be hugged.

The good people of the Environmental Protection Agency also deserve a special thanks. They put up with our visits to EPA offices, our constant irritating phone calls, and our stream of surveys. They also provided us with information in a timely and competent fashion. Having dealt with other agencies in our academic research, we can truly state that the EPA is one of the most cooperative regulatory agencies with which we have had the pleasure to interact.

Beyond the EPA, we also interacted with a number of people at the local level. State and local officials likewise seemed pleased to answer our myriad questions about water pollution control and the NPDES program. As with their federal counterparts, they were also willing to subject themselves to countless surveys and other forms of academic torture.

In putting together our data sets, we were helped by a large number of students, unfortunately too many to list. Over the past eight years a number of students helped us with the tedious tasks of coding and data entry. We would like to thank Kent Woodson, Maria Goldcamp, and Michael Goldcamp. Two others were Amelia Rouse and Robert Wright, who have received notice for their many contributions to this book (see Chapters 4 and 5).

We also would like to thank the U.S. Geological Survey for its financial support of this project. Its funding provided us with the means to acquire, code, and enter much of the data that is included in this book. Our respective departments also provided us with necessary support materials for this project, for which we are indeed grateful.

Finally, we would like to thank our colleagues in the academic field who provided us with many useful comments on this project over the years including Joseph Stewart Jr., and Kenneth Meier. An earlier version of Chapter 3 was published in the *Western Political Quartely*. The reviewers for that manuscript provided many useful comments that helped us to improve it immeasurably. We also presented early versions of several chapters at the Southwest Social Science Meetings in Fort Worth and New Orleans, and the Midwest Political Science Meetings in Chicago. Amelia Rouse and Robert Wright also presented an earlier version of their chapter at the Southwest Social Science Meeting in Dallas. We are grateful for the many useful comments provided at these meetings.

We would also like to thank Evan Ringquist, who provided a thorough reading of the manuscript and many, many useful comments. Although I am sure we have not satisfied all of his recommendations, we are indeed indebted for his extraordinary efforts. We also wish to thank the editor of this series at M.E. Sharpe, Ken Meier, for his interest and confidence in our project and the many people at M.E. Sharpe who have helped to guide this project toward its completion. Needless to say, without their help this book could never have been completed.

Enforcing
the Law

Introduction

In general usage, "enforcement" appears to be a very popular word. For example, a common theme of politicians on the campaign trail today is how they intend to get tough with criminals. Campaigns stress the need for tougher laws against a variety of potential offenders and stricter penalties against those who are ultimately convicted. Candidates who are considered weak on criminal enforcement, such as the Democrats' 1988 presidential nominee, Michael Dukakis, are ridiculed as being weak and ineffectual. Such attacks in 1988 on Dukakis led many Democrats, including his successor, Bill Clinton, to make law enforcement a major component of their domestic agendas. Not only did Bill Clinton remind voters that he was for the death penalty, but also two convicted felons were executed in Arkansas during the 1992 presidential campaign. After he was elected, Clinton managed to get a tough crime bill through Congress. Republicans were not deterred by Clinton's move to the right. After the Republican sweep in November 1994, the new majority party in Congress promised to be even more vigilant in enforcing the law and to pass a new and even sterner crime bill. The message, then, is that law enforcement should be strict and severe.

The message is clear when it comes to crime prevention. But what about other types of enforcement? This book examines enforcement of the Federal Water Pollution Control Act of 1972, more commonly known as the Clean Water Act, and its various amendments. Should enforcement of environmental standards be strict and severe? The message that is so emphatic in the area of law enforcement does not seem to resonate as clearly when we turn our attention to the behavior of federal regulatory agencies. For one thing, there is clear evidence that regulatory enforcement has not been very effective, especially in the area of environmental protection. As Ashworth (1995: 31) wrote,

> Polls may show that Americans support environmental legislation, but the record of compliance speaks otherwise. Indeed, there is probably no other class of laws that is so routinely evaded, violated, and ignored as those that have to do with environmental protection. On paper, our environmental protection mechanism is regulated as tightly as a fine watch. In practice, it is more like a wind-up clown with a drum—making a lot of noise, running around in circles, and running down almost immediately.

Although such a devastating report in the area of law enforcement would lead to calls for a more aggressive federal and state response, when it comes to regulatory enforcement such evidence meets with a mixed response. Here two different views of enforcement conflict. Adherents of one model, the enforced-compliance model, or what Hawkins (1984) called the "sanctioning" or "penal" style, have advocated limited bureaucratic discretion and a strict application of the law (see Freeman and Haveman 1972; Viscusi and Zeckhauser 1979; Keiser 1980). This model in many ways reflects the tough rhetoric of the crime-prevention debate. As Shover, Clelland, and Lynxwiler (1986: 11) wrote, the major components of the enforced-compliance model include "a reliance on formal, precise, and specific rules; the literal interpretation of the rules; the reliance on the advice of legal technicians (attorneys); the quest for uniformity; and the distrust of and an adversarial orientation toward the regulated." In other words, the enforcement of regulation should be aggressive so as deter violations of health, safety, environmental, and other social regulatory legislation (i.e., in order to protect the public interest). As the Council on Environmental Quality (1993: 81) reported,"Strong enforcement supports environmental progress in two ways: by correcting specific violations of environmental law and, more generally, by deterring potential violations. Firm and fair enforcement ensures a level playing field for private-sector competitors and spurs polluters to look beyond mere compliance to preventing pollution in the first place."

In short, it is argued that without a system of strict enforcement the regulated industry would have a clear incentive to avoid enforcement. Furthermore, it is expected that industry and other potential violators would freely violate the law. As one regional Environmental Protection Agency (EPA) enforcement officer told us, "We are the only thing that stops polluters from violating the law."

In the view of the strict model, vigorous enforcement is a vitally necessary means of preventing legal abuses from occurring. Likewise, regulation is characterized in positive terms. For example, Bollier and Claybrook (1986: vii) wrote,

> Quick: What's the first thing that comes to mind when you see the word regulation? Chances are you did not envision a man saved from cancer death, a woman spared a miscarriage, a teenage girl avoiding disfigurement from an automobile crash or a healthy baby born without defects. It is one of the unfortunate ironies of modern politics that the images most triggered by the word "regulation"—"red tape," "bureaucracy," "attacks on freedom"—are rhetorical abstractions that obscure the documented successes of federal health, safety and environmental regulation.

In summary, supporters of the strict-compliance model believe that regulation plays a positive role and therefore should be enforced with considerable vigor (see Claybrook 1984). Whereas most politicians today voice similar opinions about the need for vigorous criminal enforcement, opinion is widely distributed on the issue of regulatory enforcement. On the other side of the debate are the supporters of the negotiated-enforcement approach, or what Hawkins (1984) called the "conciliatory" model. Proponents of this approach have argued that strict enforcement of a variety of health, safety, and environmental laws has resulted in a pattern of "regulatory unreasonableness," which is "the imposition of uniform regulatory requirements in situations where they do not make sense" (Bardach and Kagan 1982: 58). By applying the law strictly and equally to all firms under the jurisdiction of a particular agency, Bardach and Kagan argued that certain cases will inevitably arise in which a firm will be forced to comply with a regulation when both the industry and society would be better off if the regulation were not applied. In order to avoid "regulatory unreasonableness," Bardach and Kagan recommended that enforcement personnel should adopt the more flexible negotiated-enforcement style. Like these authors, a number of other scholars have either advocated a negotiated-enforcement style or have been highly critical of traditional command-and-control regulation (see Muir 1977; Weaver 1978; Mendeloff 1979; Kagan 1980, 1989; Braithwaite 1985; John 1994). Flexibility in criminal enforcement has been reduced in recent years by legislation incorporating the "three strikes and you're out" provision. Likewise there appear to be increasingly frequent calls for mandatory sentencing and longer jail terms. Flexibility is on the decline in criminal enforcement, but it plays a central role in the debate over the appropriateness of regulatory responses. As Bardach and Kagan (1982: 3) wrote,

> The basic techniques of . . . regulatory programs have been the legislation of rules of law specifying protective measures to be instituted by regulated enterprises and the enforcement of those rules by government inspectors and investigators, who are instructed to act in accordance with the terms of the regulations, not on the basis of their own potentially arbitrary judgment. But uniform regulations, even those that are justifiable in the general run of cases, inevitably appear to be unreasonable in many particular cases.

Because of this perceived pattern of "regulatory unreasonableness," Bardach and Kagan argued that a looser, negotiated regulatory approach will best serve both the regulated industry and the public. Under a negotiated style, enforcement is selective and involves a due consideration of the details of the particular case at hand. Enforcement relies on such informal techniques as meetings with violators, including conferences, and other strategies designed to resolve problems without resort to formal, punitive action. Fundamental to the use of these techniques is the idea that "regulatory unreasonableness" can be prevented only if enforcement personnel have the discretion to work out solutions with individual companies, rather than apply regulations blindly and uniformly. In defense of these conclusions, supporters of a more flexible regulatory style point to the experiences of many European nations and Japan, which have had considerable success with a more consensual regulatory style (e.g., Lundqvist 1980; Kelman 1981; Brickman, Jasanoff, and Ilgen 1985; Vogel 1986).

A major component of the negotiated approach is a more benign interpretation of the motives of the regulated. Whereas Bollier and Claybrook (1986: 94) perceived the regulated industry in highly suspicious terms (e.g., the Environmental Protection Agency's "mission of carrying out environmental statutes is checked at every turn by opposing corporate pressures"), Bardach and Kagan (1982: xv–xvi) described the regulated industry in much more positive terms: "We began thinking of regulators and regulated as predator and prey. We wondered how the regulated attempt to evade the regulators, how the regulators adapt to tactics of evasion, and what environmental conditions favor successful adaptations by the regulators. But the prey/predator metaphor, we came to see, does not always work. The interaction may be more like two species that achieve a more harmonious pattern of mutual adaptation." The enforced and negotiated-enforcement approaches are essentially dichotomous, each representing the flip side of the other model. Where the enforced model calls for vigorous enforcement by the book, the negotiated approach envisions a more conciliatory regulatory environment in which regulators seek to understand the needs of the regulated in diverse circumstances. Where the enforced-compliance model envisions a positive role for government regulation, the negotiated approach characterizes regulation as blindly and inefficiently pursuing regulatory objectives, even when they can be better achieved in a less stringent manner, and even when they produce outcomes that clearly serve no benefit to society at all, while simultaneously exerting a high cost on the regulated industry. The enforced-compliance model also views the regulated industry as an enemy to be distrusted and carefully monitored, whereas the more conciliatory negotiated approach perceives industry and other regulated entities in much more benign terms. In conclusion, there is little room for compromise between these two divergent approaches to governmental regulation.

What is particularly curious about the debate over regulatory enforcement is that the political lines are drawn differently from the debate over criminal enforcement. Whereas "liberals" are usually considered to be supporters of alternatives to strict sentencing and "conservatives" are seen as tough on crime, "liberals" as a whole tend to favor more aggressive enforcement of regulatory statutes, whereas "conservatives" are more likely to favor the negotiated approach. Furthermore, although the call for tough enforcement has won the debate in crime prevention, increasing calls for more flexible approaches to regulatory problems appear to be concomitantly winning favor in the regulatory debate. Furthermore, we are not aware of any attempt to try to reconcile these two divergent approaches to enforcement.

As we write this book (April 1996), congressional Republicans are attempting to place a ban on the promulgation of all new regulations, and a Democratic president, Bill Clinton, appears to favor a move toward a negotiated style. Environmentalists, however, continue to call for tougher laws and stricter enforcement. Consequently, there appears to be no end in sight to the debate over what is the best way to enforce government regulation.

The debate between the enforced-compliance and negotiated schools of regulation continues to surge ahead, and there has been an attempt in recent years to provide some empirical analysis on the subject. Specifically, a few scholars have examined the proclivity of governmental actors (e.g., bureaucrats) to use one approach or the other. For example, Shover, Clelland, and Lynxwiler (1986) empirically analyzed enforcement data from the Office of Surface Mining and Reclamation (OSM) to determine what approach is used by OSM bureaucrats. They concluded, "The new OSM leadership [under the Reagan administration] generally adopted a negotiated compliance approach to inspection and enforcement. The agency's new executives and Interior officials made it unmistakably clear that they wanted a diminished federal effort" (1986: 152). Their findings, however, were at least in part the result of a change in presidencies from the more environmentally minded Carter administration to the vigilantly antiregulatory Reagan administration (ibid., 155). As a result, there is clearly a need for a longitudinal study of the enforcement of government regulation. To this effect, in an earlier work we examined the enforcement policy of the Environmental Protection Agency's (EPA) National Pollutant Discharge Elimination System (NPDES) to determine what approach officials in that agency had adopted. We concluded (Hunter and Waterman 1992: 416), "The enforcement style of EPA water personnel is clearly best represented by the negotiated compliance model." Other scholars (e.g., Downing and Kimball 1982; Downing 1983; Downing and Hanf 1983) also found similar evidence of administrative bargaining in water pollution control and other environmental regulatory activities.

Such studies have suggested that a negotiated enforcement style may better explain the activities of regulatory agencies, at least during the more conservative Reagan era, but they tell us very little indeed about why agency personnel adopt a negotiated or conciliatory approach in the first place. Is it, for example, because the findings of past research were largely an artifact of the Reagan administration's conservative regulatory philosophy, or are there other reasons why agency personnel adopt a bargaining style of enforcement? In short, we were interested in determining the actual motivations of enforcement personnel.

To pursue this question in greater detail, we extended the time frame of our analysis of the EPA's NPDES program to two decades and several different presidents. We examined diverse data sets provided to us by the EPA on various aspects of the enforcement process (e.g., permit issuances, compliance monitoring, enforcement actions) as conducted by both the EPA and state environmental personnel. We also spent much of the past seven years conducting extensive interviews with various players in the enforcement process, from EPA officials in Washington to regional EPA personnel, state personnel, and various interest group participants (e.g., industry, environmental group members, etc.). In the pages that follow we intend to move beyond the ideological and philosophical questions related to enforcement, which are often presented with much conviction but with little empirical evidence. Instead, our goal is to determine specifically how environmental personnel have enforced the law (through the analysis of actual data) and then to determine why they enforce the law the way they do (largely through copious interviews with environmental personnel). In so doing, we do not intend to answer the question of which of the two enforcement approaches is better. We will leave this normative judgment to others. Instead, our focus will be on explaining how the enforcement process works: What are the motivations of regulatory personnel? What constraints do they face? How do they perceive the entities they regulate?

In addressing these questions we will argue that the approach employed in the enforcement of the Clean Water Act of 1972, and subsequent legislation, can best be conceptualized as a nonsystematic process in which practitioners attempt, often ad hoc, to deal with a multitude and wide array of problems as they arise. As Kagan (1980: 87) noted, enforcement in any agency at any time is not necessarily based on a formal and rational process in which actions are deduced from rules. As we shall argue, enforcement personnel may choose to comply strictly with regulations, to use their own discretion within the framework of the law, to rely on a supervisor's judgment, or to employ completely unauthorized discretion. The choice of which approach to adopt may have more to do with the particular case at hand and with the nature of the regulatory environment than it does with any deeply felt philosophical attachment to a particular regulatory style. We will call this approach to implementation the "pragmatic enforcement style." This is a regulatory approach that places results as the primary goal of enforcement personnel, rather than either a strict adherence to the law or negotiation.

We will also argue that pragmatic enforcement necessarily involves the employment, by state and federal agency officials, of considerable bureaucratic discretion. Because many scholars have asserted that bureaucratic discretion represents a critical threat to democracy (e.g., Lowi 1979 in his comments on "policy without law"), we shall also examine the ramifications of bureaucratic discretion by agency personnel, as well as providing a clearer conceptualization of the concept. Finally, our guiding theory throughout this book will be that the adoption and implementation of a pragmatic enforcement style, and the accompanying growth of bureaucratic discretion, is not merely a choice that is left up to the good judgment of agency personnel. Rather, in many cases it is dictated by the nature of the regulatory environment with which they interact daily. The more diverse the nature of the regulatory environment (e.g., the more diverse the nature of the regulatory problems, the more diverse the set of regulatory actors governmental personnel interact with, the more diverse the geographical environment under which regulation occurs, the less specific the sources of the externality to be regulated, and so on), the more likely it is that governmental personnel will adopt a pragmatic enforcement approach and employ considerable bureaucratic discretion. We will argue and empirically examine the hypothesis that the diverse nature of water pollution problems across the fifty states has created the essential circumstances under which pragmatic enforcement is most likely to occur. In so stating, we will also hypothesize that in other agencies where the regulatory environment is less diverse—such as the regulation of nuclear power (e.g., the source of the externality is easily identified, the regulated industry is more homogeneous, etc.)—a stricter enforced-compliance style (and lower degrees of bureaucratic discretion) is more likely to occur.

Because our analysis is almost entirely focused on one program within one agency, we will lay the groundwork for what we hope will be further analysis of the influence of the regulatory environment on the behavior of bureaucratic personnel. Clearly, we will not be able to address this in a more generalizable manner in this work. We do, however, intend to provide considerable support for it so that other scholars can pick up where we leave off. Of course, we encourage such a continued empirical study of the nature of regulatory enforcement. Finally, we will not answer the question of what style is better: a strict compliance or negotiated enforcement approach. Instead, by shedding light on the motivations of the bureaucrats involved in enforcing the Federal Water Pollution Control Act of 1972 and other subsequent legislation, we hope to demonstrate why this question cannot readily be answered. Like most questions involving government, we believe the answer to that question is much more complicated than the politicians and pundits would lead us to believe.

1

The Water-Quality Problem: A Study in Diversity

In this book we argue that the level of the bureaucratic response is directly related to the diversity of the regulatory environment. This statement leads us to our first question: What is a regulatory environment? A regulatory environment involves the various actors (e.g., politicians, other bureaucrats, the courts, the regulated industry, other interest groups, and so on) that agency personnel deal with on a regular basis. But it is more than just an issue network, for it also involves economic conditions relevant to the problem being regulated, the organizational structure employed by the various regulating agencies, the manner in which these agencies interact with each other, the way in which relevant legislation is written (e.g., clear and concise, obtuse and general), the demographic composition of the target population for the regulatory action, and, perhaps most important of all, the nature of the externality being regulated. In this latter category we are interested in such criteria as who is affected by the regulation, what do agency personnel regulate, how tractable is the regulatory problem, and in what setting or different settings does the regulatory enforcement occur. As we noted in the introduction, we believe that agencies that operate within the framework of a highly diverse regulatory environment will employ a negotiated, or what we will later call a pragmatic, enforcement style. They also will employ considerable bureaucratic discretion in enforcing the law.

We demonstrate that surface-water pollution control occurs within a highly diverse regulatory environment. The number of relevant policy actors is high. Relevant economic conditions can have a direct impact on the enforcement of the law. Diverse types of organizational structures are employed to address surface-water pollution problems. A large number of agencies at the federal, state, and local level are involved in water pollution regulation, and the methods of interaction have clear implications for the manner in which the law is implemented. The laws and regulations applying to surface-water pollution control provide agency personnel with the opportunity to exert considerable discretion in enforcing the law. The demographic composition of the target population is highly diverse, involving every citizen of the United States (inasmuch as all citizens are potentially affected by water pollution problems). Finally, water quantity and quality issues vary considerably from state to state and region to region.

We begin our analysis of surface water's regulatory environment by examining the broad variations in water pollution problems across the nation. As Rogers (1993: 3) wrote,

> The United States is at least two countries hydrologically, split down the middle (almost exactly along the 100th meridian) from Rugby, North Dakota, to Laredo, Texas, by the 20-inch annual rainfall contour (isohyet). The water problems on either side of this line are radically different from each other and require different solutions. The 20-inch isohyet is the physiographical line distinguishing between the "moist East" able to grow rain-red crops and the "arid West" needing irrigation to guarantee crop yields.

Water quantity, then, differs greatly across the nation. So, too, do issues related to water problems (i.e., water quality). Rogers concluded that because of the differences in water quantity across the nation, "federal policy must be able to deal with specific regional problems and not with 'national' water problems." There are wide variations in the types of water problems that regulatory officials in different regions and states confront on a daily basis. These differences mean that some agency personnel will be more concerned with municipal discharges while others are worried about urban runoff or drainage from mines. As the nature of the externality being regulated becomes more diverse, identifying an ameliorative response to the externality becomes more problematical. This has clearly been a problem for the EPA, officials of which described the problems with developing water-quality standards in their 1973 document "The Economics of Clean Water" (Battle 1986):

> No one has described completely the quality of a body of water. To do so would entail chemical analyses of a near-infinite number of solid, liquid, and gaseous compounds, as well as a complete identification of all biota present in the water from viruses to vertebrates. Thus any practical description of water quality can only be concerned with a very limited subset of all conceivable physical, chemical and biological aspects of actual waterbodies. Typical water quality measurements are, in fact, oriented toward a small group of commonly observed pollution problems.

The report goes on to say that the effects of many chemicals are poorly understood, that natural substances in the water can be harmful, and that the cumulative effect on aquatic life from some relatively innocuous pollutants can sometimes be severe. Pollution that would not be harmful to one water system could be very harmful to another due to the other physical characteristics of the systems. Stormwater runoff, soil erosion (both natural and caused by construction and agriculture), thermal discharges, dams and impoundments that affect stream flows, atmospheric deposition, discharges of pollutants from point sources, agricultural runoff, and natural eutrophication are all activities which affect the quality of surface water. The EPA report also described the frustration of trying to pinpoint causes of observed pollution in waters: "Detecting any chemical and tracing it back to its sources can be difficult, particularly in the case of widely used and highly persistent substances such as mercury, dieldrin, or PCB's" (Battle 1986).

This chapter examines the broad diversity of water problems found across the United States, and then describes the legislative attempts to resolve these problems through the passage of the Federal Water Pollution Control Act amendments in 1972, 1977, and 1987. This set of amendments became officially the Clean Water Act in 1977. The text primarily describes enforcement under the 1972 and 1977 amendments.

Overview

As we have noted, surface-water pollution control's regulatory environment is highly diverse. The United States has more than two million miles of rivers and streams. There are forty million acres of lakes, ponds, and reservoirs, and close to one hundred million acres of wetlands. The EPA estimates that 54 percent of the nation's wetlands have been lost over the past two hundred years (USEPA, OPA-87-016). The Great Lakes contain 20 percent of the earth's fresh water, but a 1990 study found only 3 percent of the shoreline to be capable of supporting designated human uses (Valente and Valente 1995: 261).

Surface waters are polluted by a wide diversity of pollutants. These include: (1) nutrients from soil runoff, phosphates from detergents, nitrates from fertilizers, and natural processes; (2) silts and suspended solids from logging, strip mining, soil erosion; (3) pathogens from inadequately treated sewage, storm water, livestock-habitat runoff; (4) toxic and hazardous chemicals and metals from industrial discharges, runoff from mining sites and leachate from landfills; (5) organic wastes from garbage, sewage, feedlots and pastures; (6) pesticides and herbicides; (7) thermal discharges; (8) atmospheric deposition; and (9) petroleum in oil spills (Valente and Valente

1995: 270). Water moving over or through contaminated soils or pavements, direct discharges of pollutants into water systems, and discharges from sewage treatment facilities are the sources of this surface-water contamination.

Industrial processes create waste by-products that are discharged into water systems through discharge points; agricultural activities use water in ways that increase salinity and add metals, pesticides, herbicides, and fecal matter to water through nonpoint means. This includes runoff from storm sewers, if not channeled through a sewage treatment facility add urban runoff, animal waste, oil, and chemicals to the waterways; small, publicly owned sewage treatment facilities often lack the resources to remove all contaminants; construction, mining, timbering, drilling, land disposal of wastes, and dams or other stream modifications all increase the flow of sediment and other materials into the nation's waterways.

More than 95 percent of the earth's fresh water is groundwater, and half the U.S. population relies on groundwater for drinking and household use. Groundwater is extremely difficult to clean, once it is polluted, because of the movement of the plumes (Valente and Valente 1995: 267). Leaking underground storage tanks, septic tanks, landfills, hazardous-waste sites, agricultural runoff, irrigation, and feedlot activity are all sources of groundwater contamination.

In the face of these diverse threats to America's waterways, the *Twenty-fifth Environmental Quality Index,* published in 1993 by the National Wildlife Foundation, concluded that two-thirds of all surface waters now meet water-quality standards. The NWF report, however, also noted that a 1992 survey conducted by American Rivers found rivers to be in worse shape than ever before. These differences may be due to the data used to develop these results.

Data from NPDES permits and compliance reports show high rates of compliance and ultimately fewer discharges of permitted pollutants from point sources. Dams and irrigation projects, however, which draw water out of the streams and thereby reduce diffusion ability, lead to degraded water (particularly among western states), even with far fewer pollutants going into the system. In addition, agricultural runoff from these irrigation projects contributes pesticides, herbicides, and leached metals to the systems (McCann 1993). This problem has been recognized by the Department of the Interior, which has established a National Irrigation Water Quality Program to address water-quality problems in seventeen western states (Nichols 1993). NIWQP is required to develop a comprehensive inventory of water quality in systems affected by six hundred irrigation projects, including the Central Arizona Project and San Joaquin Valley project. They are currently working on the cleanup of selenium from the Kesterson Wildlife Refuge, and increasing in-stream flows in order to increase the diffusion of pollution.

Regional Differences

In addition to its diverse sources of water and equally, if not more so, diverse sources of pollution, the United States is a conglomeration of geographical regions with differing environmental situations and problems. Each region has different geography, economic basis, population densities, and political pressures. In this chapter, we examine the diversity of problems that affect water quality in the United States and describe the relative importance to water quality of NPDES permits across the states and regions. In addition to data on water-quality problems collected through various sources, we also include data from a mail survey of governors' offices conducted in 1992 and a telephone survey of state water-quality officials conducted in 1994; both include open- and close-ended questions, thus allowing for more detailed responses. These data reflect the priorities placed on various problems by the state officials who must allocate their scarce resources to a variety of environmental problems.

A quick overview of regional differences indicates a major change in focus as we cross the Mississippi River. East of the Mississippi River we find fairly high average rainfalls (usually above forty inches per year), a high water table (sometimes only inches below the surface), and old industries with outdated equipment (the so-called Rust Belt). The Great Lakes region has problems ranging from industrial pollution to zebra mussels, which are destroying water systems in the entire region. In the coal mining areas of Ohio, Pennsylvania, West Virginia, Kentucky, and Tennessee, acid mine drainage, especially from old, abandoned mines, is a serious threat to aquatic life. In the Southeast, paper mills have become a major industry, spewing toxins into the rivers on which they are located. In the north-central states, coal mining is the basis for the economy, but it is responsible for acid mine drainage and acid deposition. Northeastern states have population pressures that place a severe strain on sewage-treatment and waste-management facilities. Old landfills have begun to contaminate groundwater, requiring immediate action. Communities along the Ohio, Mississippi, and Missouri rivers have been hard hit by floods that devastated farmlands, overran sewage-treatment facilities, and created massive water pollution problems.

In addition, many of the water systems east of the Mississippi are navigable and are used to transport materials. Canals were used extensively to link areas of the East together before railroads and later trucks took over much of the transport of goods. Oceangoing vessels reach ports on the Great Lakes, and barges are used to transport coal, steel, and other materials through the East. The U.S. Army Corps of Engineers maintains waterways for navigation throughout this area and has built dams, engaged in dredging activities, and developed flood-control programs. These activities often contribute to water pollution, through artificial changes to the streams and their banks and through the leakage of oil that occurs from shipping.

West of the Mississippi the differences may best be described by the importance of the Bureau of Reclamation over the Corps of Engineers. The Bureau is responsible for irrigation projects and activities designed to assist farmers in maintaining production levels (e.g., the Central Arizona Project). Drought is often a problem, but it is countered by flash floods that can cause contamination of drinking-water supplies. Most rivers have insufficient flows to support transportation activities and have never been used for this purpose. Rivers in the west are far more important for irrigation purposes.

State Differences

Just as there are major differences from region to region regarding issues of water quantity and water quality, there are major variations from state to state. We examine state differences in this section. To bring some order to the analysis we examine the states by region, beginning with the western states.

The Western States

In the far western states of Hawaii, Alaska, California, Oregon, and Washington, water was identified in the 1992 survey of governors' offices as being fairly low on the list of environmental priorities. If water quality was mentioned at all, it was in reference to groundwater. Even the state water-quality officials interviewed in the 1994 survey said drinking water or groundwater was a higher priority than surface water, and most suggested that air quality was a more serious problem. An official from Nevada bluntly told us that his state was "coming out of an economic slump" and thus "economic growth would have more importance attached to it" than concerns with water quality.

These views do not mean that surface water is unpolluted within these states. They reflect instead a concern with other goals or the fact that discharges into surface waters by point sources are relatively uncommon. Nonpoint discharges from agriculture are more common and more serious in these states. In Alaska, officials replied that Anchorage was the only place where point source pollutants represented a problem. Alaska officials did, however, suggest that nonpoint sources were of great concern. In the 1994 survey, pulp mills, forest practices, hard rock mining, and placer mining (for gold) were listed, as well as urban runoff in Anchorage, as the major sources of water pollution. Most of these result in nonpoint source pollution.

California officials said industries and sewage treatment facilities are more likely to discharge into land-based lagoons, because they have so few surface waters to absorb discharges. In recent years, the problems in California have been a lack of water in the southern half of the state, leaching of metals from agricultural lands into water systems (most notably, the leaching of selenium from San Joaquin Valley agriculture into the San Luis Drain and into the Kesterson Wildlife Reservoir; the reservoir had to be covered for some time to prevent migrating birds from landing there due to the high level of birth defects found among hatchlings in the area). Although the climate in California promotes agriculture, the distribution of water in the state does not. The average rainfall in southern California promotes agriculture, whereas the distribution of water in the state does not. The average annual rainfall in southern California is nine to ten inches. North of San Francisco the landscape becomes more mountainous and less conducive to agriculture, but it also has adequate rainfall and water supplies. Diversion of water to agricultural uses to the south has created problems for San Francisco, which lacks sufficient water to flush out pollution from sewage, oil refineries, and other activities along the Bay. Most of the problems in California are, however, from nonpoint sources of pollution. As a result the NPDES permits or enforcement would have little effect on the quality of the water in the state.

Officials in Oregon, Washington, and Hawaii were more concerned about groundwater contamination than they were with surface water. They also were concerned about pollution of their coastal waters by shipping, oil spills, and similar causes. Hazardous waste is another concern of officials in Washington and Oregon.

Idaho, Arizona, Nevada, New Mexico, and Colorado provide another perspective. In Idaho agricultural and timber industries were cited as the major sources of nonpoint source pollution. In Colorado, air quality is a serious concern, but water is not an important issue according to most state officials. Little rainfall means that the supply of surface waters is not plentiful. As a result, the quantity of water is generally more important than issues of water quality. In this regard, the Central Arizona Project is now completed and is diverting Colorado River water into arid regions to increase agricultural production. The Bureau of Reclamation, which was responsible for its development, now is responsible for resolving many of the water-quality conflicts caused by irrigation projects and the loss of water from streams.

Far western concerns are air quality and drinking water, so state resources tend to be directed toward these activities. Because of their low water tables, these western states have been the recipients of nuclear and hazardous wastes. As a result, they find these issues to be of greater importance to them than most other states. Water is, of course, a problem, especially for coastal states, but their problems stem from offshore oil spills, sewage-treatment problems, and overflows of sewage into storm sewers when the occasional heavy storm hits. California officials, for example, explain that NPDES is a minor issue for them because they give very few permits for discharging into water systems. Most of their discharges go into on-site lagoons or into the air, because they lack the water systems for dispersing pollutants.

The Midwestern States

In the midwestern states of Oklahoma, Kansas, Iowa, Arkansas, Missouri, and Nebraska, hazardous and solid waste products are given high priorities in our surveys. Nonpoint source pollution from agriculture is the most serious water problem. In this region, agriculture (huge poultry farms in Arkansas and commercial agriculture in Nebraska and Iowa) has led to serious problems with surface waters. Paper and pulp mills are another problem for Arkansas, but the political environment in these states has been pro-industry/agriculture, making it very difficult for water-quality enforcers to make much progress.

Officials in North Dakota reported drought as a more serious problem than water pollution. Rainfall is haphazard in these states, leading to a mixture of floods and droughts that makes careful surface-water control difficult. Floods damage sewage-treatment facilities and pull pesticides from the fields, whereas droughts reduce the stream flows to the point that little diffusion can take place.

The western section of the Midwest is a farming area with low rainfall. In these states, the economies tend to dictate consideration of farming activities. Nonpoint source pollution from agricultural runoff is a particular problem. Illinois is the only state west of the fall line where point source pollutants were described in our surveys as a serious water problem. Officials in all other states felt that agricultural runoff, droughts, and floods were more important. In Illinois, however, old sewage-treatment facilities and old industries—especially utilities—are seen as a major source of water pollution. Upgrades are needed in many areas in order for communities and utilities to remain in compliance with clean water legislation.

Another midwestern state, Wisconsin, had to deal with water pollution in 1993 that made 400,000 people sick (Gurwitt 1994). A microbe, *Cryptosporidium* (mystery spore), infected their drinking water. As a result, the city of Milwaukee is considering a $90 million project to change its system for disinfecting its water. Although the problem is best known for afflicting Milwaukee, researchers have found the spore in about 80 percent of U.S. surface water and in about 25 percent of the drinking water surveyed.

The Great Lakes

While the citizens of Milwaukee have dealt with a costly and mysterious spore, the denizens of Ohio have been forced to confront the zebra mussel. State officials and citizens surveyed in 1990 agreed that the zebra mussel was their top water-related problem. This is an extremely small barnacle-type mussel that came into the Great Lakes on ships and then migrated into water intake systems. The mussel reproduces rapidly, and its progeny completely block the intake systems, effectively destroying the water supply to the area's residents and businesses. Millions of dollars are being diverted from other problems to try to halt the spread of the zebra mussel before it gets into rivers and streams.

Ohio officials indicate that chemical industries and small municipalities contribute the most to their surface-water problems. Like officials in many western and midwestern states, they are beginning to face groundwater contamination problems from facilities built in the 1940s and 1950s. These facilities are outdated and rusting. As a result, they have breaks and leaks in their discharge pipes. Ohio also has several nuclear-fuel production facilities, that are now leaking into the groundwater. At Fernald, the Department of Energy is constructing a massive wastewater treatment facility in order to pump contaminated water out of the ground and remove uranium and other radioactive contaminants from the water. DOE was ordered to pay $78 million to a fund to be used for monitoring the health of residents and workers who may have been affected. A similar situation exists in Portsmouth, Ohio, and Paducah, Kentucky, where nuclear facilities have begun to contaminate surface and groundwaters.

Agricultural runoff and acid mine drainage also are problems in the Great Lakes states and contribute to the nonpoint and drinking water problems. Officials in Ohio say that small businesses with little understanding of the legislation and marginal profits are their biggest problems related to surface-water pollution, because they lack the capacity to respond.

The Northeast and East Coast

In the Northeast, coastal areas are beginning to see zebra mussels affecting their water treatment facilities. There are few industrial polluters in most areas, but drinking water and contamination of groundwater from inadequate solid-waste disposal have become major concerns. Most landfills in the area are closed, but continue to leach contaminants into the groundwater. As with other areas, violators of NPDES permits are usually marginal businesses who lack either the knowledge or capacity to comply with clean water regulations.

Along the East Coast, cleaning the bays, estuaries, and harbors is a major concern. George Bush was able to make political gains over Massachusetts governor Michael Dukakis in the 1988 presidential election by raising the condition of Boston Harbor as a campaign issue. Given their greater concern with surface waters, unlike state officials from the West and Midwest, it is not surprising that Massachusetts state officials say nonpoint and point sources of pollution are equally important contributors to water problems in their state. They cite the growth of the state's population as a major cause.

Other East Coast states have different problems. Officials from Connecticut are concerned with protecting Long Island Sound; Delaware is concerned with Chesapeake Bay, as is Maryland. Delaware officials are also concerned with overfishing, cleanup of estuaries, and the prevention of runoff from residential and agricultural areas that is adding nutrients and depleting oxygen from their water systems.

Officials in Maine and Rhode Island say NPDES is the major water priority in their states, but neither identifies any particular problems either with surface water or groundwater. In the past, paper and pulp mills created water pollution problems, but state officials indicate most of these problems have been resolved.

The Southern States

Interestingly, the paper mills have not responded in such a positive manner in many Southern states. Environmental Protection officials in Virginia say that pulp and paper mills are their most serious problem, but that the mills use political pressure to prevent any action from being taken against them. Officials from Georgia are also concerned about pulp and paper mills, citing them as their state's worst NPDES problem. They also said they had no real water problems, however. One problem in the state is related to the issue of wetlands. Okefenokee Swamp, which is home to many different species— including ospreys, sand cranes, ibises, and many other birds, along with alligators and snakes—is a self-contained ecosystem that is extremely vulnerable to rainfall, development that draws water from the system, and pollution.

Officials in Florida are relatively unconcerned about point source discharges. Agricultural runoff is identified as a serious problem there, as are inadequate sewage-treatment facilities. Because of the extremely high water table (sometimes inches below the surface), *all* discharges of any kind require treatment. Even minor problems can affect the drinking water. Industrial and urban growth also create problems. Whenever water is drawn from the ground, intrusion of salt water occurs. This has been true in Virginia, the Carolinas, and Georgia, but it is especially serious in Florida. State officials want to focus their attention on the drinking water and agricultural runoff and are therefore happy to leave the enforcement of the NPDES program to officials from the EPA.

Protection of drinking water is an important problem along the East Coast. Many areas, such as Virginia Beach, have drawn so much water from their water tables that seawater has encroached, creating a nondrinkable brine. Population pressures and manufacturing activities have been responsible, although actual NPDES permit violations are not the biggest issue.

For many southern states, the incredible growth in population over the past twenty years has created pressures on their sewage-treatment facilities, which they have been unable to meet. Many communities lack a central sewage-treatment facility, but septic systems are unable to handle the wastes generated by growing populations.

In summary, then, this encapsulated analysis of the states indicates that there are broad differences in water pollution problems and priorities across the fifty states. In the rest of this chapter we examine the legislative approach the federal government has adopted in attempting to ameliorate these water pollution problems.

A Brief Legislative History

The federal role in water-related legislation can be traced back nearly to the founding of the nation (see Rogers 1993). Most of this legislation, however, was concerned with issues of water transportation and water quantity, rather than water quality. In fact, water quality has been a relatively recent federal concern. The Water Pollution Control Acts of 1948 and 1956 did modestly attempt to define a federal role in this area. This attempt was unsuccessful, however, largely because too much authority for the implementation of the environmental program was delegated to the states. Many states, at this time, did not demonstrate a commitment to water pollution control or lacked the financial resources to administer the program adequately. As a result, implementation was sporadic at best (Davies 1970: 38–43). Other congressional attempts at environmental management, specifically the Clean Water Quality Act of 1965, similarly delegated a great deal of authority to the states (ibid.: Chapter 2). The 1965 act was, however, the first federal law to actually mandate that the states develop "quantitative water quality criteria for interstate waters within their borders and to develop implementation plans to meet these water quality standards" (Ringquist 1993: 53). It also allowed for the regulation of point sources of pollution. Regulatory action, however, was based on a "prediction of ill effect." Further, it required that the pollution official calculate many complex variables in order to make an ecologically valid prediction. The 1965 act also left the lion's share of regulatory responsibility in the hands of the states. As the Conservation Foundation (1976: 19) reported,

> The 1965 Act held that the Federal Government could initiate general enforcement procedures only when pollution in one state endangered the health or welfare of persons in another state, or where pollution was damaging the interstate marketing of fish or shellfish. Where pollution was wholly in-state, the Federal Government could enforce only when a state expressly requested it to do so. Agencies that set out to enforce the law found that procedures and requirements were heavily weighted in favor of the polluter.

The 1966 Clean Water Restoration Act overcame some of these problems. It did include provisions for greater federal funding and transferred the Federal Water Pollution Control Administration from the Department of Housing and Urban Development to the Interior Department (Lowry 1992: 21). Still, the federal role in water pollution control was limited. Because of the failure of these acts, environmental groups began to lobby Congress to adopt legislation that would give the federal government a more prominent role in environmental protection. By 1970, a growing number of influential politicians with environmental sensitivities had been elected to office. In addition, Senator Edmund Muskie (D.-Maine), who had shown considerable interest in environmental issues in the past, now adopted a major interest in environmental policy, becoming an important policy entrepreneur for the issue. Consequently, the environmentalists' call for increased federal participation in the areas of air and water pollution control received a more favorable reception in Washington than it had in the past.

Another factor contributing to the expansion of the federal government's role in environmental politics was the emergence of greater public concern. In 1965 only 25 percent of the public thought that water pollution was a very or somewhat serious problem. But by 1968 this percentage had increased to 58 percent (Erskine 1972: 121–23). The giant Earth Day demonstrations of 1970 were yet another clear indication that a growing number of Americans were committed to stricter environmental regulation. As public support for environmental protection proliferated, there was an inevitable rush by politicians to curry favor with this new constituency. Unfortunately, popular support for environmental protection was largely unfocused. Politicians had no clearly delineated program for dealing with environmental problems; rather, as Jones (1975: 175) wrote, the mood was reflective of "a majority in search of a policy." The Clean Air Act of 1970 was written, and the Environmental Protection Agency established, under these frantic circumstances. By the time the Federal Water Pollution Control Act of 1972, now popularly known as the Clean Water Act, was written legislators had a little more experience creating regulatory solutions to environmental problems. Still, the resulting legislation reflected more of a concern with responding to the growing environmental movement, rather than providing a clear blueprint for dealing with water pollution problems. One key to the congressional response was to expand the federal government's role over water pollution control. As the Conservation Foundation (1976: 20) concluded, the "1972 Act completely overhauled the 1965 program."

The Clean Water Act

Congress, in developing the 1972 amendments to the Federal Water Pollution Control Act, changed its focus from the maintenance of ambient water quality, to the limitation of discharges by individual polluters. This change occurred to resolve two problems. First, the focus on maintaining ambient water quality meant that waters used primarily for industrial purposes were allowed to be heavily polluted (Battle 1986: 7). The earlier legislation had as its goal the prevention of further degradation and, as a result, virtually abandoned some waterways. Attitudes after Earth Day in the nation reflected a desire to return to a more pristine, less industrialized environment. Second, because of the difficulty of tracing pollution back to its source, there was often little the states could do to improve their water systems. Congress determined that discharge limits, based upon the capability of current technology, would be easier to enforce and would ultimately lead to the desired outcomes.

The legislation had several parts. Some of the stated goals of the 1972 amendments were (Battle 1986: 8):

    a) That discharge of pollutants into the navigable water be eliminated by 1985;
    b) That the interim goal of nationwide water quality providing for protection

of fish and wildlife and for water recreation users be achieved by 1983;
c) That discharge of toxic pollutants in toxic amounts be prohibited.

It was recognized that technology did not exist to accomplish all of these goals. Therefore existing facilities were required, for point sources, to use the "best practical control technology currently available" (BPT) by July 1, 1977, and the "best available technology economically achievable" (BAT) by July 1, 1983. By 1977 it was clear that many facilities would not be able to meet these goals, so Congress authorized the EPA to grant case-by-case extensions when good-faith efforts were being made. Effluent discharge limitations were to be established by the EPA for different industries on the basis of available pollution-treatment technologies. All discharges were also made subject to the same standards. The act made all point-source discharges of pollutants illegal without a permit.

Title I of the amendments provided primarily for research, grants, and the development of comprehensive programs for the protection of surface water and groundwater. Section 104 provided for the establishment of a water-quality surveillance system, funding of research on the causes of water pollution, on the effects of pollution, and the development of technologies to clean up polluted waters. Section 105 authorized the EPA to make grants to states, municipalities, or agencies for the purpose of developing pollution prevention, reduction, or elimination technologies and waste treatment or water-purification systems. Section 109 provided for training grants to universities to prepare students for jobs in water-quality control.

Title II dealt with grants for the construction of treatment works. The purpose of this title was to "require and to assist the development and implementation of waste treatment management plans and practices which will achieve the goals of this Act" (Clean Water Act: 252). The EPA was authorized, under the provisions of this title, to provide grants to states, municipalities, or agencies for the construction of waste-treatment and water-treatment facilities. These facilities were required to use the best practicable technology available and were encouraged to provide for the "recycling of potential sewage pollutants through the production of agriculture, silviculture, or aquaculture products; the confined and contained disposal of pollutants not recycled; the reclamation of wastewater; and the ultimate disposal of sludge in a manner that will not result in environmental hazards." Title II made it possible for communities to improve their waste treatment facilities or, in many cases, to build their first one. It provided matching funding, so communities had to raise 25 percent of the funding for projects completed before October 1, 1984, and 55 percent for projects beginning on or after that date. These funds were allocated over the period covering 1973–1982 and reached a level of $7 billion for fiscal year 1975. Because this title carried such a high budget, it was the first target for rescissions, and the Reagan administration reduced the budget to approximately $2.4 billion per year.

Title III set standards, timetables, and enforcement procedures for point source pollutants (effluent discharges) and specified that states must establish standards at least equal to federal standards. Under this title, states must submit standards to the EPA every three years for review and must submit any revisions to their standards upon completion of the revisions. The EPA may require states to develop stricter standards or may impose federal standards when they deem it to be necessary in order to achieve the goals of the Act. Section 304(f) deals with nonpoint source pollution, Section 308 establishes inspection and monitoring standards, and Section 309 provides for EPA oversight of state activities, allowing the EPA to step in and take action if the state does not act within thirty days on a violation. Section 311 prohibits the discharge of oil and hazardous substances in harmful quantities into navigable waters and shorelines, whether from point or nonpoint sources. The National Pollutant Discharge Elimination System (NPDES) (see Chapter 2) was established under Title IV, Section 402. This section authorizes the EPA (and states with authority delegated to them) to issue permits for effluent discharges, based upon the standards established under Title III. Section 404 provides for wetland protection. Under Title IV the EPA administrator is authorized to enforce the standards established under Title III. Title V, Section 505, provides standing to citizens for suits against violators and against the enforcing agency if timely action has not been taken against violators. It also covers the establishment of a Water Pollution Control Advisory Board to advise the EPA administrator on policy relating to the activities and functions of the EPA under this Act.

In the next chapter we turn our focus to the institutional environments under which the 1972 Act and its subsequent amendments have been enforced. We discuss the organization and functions of the Environmental Protection Agency and the National Pollutant Discharge Elimination System. We also discuss the specific procedures established for enforcing these laws.

2

The Institutional Setting

In this chapter we examine the institutional setting under which surface-water pollution control is conducted. First we examine the role of the Environmental Protection Agency (EPA). We then focus on the purposes and methods of the National Pollutant Discharge Elimination System (NPDES), which enforces the surface-water pollution control program for the EPA. In so doing, we both delineate the process under which enforcement occurs and identify the multiple opportunities for the exercise of bureaucratic discretion by agency employees.

The Environmental Protection Agency

The Environmental Protection Agency is the largest of the federal regulatory agencies. It administers more than two dozen statutes. As of 1992, prior to the major budgetary reductions proposed by the Republican controlled Congress in 1994, the EPA had eighteen thousand employees, approximately twelve thousand of whom work in one of its ten regional offices. It also had a budget of $6.5 billion (Ringquist 1995c: 149). As was the case in 1981, however, when the newly elected Reagan administration severely reduced the agency's budget and personnel levels (see Wood 1988; Waterman 1989), by 1994 the EPA was again identified as a primary target for budgetary reductions, this time by the newly elected, Republican-controlled Congress. Once considered an agency with considerable bipartisan support, by the 1980s and 1990s environmental protection, and the role of the EPA, had clearly become increasingly more divisive political issues.

This was not always the case. The EPA was established via executive order on December 2, 1970, by a Republican president, Richard Nixon, combining a number of existing federal pollution programs into a single agency. Among these were programs dealing with air pollution from the Department of Health,

Education, and Welfare (HEW); water pollution from the Department of the Interior; pesticide control from the Departments of Agriculture, Interior, and HEW; solid waste management from HEW; and radiation standards from the Atomic Energy Commission (Jones 1975: 238). The new EPA also replaced the National Air Pollution Control Administration, which had been the primary federal agency responsible for environmental management.

As Ringquist (1995c: 149) noted, "The EPA is unique structurally; it is the only regulatory agency (as opposed to a commission) that is not located in an executive branch department." Structure was very much on the minds of the policymakers who created the EPA. In establishing it, one of their primary concerns was that the new agency would not become a pawn of the regulated industry. For this reason the idea of creating a federal regulatory commission was rejected. In the academic literature, regulatory commissions were synonymous with the word "capture." It was argued that the new environmental agency could avoid capture if it were established as an independent agency, with its administrator selected by and serving at the pleasure of the president. To increase presidential influence, the administrator's term was designed to run concurrently with the president's, and at the pleasure of the president, meaning the president could remove the administrator at any time. In an attempt to ensure that the administrator would be accountable to the public and environmentalists, Senate confirmation was also required (Marcus 1980: 267).

In practice it is questionable whether the EPA administrator has really been accountable to the public. Instead, the empirical evidence to date suggests that the primary loyalty of administrators has been with the president (e.g., Wood 1988; Waterman 1989; Wood and Waterman 1991, 1993, 1994; Waterman and Wood 1993). For example, during the presidency of Ronald Reagan, a sternly anti-environmental agenda was pursued by his first administrator, Anne Gorsuch Burford. Her administration of the EPA ended in controversy. Burford was cited for contempt of Congress for refusing to turn over relevant documents to a House committee. There were also allegations that EPA officials during her tenure had put together a so-called hit list of EPA employees who were considered unsympathetic to the Reagan administration's environmental agenda. Many of these agency officials were then transferred to less desirable assignments within the EPA or to more distant regional offices. The end result was that morale within the agency sank to an all-time low, Congress and the media intensified investigations of the EPA, and eventually Burford and many other top Reagan-appointed officials were forced to vacate their offices (Waterman 1989: Chapter 5). This episode raised the question of whether strict accountability to the president, even with Senate confirmation, protects the public interest in the area of environmental protection.

Ackerman and Hassler (1981: 6) argued that a New Deal–style regulatory commission would have better served the environmental movement than the independent EPA. First, under a commission form, it would have been more "difficult for a momentary national impulse to affect agency policy." This would be the case because commissioners are more isolated from the impact of public opinion and overt political influence than an official who is directly responsible to the president, such as the EPA administrator. The primary reason for this is that commissioners are chosen for fixed terms, generally of five to seven years. They therefore can be appointed by the president, but not removed by him. Also, the terms of the commissioners are generally staggered, so that any one president is unlikely to appoint all members of the commission during only one term in office. Wood and Waterman (1991, 1994) found that appointees to regulatory commissions are also responsive to presidential influence, but they concluded that this influence is to some extent mitigated by the more rigid organizational structure of the commission form.

A second reason Ackerman and Hassler provided for recommending a commission form of government is that a commission is a body of experts who would be less open to judicial intervention. Although the courts would have the jurisdiction to intercede, they would be less likely to do so than they have been under the liberal judicial oversight provisions of the Clean Air and Clean Water Acts. According to R. Shep Melnick (1983), the courts have been highly prone to intercede in environmental policy matters. Critics of existing regulation by the EPA have asserted that these judicial interventions have had the effect of considerably slowing the pace of regulatory enforcement. On the other hand, pro-environmental organizations such as the Conservation Foundation (1976) have contended that public participation in the regulatory process, including judicial intervention, is a primary mechanism the public retains for holding dischargers accountable for their actions. In short, although the EPA's existing structure makes it more responsive to presidential influence and opens the door to considerable court intervention, Ackerman and Hassler believed a commission form may have been better suited to the task of promoting professionalism and limiting excessive judicial intervention.

In addition to these concerns, there were also important political reasons why the EPA was established as a separate agency. As Landy, Roberts, and Thomas (1994: 32) wrote, "From the president's point of view, a separate agency had two very attractive features. First, it was a highly visible and innovative action. Second, it represented a compromise between those who wanted to totally redesign the executive branch and those who wanted to change nothing." Largely then because of the concern that a regulatory commission would be susceptible to capture by the regulated industry and the president's political need to demonstrate his concern for the environment the position of EPA administrator was endowed with considerable authority and, perhaps more important, a great deal of discretion. The role of discretion is particularly important in view of the degree to which scientific theories and evidence regarding the myriad problems the EPA faces are open to wide interpretation. The administrator can often choose between competing scientific theories in order to provide a rationalization for a particular decision. In one instance, for example, Burford supported the epigenetic theory of cell chemistry, which posited that a number of carcinogenic substances affect cell mechanisms in addition to DNA strands. In practical terms this theory meant human beings could be subject to greater exposure to known carcinogens without fear of developing cancer. As a result, Burford decided to approve higher tolerance levels for several pesticides that were known carcinogens. According to the competing genotoxic theory endorsed by the previous Carter administration's administrator, Douglas Costle, all carcinogens were thought to cause alterations in genetic cell materials, and therefore carcinogens should be strictly regulated (Rosenbaum 1985: 96). Although the genotoxic theory was more widely supported within the scientific community at large, there was scientific backing for the epigenetic theory, which provided Burford with the justification she needed for her decision.

The discretionary authority of the administrator extends beyond rule making. The administrator also has wide discretionary authority to reorganize the offices of the EPA and to develop the agency's budget. Burford used her reorganization authority to eliminate the agency's enforcement division, in an only slightly veiled attempt to weaken the EPA's enforcement capability. Likewise, under Bill Clinton's administrator, Carol Browner, a revolutionary reorganization of the agency occurred. Since Burford's tenure as administrator, the EPA had been organized into offices dealing with specific environmental sources. For example, the Office of Water was designed to handle all problems involving water-related issues, whereas the Office of Air, Noise, and Radiation dealt with all air-related issues. The problem, according to Browner, was that coordination across EPA offices was often quite difficult to achieve. There also was considerable overlap across functional offices. For example, if a transportation company was polluting both the air and the water, then both offices not only had to become involved in regulating the polluter, but also had to coordinate their activities. The problem, according to many EPA officials, was that coordination was difficult. In addition, organizational overlap led to redundant and wasteful action by the EPA, which proved overly burdensome to the regulated industry and costly to consumers. The solution was to reorganize the agency according to the type of industry involved in pollution activities. Thus, under Browner, the agency focused on a multimedia approach, rather than such specific media as air, water, or hazardous wastes. The Browner reorganization is yet further evidence of the extraordinary discretionary authority of the EPA administrator.

Although the real authority of the agency rests with the administrator, the deputy administrator has often played an important role in EPA affairs as well. Yet when the deputy administrator is not the personal selection of the administrator, as was the case with John Hernandez during Burford's term at the EPA, the authority of this office is considerably diminished. Along with the administrator and deputy administrator, various assistant administrators oversee each of the functional offices of the agency. In the past these included such offices as the Air, Noise, and Radiation; Water; Planning and Management; Research and Development; Enforcement; and Pesticides and Toxic Substances. As noted, with the Browner reorganization, the EPA's approach to enforcement has changed radically. As with the deputy administrator, the authority of each of these assistant administrators is greatly dependent on support from the administrator.

Among the EPA's more than ten thousand other employees are a large number of scientists, engineers, attorneys, and other professionals, most of whom are career civil servants. The EPA has distinguished itself for acquiring an impressive cadre of experts on environmental affairs, and many of them have been strong advocates of the environment. It would be a mistake, however, to assume that the personnel of the EPA have constituted a giant monolith in support of a specific environmental approach. EPA employees have been deeply divided over a variety of issues, such as the decision involving emission dispersion and the use of variances in State Implementation Plans (Melnick: Chapters 5 and 6). In a particularly bitter dispute, the Office of Air, Noise, and Radiation and the Office of Planning and Management argued for more than two years whether industry should be compelled to use scrubbers (Ackerman and Hassler 1981). In Chapter 4 of this volume, Amelia Rouse and Robert Wright examine data on the attitudes of officials of the EPA's NPDES program (see also Waterman, Rouse, and Wright 1994). Their analysis sheds more light on the commonalities and differences in the attitudes of NPDES personnel.

Rouse and Wright focus on the attitudes of EPA personnel in the regional offices. Most of the EPA's employees are dispersed around the country in one of the agency's ten regional offices. As Ringquist (1993: 37) wrote, "Most of the real work of the EPA is accomplished at the regional level. For example, regional offices undertake almost all federal inspections and enforcement actions, and act to coordinate different environmental policies. Regional offices are also much more important than the central office to states and regulated industries, since these entities interact with regional offices on a daily basis." The division of EPA authority into ten regional offices has the effect of geographically dispersing EPA employees across the nation, a definite decentralizing tendency which can undercut the direct authority of the administrator. As one assistant administrator told us, it also promotes serious regional differences in EPA performance, a subject we return to in Chapter 5. One major source of these regional differences, according to the same assistant administrator, is provided by the regional administrators who oversee each regional office. These administrators are technically presidential appointees, but in reality are selected on the basis of the system of senatorial courtesy. As a result, they tend to reflect the local attitudes of their regional constituencies rather than the national attitudes of the president or the federal EPA. Because EPA NPDES personnel perceive these regional administrators as exerting as much influence as the EPA administrator (Waterman, Rouse, and Wright 1994), they have a clear potential for influencing the manner in which the Clean Water Acts are enforced.

Although the regional offices can undercut direct hierarchical authority from the Central Office in Washington, their existence is necessitated by the EPA's strong intergovernmental component. Another decentralizing tendency is that the EPA is not the only agency responsible for the development of environmental policy. As Peter Rogers (1993: 4) notes, "The federal government alone has over 90,000 employees working on water problems, spread over 10 cabinet departments, two major independent agencies, and smaller agencies." These smaller agencies include "11 independent federal agencies in 10 cabinet departments, four agencies in the Executive Office of the President, five river basin commissions, the federal courts, and two bureaus. There are at least 25 separate water programs, governed by more than 200 sets of federal rules, regulations, and laws" (ibid: 15–16). In addition to these large number of federal actors, the EPA even has responsibility for regulating other agencies, such as the Tennessee Valley Authority (TVA). Although there are problems with such intergovernmental regulatory activity, the case of the TVA demonstrates that the problems of coordination are not insurmountable (see Durant, Fitzgerald, and Thomas 1983; Rechichar and Fitzgerald 1983).

Likewise, the EPA competes, and works with, other agencies in other regions of the country. The states and local governments have more than 270,000 employees working on water-related problems, and the private sector adds at least another 50,000 consultants and contractors to this list (Rogers 1993: 4). The EPA must cooperate with the fifty states in the development of regulatory policy. For example, under both the Clean Air and Clean Water acts, states must submit state implementation plans (SIPs) to the EPA. These plans delineate the method state governments will use to comply with the standards and deadlines enumerated in the enabling legislation. The EPA must then review the SIPs to determine if they satisfy federal guidelines. Although this review process gives the EPA oversight authority over state environmental agencies, it does not guarantee control over them as well. As numerous EPA personnel have told us, the federal EPA does not have sufficient personnel or fiscal resources to perform a comprehensive study of every state's environmental program. As a result, much authority is necessarily delegated to the states. Ann O'M. Bowman (1984, 1985) has argued that this intergovernmental component of environmental regulation has impeded progress in implementing environmental programs. In particular, coordination of decision making is more difficult because different levels of government are involved in the implementation process. Yet, as Gormley (1987: 285) notes, "Over the past few years, the federal government has delegated considerable authority over environmental protection to the states." In particular, during Ann Burford's tenure as EPA administrator (1981–83) "state program responsibilities grew from 33 percent of possible assumptions of responsibility to 66 percent" (ibid.). State involvement in environmental protection has continued to grow since Burford's tenure. Given this active state role, in Chapters 6 and 7 we present detailed evidence regarding the state-level commitment to environmental protection. Our results identify some clear problems in state implementation of the Clean Water Acts. They will also demonstrate that in general the states have played a much more active role in NPDES enforcement than much prior scholarly research hypothesized.

In summary, the EPA is a curious blend of centralized control by the administrator and decentralized authority over its many functional units, the other federal agencies it shares responsibility with, and the intergovernmental component of environmental regulation. Agency officials from the administrator on down also have considerable discretion to interpret and implement the law. In the next section we examine the establishment and organization of the NPDES program, which is the main topic of this book. Then we turn our focus to a detailed examination of the methods of NPDES enforcement. In so doing, we again underscore the broad potential for bureaucratic discretion in NPDES enforcement.

The National Pollutant Discharge Elimination System

The National Pollutant Discharge Elimination System program is one of three permit programs created under the provisions of the Clean Water Act of 1972. The NPDES program was designed to oversee point source discharges by municipalities and industrial firms, among others. The ocean dumping program regulated dumping of sewage sludge, garbage, and industrial chemicals at sea. The Army Corps of Engineers also was granted authority for two specifically identified pollutants: fill material and dredged spoil (Conservation Foundation 1976: 101).

The NPDES program is the subject of the three subsections to follow. Our analysis is divided into three categories: the NPDES permit issuance and review process, the compliance monitoring process, and the procedures used by NPDES personnel for enforcing the Clean Water Act of 1972.

To assist us in describing how the NPDES enforcement process is operated, we liberally cite from the EPA's Enforcement Management System (EMS) manual. The manual "constitutes a system for translating compliance information into timely and appropriate enforcement action. It also establishes a system for identifying priorities and directing the flow of enforcement actions based on these priorities and available resources." The EMS, which was originally developed in 1977, also "provides a framework of basic principles, supplemented by policies and procedures which may be modified reflecting the dynamic process of compliance monitoring and enforcement" (EPA 1986: 2–3).

According to the EMS, there are seven basic principles of enforcement. The first three relate to the permit and compliance monitoring processes. Principles 4–7 then relate to the subsequent enforcement process. They are (EPA 1986: 8):

1. "Maintain a source inventory that is complete and accurate."
2. "Handle and assess the flow of information available on a systematic and timely basis."
3. "Accomplish a pre-enforcement screening by reviewing the flow of information as soon as possible after it is received."
4. "Perform a more formal enforcement evaluation where appropriate, using systematic evaluation screening criteria."
5. "Institute a formal enforcement action and follow-up where necessary."
6. "Initiate field investigations based on a systematic plan."
7. "Use internal management controls to provide adequate enforcement information to all levels of the organization."

These seven principles are meant to provide a broad framework under which enforcement should take place. On the other hand, "the specific details of how each of these basic principles become operational in a specific State or Regional system may vary to reflect differences in organizational structure, position mixes, and State laws." The manual concluded, "As long as the basic principles are incorporated and are clearly recognizable, the resulting system is acceptable" (ibid.).

In short, the EMS guide establishes minimum standards and leaves many of the operational details of implementation to the individual EPA regional offices and the primacy states. In the following pages we delineate the NPDES process in considerable detail, demonstrating the complicated, yet fluid nature of that process.

The Permit Process

The first stage in the NPDES process involves the acquisition of a permit. Many of the EPA and state officials we interviewed described this as the most important stage in the enforcement process. A firm, such as an industry or a municipality, that intends to discharge various permissible effluents into nearby waterways must first secure an NPDES permit. This is a legal requirement of the 1972 Clean Water Act. Yet, as state environmental officials in Florida and West Virginia informed us, many dischargers in those states continue to operate without NPDES permits more than twenty years after the passage of the landmark 1972 legislation. Officials in other states also told us that requirements are often set too high by the people who write the permits; in many states the people who write the permits are not even the same people who subsequently enforce the law. The end result is that even if permittees are in full compliance with their permits, they can cause serious damage to the environment. In theory, however, all dischargers are supposed to acquire permits and these permits are supposed to protect the integrity of nearby waters. As the Conservation Foundation (1976: 101) noted, "The discharge permit is a legal instrument which binds the discharger to a specified set of requirements concerning the frequency, quantity, and location of pollutant discharges. It also prescribes, as appropriate, abatement schedules and requirements for monitoring and reporting the discharge." Without a permit, firms cannot legally discharge at all. As Section 301 of the 1972 Clean Water Act prescribes, the "discharge of any pollutant by any person" represents a violation of the law unless a permit is first obtained. Section 502 of the act defines a "discharge of a pollutant" as meaning "any addition of any pollutant to navigable waters from any point source." A point source is defined by the act (Section 502 [14]) as "any discernible, confined and discrete conveyance." The act then lists examples ranging from "pipes" to "rolling stock" (ibid.). The act, however, does not require permits for nonpoint sources of pollution (discharges for which no discernible source can be identified), which is one of the primary limitations of the 1972 act; though the Water Quality Act of 1987 has expanded the EPA's focus to nonpoint sources of pollution, while also expanding the role of the states in water pollution control.

Each NPDES permit "must contain a set of effluent standards specific to that source." The act also "provides for an upgrading of effluent limitations based on water quality standards, implementation plans, and other state-approved requirements" (ibid: 103–4). Generally, certain limits are placed on the discharge of certain effluents into nearby waters. If, however, discharges from several different pipes by the same or different firms could threaten a particular waterway's quality, then discharge standards can be tightened.

Originally, the EPA considered using this water quality-based standard for its permitting system. According to this system, "the safe carrying capacity of waterways receiving discharges is established for a number of pollutants." Permits are then issued such "that the total amount of pollutants entering the waterway does not exceed its safe carrying capacity" (Ringquist 1993: 55). This permitting system proved unworkable, however, for a number of reasons. For example, as Ringquist wrote, "Pollutant-carrying capacities vary with changes in ambient water conditions such as temperature and flow levels. These conditions make it very difficult to divide up the pollutant-carrying capacity of a body of water among a large group of municipal and industrial polluters." As a result, the EPA rejected water quality standards in favor of technology-based standards; although some states use water quality-based standards for their permits (ibid.: 58). Under technology-based standards "uniform technical requirements" are placed on "all polluters in a particular industry or all polluters using a particular manufacturing process" (ibid.: 55). The 1972 Clean Water Act set as its original technology-based standards the best practicable control technology (BPT), by 1977, with a move to the best available technology (BAT) by 1983. These deadlines, however, proved too optimistic. The BPT deadline was extended by the 1981 Clean Air Amendments until 1988, and then extended again by the 1987 Water Quality Act. As Ringquist (1993: 56) wrote, "Many industries have not yet installed BAT controls. One reason for the failure of industry to meet BAT deadlines is the snail's pace at which the EPA has promulgated BAT regulations. From 1979 to 1987, only twenty-nine BAT regulations were developed. The EPA cannot be held completely responsible for the lack of BAT standards, however, because nearly every standard proposed by the agency has been delayed in court by industry litigation."

Despite its imperfections and the serious administrative problems associated with its implementation, the technology-based permit system is now employed by the EPA. Under this approach, permits must be issued for each individual discharge source, although "several sources may be included in one permit, as, for example, when several pipes emanate from one factory" (Conservation Foundation 1976: 102). Permits are issued through two processes, regular and fast-track. The regular process involves a separate application form and a separate review process for each discharge point and medium. The fast-track process allows an applicant to apply for all permits for a facility (including permits for air and water) in one step. Permits are issued by either state or regional EPA officials, depending on which administering agency has primacy in a particular state. Permits can be issued in two basic categories: major and minor. The main distinction between the two types of permits involves the amount of water discharged into nearby waters. An example of a major municipal discharger would be a wastewater treatment facility that discharges a flow of at least one million gallons of water per day. Treatment facilities discharging less than one million gallons a day would be classified as minor dischargers. Similarly, industrial discharges who have eighty or more points are classified as major dischargers. Points are assigned on various effluent parameters including toxic pollutant potential, flow/wastewater type, conventional pollutant load, public health impact, and water quality (EPA 1986: 1–2 of Definitions for the Enforcement Management System). Points can also be assigned according to the discretion of the administering agency. As the EMS manual states, "USEPA Regions are permitted to assess up to five hundred points at their discretion, thereby placing some dischargers in the major classification which would not have otherwise been there. This provides the regions the opportunity to classify certain dischargers with local problems as majors, even though they would not be under a fixed, inflexible national scheme. Each Region's discretion is limited to 20 discretionary additions plus five percent of their total major permits" (ibid.).

The distinction between a major and minor permit is of critical importance because it has a direct impact on the subsequent enforcement process. Enforcement priority is given to major permittees, meaning that NPDES personnel generally act first on major permittees. Thus, the manual "places priority on rapid responses to instances of significant noncompliance [a term we discuss shortly], especially by major dischargers" (EPA 1986: 2). Minor permits are given a lesser emphasis. The manual continues, "As resources allow administering agencies should also address minor dischargers of concern and other instances of noncompliance." Thus, the decision to issue a major or minor permit has an important impact on the subsequent enforcement process for a discharging firm.

The process of issuing an NPDES permit under the Clean Water Act of 1972 is often highly contentious. It is at this stage of the enforcement process that potential permittees (or permittees seeking revisions in their existing permits) negotiate with regional EPA and/or state officials regarding the exact nature of their permit. They often negotiate over such factors as the allowable level of effluent, the allowable level of discharge, the time frame in which compliance will be permitted, the equipment needed to comply with the permit, and so on. At the same time, the public and environmental groups are most likely to play an active role at this stage of the enforcement process rather than at the later compliance monitoring or enforcement stages (see Heberlein 1976; Conservation Foundation 1976; Godschalk and Stiftel 1981; Rosener 1982). Because of this confluence of actors and interests, this stage tends to be the most conflictual. Because NPDES permits are issued for a period of five years and then must be reissued, there also is a regular time interval at which outside groups can become involved. The Clean Water Act encouraged this type of open debate, not only by requiring that permits be reissued but also by specifically providing for increased public participation. As the Conservation Foundation (1976: 107–8) reported, when an application for a permit is received,

> EPA must prepare a draft permit consisting of tentative determinations of the effluent requirements, monitoring provisions and schedule of compliance. . . . The regional EPA office maintains a list of all interested individuals and organizations in the region and mails to each a public notice 30 days before any final decision on the permit. Written comments or requests for public hearings may be made within this period. The public notice identifies the discharger, and the point on the waterway to which the discharge is made. It contains the tentative determination to issue or deny the permit; a description of the procedures for requesting a public hearing; and directions for getting to the location for inspecting and copying the draft permit.

Two types of hearings are then permitted under the 1972 act; public and adjudicatory hearings. The first is a public hearing, which can be held if the regional administrator believes "a significant degree of public interest is manifest in a proposed permit or group of permits" (ibid.: 108). Public hearings can also be requested by citizens during the thirty-day comment period. The report of the Conservation Foundation continued,

> Following the public hearing, the regional administrator may make modifications in the terms and conditions of the proposed permit and then issue or deny the permit. The permit will then become effective 30 days after this date unless a request for an adjudicatory hearing is granted by the EPA. . . . Adjudicatory hearings are more formal than public hearings and requests for them must "state with particularity" the reasons for the request and the issues to be considered and give the viewpoint of the person making the request. (Ibid.: 108–9.)

Once the adjudicatory hearing has been held,

> regulations provide for a sequence of procedures in which the regional administrator will issue a tentative or recommended decision, to which any party may submit exception; subsequently, he will issue a decision that will become final unless any party appeals or unless the administrator of the EPA, on his own motion, stays the regional decision pending review. . . . "Any interested person" can initiate judicial review of a decision by the administrator under Section 509 of the Water Act. Such review must take place in the United States Circuit Court of Appeals for the federal judicial district in which the person lives or transacts business. (Ibid.: 109.)

When a permit is approved it is then issued for a period of five years. Permits, however, can be "modified, suspended or revoked if a violation of the terms or conditions of the permit occurs; if the permit is obtained by a misrepresentation of fact or failure to disclose fully all relevant facts; or if a change in any condition requires a temporary or permanent reduction or elimination of the permitted discharge" (ibid.: 103). As noted, the permit specifically lists the permissible level of discharge (how many gallons, etc.), the effluents that can be discharged, and the approved discharge site. Permittees are then legally bound by the requirements specified in their NPDES permit, meaning they cannot discharge in excess of the amount permitted, discharge effluents that are not specified in their permit, or discharge into other sites.

The actual permit issuance process varies somewhat from state to state and region to region. In some states and regions the people who issue permits are not the same people who perform inspections or enforce the law. In others, the same unit is responsible for all three functions. Thus, one stark variation in the permit issuance process, from state to state and region to region, is the question of who actually issues the NPDES permit. Our interviews demonstrated that most enforcement personnel in the states and at the federal level perceive the permit issuance and the later permit-review process as highly perfunctory. We were repeatedly told that the major political action does occur at the public-hearing and comment stages. Permits can be modified considerably based on the testimony and evidence provided in these stages of the permit process. But we were also told that the decision to issue a permit is largely a technical matter. Either an applicant is qualified to receive a permit or not. In Chapter 7 we provide a test of this hypothesis when we consider various factors and their influence on major and minor permit issuances. At this point, however, we state only that many EPA and state officials noted the highly technical and nonpolitical nature of the NPDES permit issuance process.

The same can also be said with regard to the permit review process. At the permit-review process a public hearing is again held, followed by a comment period, and so on. Again, once the permit to be modified or reviewed is negotiated through these sometimes troubled waters a new permit is generally issued. It is not uncommon, however, for a permit to be rejected at this stage. This decision depends greatly on the permittee's compliance history, the level of discharge, the quality of the recipient waterway, and other relevant factors.

In our interviews with various state enforcement personnel, we learned that some states count a permit review as an actual enforcement action. State officials in West Virginia, for example, told us that when a permit expires or is modified they issue an administrative order to cancel the permit. Consequently, although no real enforcement action has taken place, it is counted as an enforcement action by the state of West Virginia. This, of course, to the untrained eye, would have the result of inflating the number of administrative orders issued by the state, thus making it appear that state enforcement officials were more vigorous in their enforcement of the law then they actually had been. West Virginia officials dispute this interpretation, however, arguing that permit reviews are among the most important activities they perform on a regular basis. Still, if this practice were widely followed in other states, it would have the effect of grossly overrepresenting the apparent enforcement zeal of the states.

Compliance Monitoring

Once a permit is issued, then the next stage in the NPDES enforcement process is compliance monitoring. At this stage state or regional EPA personnel, and sometimes a combination of the two, ensure that a permittee is complying with the provisions of its permit, and therefore with the provisions of the Clean Water Act (inasmuch as a violation of a permit is legally considered to be a violation of the act).

The compliance-monitoring process is central to the entire EMS enforcement system. As the EMS manual (EPA 1986: 9) states, "At the foundation of the EMS is a complete and accurate compilation of all pertinent information on all dischargers covered by NPDES permits. An effective program cannot exist without this information process." This means that once a permit has been issued, the next step in the enforcement process is to conduct regular compliance-monitoring evaluations. The most common method by which NPDES compliance monitoring occurs is through the self-reporting procedures of the discharge-monitoring reports (DMRs). All permittees must submit DMRs to their administering agency (either a state agency or an EPA regional office, if the state in which a permit is issued does not have primacy). These reports allow agency officials to determine "whether there are violations of the effluent limitations in the permit or in an enforcement order that is active against the permittee." These reports are provided monthly or quarterly by federally designated major permittees and by P.L. 92-500 funded minor permittees. Other permittees may be allowed to report on a less frequent basis (EPA 1986: Attachment A of the Violation Review Process, Chapter 2).

It can be alleged that DMRs are symptomatic of the paper work burden government regularly places on business, but the NPDES program simply could not function without this method of data collection. As our interviews revealed, neither the EPA nor the primacy states have the necessary resources (either monetary or personnel) to conduct on-site inspections for each permittee. DMRs, therefore, are an integral part of the compliance-monitoring process. The Conservation Foundation agreed, reporting (1976: 107), "Since neither EPA nor any state has the resources to make adequate site visits to ensure compliance with permit conditions, the self-monitoring requirements are the vital link between the NPDES and the enforcement program." To a great extent, it can also be argued that DMRs are less intrusive than on-site inspections since they allow the actual permittees to provide information to agency officials.

On the other hand, it can be argued that the DMRs present permittees with an opportunity to mislead federal officials. To mitigate this possibility, Section 308 (b) of the 1972 Clean Water Act specifies that all monitoring-related data must be made public (ibid). This ensures that environmental groups and concerned citizens can have access to these reports. In fact, twenty-two states have programs in which citizens play an active role in monitoring water quality (Ringquist 1993: 73).

The evidence suggests that environmental groups, in particular, have made ample use of the data from DMRs to bring legal action against polluters, under the citizen-suit provisions of the Clean Water Act (Greve 1989). As Ringquist (1995a: 356) noted, "Initially, these provisions were used almost exclusively to sue the EPA for failing to perform nondiscretionary duties, such as issuing regulations by a particular deadline." By the 1980s, however, with a conservative Republican in the White House, environmental groups began to use evidence from DMRs, and other evidence, to file suits directly against polluters. Following a conference held in 1983 the number of citizen suits against polluters increased substantially. As Ringquist (1995a: 357) wrote, "The number of citizen suits brought against polluters exploded from two in the third quarter of 1982 to 78 in the first quarter of 1984."

Beyond legal action, citizens and environmental groups are involved in the compliance-monitoring process in yet another way. A number of EPA officials told us that they receive many reports of violations of NPDES permits from the public. In fact, this process, which Scholz and Gray (1995) called "signaling" (i.e., citizens, or workers in the case of the Occupational Safety and Health Administration, inform or signal federal employees about existing regulatory violations), provides an important mechanism for assisting federal regulators in identifying regulatory violations. Our interviews with EPA personnel likewise suggest that signaling is indeed an important monitoring device. In short, public participation appears to be a critical step in ensuring accountability in the monitoring process.

Additionally, when we spoke to federal and state officials, as we will report in greater detail elsewhere in this book, they generally expressed a high level of trust in the permittees they regulate. They specifically stated that the information they receive from permittees is generally reliable. They did, however, note that follow-up on-site inspections are of vital importance in ensuring that permittees continue to be truthful in the information they report. Regular on-site inspections thus are the mechanism that ensure truthfulness in reporting on the DMRs. Regular inspections are mandated, but not on a monthly or quarterly basis. As the EMS manual states, "The NPDES Regulations . . . require States which administer the NPDES program to have procedures and abilities for inspecting all major dischargers (permittees) at least annually. As a matter of policy, all major NPDES permittees shall be inspected annually by a combination of Regional and State effort." These regular inspections ensure that the information provided on the DMRs is accurate. They also identify cases of noncompliance. In fact, inspections have several identified purposes. They are designed to (EPA 1986: Chapter VA, 3–4):

1. Respond to public health problems and emergency situations;
2. Support enforcement and possible enforcement actions;
3. Verify data and follow up on Discharge Monitoring Reports in order to assure quality;
4. Support the development of major permits, but this should be limited to only those cases where the applicant's data collection techniques are a matter for contention;
5. Perform routine compliance monitoring.

Inspections at regular intervals are mandated by the EMS manual, but all inspections are not alike. They differ widely, with regard to the type of information collected and the vigor of the inspection oversight (EPA 1986:

Chapter VA: 1–3). For example, the least vigorous inspection type of all is the reconnaissance inspection (RI), "used to obtain a preliminary overview of a permittee's compliance program. The inspector performs a brief visual inspection of the permittee's treatment facility, effluents and receiving waters. RI utilizes the inspector's experience and judgment to quickly summarize a permittee's compliance program. . . . It is the briefest of all NPDES inspections" (ibid). Somewhat more vigorous is the compliance evaluation inspection. This is a nonsampling inspection, which means that neither EPA nor state officials actually test the water quality at a particular site. These inspections are "based on record reviews and visual observations and evaluations of the treatment facilities, effluents, receiving waters, etc." (ibid.). A performance audit inspection is somewhat more vigorous than the CEI. It is

> used to evaluate the permittee's self-monitoring program. The PAI incorporates the same objectives and tasks as a CEI, but in a PAI, the laboratory procedures, data quality, and data handling are examined in greater depth. In a PAI, the inspector actually observes the permittee going through all of the steps on the self-monitoring process from sample collection and flow measurements, through lab analyses, data work-up and reporting. . . . The PAI is more resource intensive than a CEI, but less than a CSI, because sample collection and analyses by EPA or the State are not included. (Ibid.)

A diagnostic inspection (DI) "focuses primarily on municipal [Publicly Owned Treatment Work] POTW's that are not in compliance with their permit requirements. . . . An objective of the DI is to identify causes for noncompliance which can be corrected in a relatively short period of time and without large capital expenditures. The DI will also have as an objective the identification of major plant deficiencies in operation, design, and/or construction" (ibid). Although each of these inspections are of a lower level of rigor, several other inspection types involve considerably greater vigor.

The compliance sampling inspection (CSI) involves actual sampling. In short, "representative samples of a permittee's influent and/or effluent are collected. Samples that are required by the permit are also obtained. Chemical analyses are then performed and the results are used 1) to verify the accuracy of the permittee's self-monitoring program and report and 2) to determine the quantity and quality of the effluents, 3) to develop permits, and 4) where appropriate, as evidence for enforcement proceedings" (ibid).

A toxics sampling inspection (XSI) "has the same objectives as a conventional CSI, however, it places an increased emphasis on toxic substances (i.e., the priority pollutants) other than heavy metals, phenols, and cyanide, which are typically included in a CSI. Increased resources over a CSI are needed because highly sophisticated techniques are used to sample and analyze for toxic pollutants" (ibid). The compliance biomonitoring inspection (CBI) "evaluates the biological effect of a permittee's effluent discharger(s) on test organisms through the utilization of acute toxicity bioassay techniques. In addition, this inspection includes the same objectives and tasks as CEI" (ibid). Finally, the legal support inspection (LSI) is described by the EMS as "a resource intensive inspection conducted when an enforcement problem is identified as a result of a routine inspection or a complaint. For an LSI, the appropriate resources are assembled to effectively deal with a specific enforcement problem" (ibid).

As can be seen, there are a number of different types of inspections that the EPA or state officials can conduct. The choice of inspection type obviously matters greatly. A compliance evaluation or a reconnaissance inspection would obviously be much less rigorous than a compliance sampling inspection. Because of the EPA's and the states' limited fiscal and staff resources, it simply would not be possible for them to conduct regular sampling inspections in every case. These inspections are highly resource-intensive, requiring inspectors to take water samples and for in-house or contract laboratories to do the analysis. Largely because of these cost factors, most inspections are of the nonsampling variety.

As the EMS manual states, "The objective of the RI is to expand inspection coverage without increasing inspection resources." Because it is not resource intensive it is a commonly employed inspection type. Similarly, "As the CEI does not involve sampling, it is frequently used as a 'routine' inspection." On the other hand, "the CSI inspection, because it is more resource intensive, must have a more limited use. The CSI is most often conducted when there is 'cause' to suspect major violations of permit requirements and effluent limits" (ibid).

Thus, the likelihood of having a sampling inspection conducted on a permittee's premises increases if a violation is suspected, particularly if committed by a major permittee. In point of fact, all major permittees are expected to undergo at least one sampling inspection every two years. The likelihood of a sampling inspection also is greater for a municipal permittee. In addition to these likelihood factors, the EMS manual (EPA 1986: Chapter VA, 5) also provides instruction regarding which type of inspection is appropriate under different circumstances. It states:

> The type of inspection will be tailored to the individual purposes to be achieved by the inspection. The mix of inspections within each State in turn will be tailored to the needs in each state. . . . The individual State inspection

mix will be tailored to the particular needs of the state such as: a disproportionately large number of self-monitoring and laboratory problems
among permittees that need to be addressed with performance audit inspections, or a large number of dischargers with toxic limits problems that require
toxics sampling inspections. . . . The type of inspection selected depends on
the compliance status, type of facility, and the nature of the information
needed from an inspection.

The EMS manual also states that regional EPA offices can allow states to
use reconnaissance inspections as "an integral part of . . . [their] inspection
mix" (3). It then continues, "The RI's may be used on a selective basis to
satisfy the coverage requirement, but may not be used for any major permittees" who have been in significant noncompliance during any quarter during the past year or a facility involved in pretreatment. The manual states,

The purpose of allowing RIs to be used to satisfy the routine compliance
inspection coverage requirements for major facilities is to focus more intensive inspections on problem facilities. It would be appropriate to allow an RI
to satisfy the coverage requirement when the facility is subject to frequent
visits and its operational characteristics are well known to the permitting
authority. It would be generally inappropriate to use an RI to satisfy the
annual coverage requirement for a major facility in two successive years. It
should also be noted that if the results of an RI indicate significant problems
in a facility's operations or discharge, the problems will be addressed as soon
as possible by conducting a more comprehensive inspection or followup
action. (Ibid.)

The EPA also establishes "a recommended mix on inspection types
through the budget workload model." As the EMS manual states, "The
model generates a mix that reflects the level of EPA resources, the number
of permittees to be inspected, and the emphasis of that National program on
various groups of permittees during the budget year" (2). In short, although
the EMS manual provides some direction with regard to which type of
inspections should be employed, it is clear that the manual permits both
state and regional NPDES officials to employ considerable discretion in
their choice of inspection type. Because, as we argue in Chapters 6 and 7 of
this book, some states have clearly been more vigorous in their enforcement
of the Clean Water laws than others, this discretion obviously means that
inspections in some states will be more intensive than in others. We recognize this as a problem but have no ready solution, for without adequate
fiscal and staff resources, considerable flexibility in terms of the choice of
inspection will clearly continue to be necessary.

In an attempt to provide more effective oversight, each primacy state is required to submit a state inspection plan to its administering regional office. These plans "should establish that a quarterly list of candidates for inspection will be developed within thirty days prior to each quarter." The EMS manual continues,

> The quarterly list should contain names of major and PL92–500 minor facilities to be inspected and the estimated number of other inspections to be conducted, grouped by inspection type and/or facility category. . . . The Annual State/EPA Inspection Plan will contain procedures for communications between EPA and the State on conducting NPDES inspections within a given State. . . . The Plan should provide detailed procedures and specific workload projections to support these national objectives. In addition to the national objectives, the Plan should allow the State and EPA to address specific local and regional concerns. (7)

In this process, "EPA's primary role . . . will be to: provide enforcement support; overview State inspection programs to ensure they are consistent with national guidance manuals; provide quality assurance, technical assistance and training, and augment State routine compliance programs" (EPA 1986: NPDES Inspection Strategy). The EPA also provides financial assistance to aid state inspection programs. State inspection programs also are funded through the Clean Water Act's S106 grant program. In addition, the regional offices provide "ongoing evaluation of the State Inspection program, including periodic random audits of inspection reports and case files." Additionally, regions "conduct at least an annual audit of the State inspection records and management system." The level and frequency of this overview process, however, "should be tailored to the State's overall performance in the inspection activity category" (EPA 1986: Chapter VA, 3).

As a further oversight mechanism, regional offices also provide joint inspections with the states. The EMS manual continues:

> The number of joint EPA–State inspections and the number of EPA and State independent inspections will be negotiated between the EPA Region and the State, and included as part of the State/EPA Annual Inspection Plan. Each Region of EPA will maintain an independent inspection program to carry out its enforcement and overview responsibilities. The Region will normally provide prior notice to the State before conducting independent inspections. The only limited exception would be where investigative inspections would be jeopardized by the prior notice. The coverage to satisfy the total inspection needed in a State will be a responsibility that is shared by both the Region and State. However, direction is provided by the lead agency. In NPDES States, the State should take the lead in operating the inspection program. . . . In non-NPDES states, EPA has the lead responsibility for operating the inspection program. (4)

Thus, states are subject to oversight regarding who they inspect, how often they are inspected, and which type of inspection is conducted. Despite the oversight mechanisms, states still retain considerable discretion in carrying out the law. As we argue in the section of this book on state enforcement of the Clean Water laws (Chapters 6 and 7), this has produced both desirable and unsatisfactory outcomes. From an examination of the EMS manual, however, it is clear why variations would exist in state-level compliance-monitoring activity.

The Enforcement Process

Following an inspection, in most cases the compliance-monitoring process concludes with a determination that permittees are in compliance with NPDES guidelines. One head of an EPA regional office told us that 95 percent of all permittees in his region are in compliance at any given time. In the other 5 percent of cases, however, permittees are found to be in noncompliance. This means, according to principle number 4, of the seven principles of enforcement delineated above, "When an instance of noncompliance is identified by the pre-enforcement screening, the appropriate follow-up action must be determined. This is a determination that should be made by technical personnel with legal consultation, when necessary" (EPA 1986: 17).

According to Attachment B of the Enforcement Response Guide,

> There are three levels of response to all violations. For any violation the administering agency must review the violation and determine the appropriate response. For some violations, the response may be no action necessary at this time. The informal enforcement response can be an inspection, phone call, a violation letter, or a Federal Notice of Violation to the permittee with a copy to the administering State agency. The violation letter can be limited to a notification of the violation or to requiring certain steps to be taken within specific time frames. The formal enforcement response must be one of the following:
>
> 1. An Administrative Order or State equivalent action; or
> 2. A judicial referral to the State Attorney General or to the Department of Justice. (EPA 1986.)

Determining the appropriate response level in a particular case of noncompliance is complicated by a number of factors including the seriousness of the violation: for example, does it present a direct threat to the health of the surrounding community, does it represent an aesthetic threat to the environment, did the violation occur in a pretreatment facility, did the permittee fail to report the violation, did the permittee try to bypass the problem improperly, are there suspected operation and maintenance problems at the facility where the violation occurred, what is the permittee's compliance history, and what is the permittee's ability and willingness to comply with the Clean Water Act (EPA 1986: Attachment A of the Violation Under Review Process, Chapter 2, 2)? As many NPDES enforcement personnel have told us, in many cases of noncompliance the solution is direct. They sit down with the permittee and discuss a plan of action to correct the problem. NPDES personnel told us that many violations can be handled in this informal manner. Often, for example, an equipment failure can lead a permittee to be temporarily out of compliance. Under these circumstances, a timely repair of the damaged equipment is all that is required. As a result, in many cases of noncompliance EPA officials do not employ the most direct formal sanctions available to them. These, we were repeatedly told, are saved for cases involving permittees who do not willingly comply with the law or who ignore plans for a return to compliance. In short, only a small percentage of all total violations are later classified as being in significant noncompliance (SNC).

Cases of noncompliance are reported in the quarterly noncompliance report (QNCR). From all of these instances identified in the QNCR only a subset will be identified as being in SNC. As the violation review action criteria state, all violations do not require a formal enforcement response, although all do require a professional review. On the other hand, SNCs "must receive a formal enforcement response or return to compliance within a fixed period of time unless an acceptable justification is established for not taking action (ibid.: 6). Administering agency performance in addressing SNCs is then reported in the Agency Strategic Planning and Management System.

If a permittee is found to be in significant noncompliance with the law then a formal enforcement action must be taken before the violation appears on QNCR for a second time. This means that an enforcement action generally is taken within sixty days. If a primacy state is the administering agency, and it does not act within the sixty-day period, then the administering regional office is expected to step in and take action. In these cases the state agency must then provide a written justification why an alternative (informal) action or permit modification was considered to be appropriate (EPA 1986: Attachment B, Enforcement Response Guide, Chapter 2, 2).

In those cases in which a formal action is taken, but compliance is not achieved, the EMS (Attachment 3, Chapter 2) states, "successive AO's [Administrative Orders] for the same noncompliance problems should normally be avoided and the case should be escalated to the referral process."

At the federal level, this means that a referral for civil action can be made to the Justice Department. At the state level the laws vary. All states allow for civil action, but some also allow for criminal penalties against the most egregious of violators. Some states have representatives from the attorney general's office assigned to them, whereas in others these officials work for the environmental departments themselves.

At the federal level, civil penalties can be brought against a violator up to but not to exceed $10,000 per day for a violation. The manual (EPA 1986: Chapter VI, 1) even states, "The Agency will vigorously pursue penalty assessments in judicial actions to ensure deterrence and to recover appropriate penalties." As we will demonstrate in the next chapter, however, vigorous pursuit of civil penalties has not occurred at the federal level. The four avowed goals of the civil penalty program include: "(1) penalties should, at a minimum, recover the economic benefit of noncompliance; (2) penalties should be large enough to deter noncompliance; (3) penalties should be more consistent throughout the country in an effort to provide fair and equitable treatment to the regulated community; and (4) there should be a logical basis for the calculation of civil penalties for all types of violations, industrial and municipal, to promote a more swift resolution of environmental problems and of enforcement actions" (ibid.).

Penalties are to be assessed through an explicitly delineated formula:

$$\text{Civil Penalty} = (\text{Economic Benefit Component}) + (\text{Gravity Component}) + 1 - (\text{Adjustments})$$

The economic benefit component is calculated using an EPA computer program—BEN—which "produces an estimate of the economic benefit of delayed compliance, which is calculated to be the sum of the next present value of: delayed capital investment, one-time non-depreciable expenditures, and avoided operating and maintenance expenses." The gravity component then incorporates a penalty parameter into the model. This component is "based on the significance of the violation, health and environmental harm, number of violations, and the duration of noncompliance." Adjustment factors then include the "history of recalcitrance, ability to pay, and litigation considerations."

As can be seen, the enforcement process, as adumbrated in the EMS manual, is hierarchical, meaning that there is a process for escalating enforcement actions from a lower to a higher level. But as several EPA officials have told us, the process is often not hierarchical at all. A perfunctory inspection of the EMS provides one important reason for this outcome. EPA and state personnel have considerable discretion in carrying out the provisions of the NPDES program. In the next three chapters we examine the influence of this discretion at the federal level. In Chapters 6 and 7 we then examine how the NPDES system has been enforced at the state level. In both the federal and state cases we demonstrate that there has been considerable variation in enforcement activities. To understand why this is so, we now turn our attention to the concept of "pragmatic enforcement."

3

Pragmatic Enforcement

In the last two chapters we examined the nature of water problems in America and the enforcement process that has been established to deal with them. In this chapter we begin to focus on the behavior of the bureaucrats who enforce the Clean Water Acts. This is our objective throughout the remainder of the book. In this chapter we ask a series of fundamental questions: How do EPA NPDES personnel enforce the law? Why do they enforce it the way they do? Which factors motivate their enforcement behavior? We argue that NPDES personnel respond to the diverse nature of the regulatory environment that is characteristic of surface-water–related issues in America. We argue that their enforcement behavior is motivated largely by pragmatic concerns. We call this bureaucratic style "pragmatic enforcement."

Pragmatic enforcement is not the goal of NPDES enforcement, but rather a natural response to the diversity of the surface-water regulatory environment. According to the NPDES enforcement manual, the primary goal of NPDES enforcement has been to achieve and maintain "a high level of compliance with environmental laws and regulations." The manual states, "The United States Environmental Protection Agency (USEPA) has stressed consistently the need for a systematic administrative approach to compliance monitoring and enforcement with the objective of achieving a consistent, uniform national posture in the implementation of the National Pollutant Discharge Elimination System (NPDES) program established by the Clean Water Act (CWA)" (EPA 1986: 1).

Such terms as "systematic administrative approach" and "uniform national posture" suggest that the EPA's objective has been to establish an enforcement system that operates by the book, with clear, consistent procedures. After all, uniformity has been the goal of other regulatory agencies. For example, the Nuclear Regulatory Commission (NRC) has established precise criteria for the identification of various violations and has similarly delineated specific measures for ameliorating those situations. As such, the NRC enforcement manual provides agency enforcement personnel with limited discretion. The manual provides an unusual degree of specificity with regard to what an inspector must do if a particular type of violation is identified and who should make a determination in those cases in which ambiguity exists (see NRC 1986; Goodman and Wrightson 1989; Waterman 1989; Wood and Waterman 1994).

Although the NRC has been able to achieve a remarkable degree of regulatory consistency, essentially operating by the book, its functions and clientele are much different from those of the EPA. For example, the NRC regulates nuclear power plants. Both the location and the source of potential regulatory problems are easily identifiable. Whereas nuclear plants use different designs and technologies, NRC personnel deal with a largely monolithic industry. Exogenous factors, such as variations in the setting of nuclear power plants and geographical diversification, play a less important role in the enforcement process than they do in the case of surface-water pollution. In short, with a less diversified and more predictable regulatory environment, it is possible for NRC personnel to adopt a by-the-book approach. It is also possible for the NRC to greatly limit bureaucratic discretion at the enforcement level.

The same cannot be said for the EPA or the NPDES program. Rather than monitor a monolithic industry, EPA water personnel deal with a wide range of potential violators, including industry, agriculture, municipalities, and other government facilities. Likewise, as we discussed in Chapter 1, differences in water-related problems across geographical regions play an important role in surface-water enforcement, clearly more so than similar variations play in the enforcement of nuclear-power regulation. Furthermore, EPA personnel do not have primacy over all violators, as do NRC personnel. In the case of the NPDES program, much of the actual enforcement task is performed by state-level personnel, with EPA officials acting in a supervisory capacity. As a result of these types of factors, it is more difficult for EPA than NRC personnel to identify a priori the types of violations that may occur or to delineate specifically the ameliorative measures most appropriate to each case. In other words, a strict regulatory approach may be less feasible given the diversified regulatory environment in which surface-water regulations are implemented.

As a result of this more diverse regulatory environment, we will argue throughout this book that the EPA has been forced to adopt a greater degree of regulatory flexibility than agencies with less diverse regulatory environments, such as the NRC. This does not mean that the EPA has given up on the goal of a uniform approach. The NPDES manual states that enforcement should be related to the severity of the violation; a clear recognition that some actual hierarchy of enforcement should exist. As the manual (EPA 1986: 5) states,

> While it would be difficult, but not necessarily effective, to have identical enforcement responses for identical violations in different States, the enforcement response should be directly related to the severity of the violation. Given the decentralization of authority and responsibility in carrying out the NPDES program, implementation of the basic EMS principles should produce national consistency, while still accommodating differences between Regions and States.

The question for the EPA's water enforcement personnel has been how can they successfully satisfy two contradictory goals: national consistency and the accommodation of regional and state differences. In reconciling these two contradictory goals, the EPA has most often chosen to sacrifice uniformity on the altar of necessity. In other words, the goal of consistency has been superseded by an emphasis on finding workable and reasonable solutions to existing problems in a diverse regulatory environment. Rather than rely on an ideological or political approach to enforcement, EPA water personnel have adopted pragmatic strategies for dealing with a diverse regulatory environment.

Our Data

To demonstrate how and why the EPA has adopted a pragmatic enforcement style, in this chapter we analyze data provided by the EPA from the NPDES program for the years 1975–1988 and January 1986–July 1994. The reason why the data are divided into two cohorts is because over time the EPA itself has altered the manner in which it compiles and stores its data. As a result, the data are provided from at least two computers in different and noncomparable formats. The data for the earlier period, which we rely on the most in this chapter, consist of more than twenty-seven thousand individual enforcement actions conducted by EPA officials. The data in this chapter therefore do not include actions conducted by the states. These data consist of more than seventy enforcement categories, but we have collapsed them into a manageable typology of eight enforcement types. We accomplished this by referring to the EPA's "Water Management System" enforcement manual and the EPA "Enforcement Response Guide" (Supplement B of the manual), and through interviews with numerous EPA personnel. Our hierarchical typology ranges from level 0 action, so called because virtually no real enforcement whatsoever actually occurs, to level 7 (the most aggressive form of enforcement). We provide an outline of the specific types of enforcement actions that fit into each of these categories in Table 3.1. These data include the date each enforcement action was conducted, the permit number, the identity of the violator, and the state and region in which the violation occurred. The data for the second period unfortunately are not as rich in detail. They consist of aggregate enforcement outputs from January 1986 through July 1994. They do not allow us to examine each specific enforcement action conducted by NPDES personnel; still, they do provide an important check to determine if NPDES personnel have, in recent years, markedly altered the manner in which they enforce the law.

In addition to these two main data sets, two additional data sets from June 1988 through June 1989 and July 1989 and through July 1992 allow us to examine the type of violator (e.g., industry, municipality) involved in a particular action. As is typical of much of the data we received from the EPA, the data were provided to us in noncomparable formats. This means that the category of type of violator differs somewhat between the two data sets. Both data sets, however, still allow us to compare municipalities and industry, the violators of most concern to us.

A Limited Judicial Role in NPDES Enforcement

As can be seen in Table 3.1, a wide range of diverse enforcement mechanisms are available to NPDES personnel. Leaving aside permit issuances and inspections, which we examine in greater detail later in this book, EPA personnel employ such diverse enforcement techniques as phone calls, conferences, comments, warning letters, notices of violation, administrative orders, and civil penalties. Even a determination that "no current action is warranted" is considered to be an enforcement action. This vast number of enforcement mechanisms available to NPDES personnel is important. As Ayres and Braithwaite (1992) argued, the larger the range of enforcement mechanisms available to regulatory personnel, the broader the flexibility they are likely to employ in enforcing the law. On this basis alone, then, we would expect NPDES personnel to exhibit broad levels of bureaucratic discretion.

A careful examination of the results presented in Table 3.1 also make it quite apparent that the vast majority of the enforcement actions conducted by the EPA have been engaged at relatively low levels. For example, only 102 of more than 27,000 enforcement actions conducted between 1975 and 1988 involved civil penalties or contempt actions, what we categorize as a level 7 enforcement action. That is less than one-half of 1 percent (0.4) of

Table 3.1

Types and Frequencies of Enforcement Actions Conducted by EPA Officials, 1975–1988

Action	Frequencies	Percentage
(0) Comment, no action warranted, permit modification requests, or reissue	5,927	21.6
(1) Telephone calls, director's letters, enforcement notice letters, permit modifications, meetings with the permittee	2,282	8.3
(2) Warning letters, notices of violation, final orders of the board, and other state orders	11,031	40.2
(3) Plans for administrative orders, MCP and CCP actions, and other formal letters	2,201	8.0
(4) Enforcement conference agreement, show cause hearing	122	0.4
(5) Administrative orders, referrals to higher level review, judicial action planned, and penalties recommended	3,870	14.1
(6) Civil action filed, consent decrees, judicial action pending, judicial decrees, sewer bans, NPDES penalties pending, stipulation orders	1,904	6.9
(7) Contempt action, civil action, and NPDES Penalty Category II penalties filed	102	0.4
N = 27,439		

all enforcement actions conducted during this time period. Even when we consider level 6 enforcement actions, which include filings for civil actions, consent decrees, judicial decrees, and other enforcements designed to initiate the legal process, the EPA appears reticent to act. Just under 7 percent of all activity was conducted at level 6. Thus, when we consider the two highest levels of enforcement activity, the picture that emerges is of an agency that is reluctant to move the regulatory process into the judicial realm.

Having examined these results, we were understandably concerned with the limited number of level 6 and 7 cases conducted by EPA personnel. We therefore sought out explanations for the agency's apparent reluctance to move into the judicial realm. Part of the reason for the low level of judicial activity can be derived from the NPDES EMS manual. It states (EPA 1986: Chapter IV, 6) that in deciding whether to litigate,

> The government should evaluate every penalty with a view toward the potential for protracted litigation and attempt to ascertain the maximum civil penalty the court is likely to award if the case proceeds to trial. The [EPA]

Region should take into account the inherent strength of the case, considering for example, the probability of proving questionable violations, the probability of acceptance of an untested legal construction, the potential effectiveness of the government's witnesses, and the potential strength of the defendant's equitable defense.

In short, a number of diverse factors go into the calculation of whether to litigate in a particular case. The EMS manual doesn't merely instruct its enforcement personnel to proceed legally if a certain type of violation of the law has occurred, or if all other lower-level procedures have been attempted, but rather if a willful violation can be proved. Litigation, then, is limited to only certain types of cases. It is not simply determined by the severity of the violation, but also by the likelihood of deriving adequate compensation and pragmatic notions of the rules of evidence.

These factors became even more clear in our interviews with NPDES officials at the state and federal level. We asked them if they could explain why the EPA has been so reluctant to move against violators in the courts. These interviews suggested that even when the EPA has primary authority over the NPDES program, which it does in twelve states, its personnel prefer to employ administrative actions rather than legal remedies. Court cases require intensive effort and a large expenditure of scarce agency resources. Seldom are the costs of legal action ever recovered, even if a guilty verdict is determined. Beyond these cost factors, the rules of evidence also make legal action less attractive. EPA personnel must prove not only that violations have occurred, but they must also prove intent on the part of the violator to willfully disregard the law. The probability of securing an actual conviction under these circumstances is considered unlikely in all but a few egregious cases.

Even in those cases in which a guilty verdict is secured, there is an exceedingly high likelihood that the fine actually paid will be far less than the fine assessed by the courts. Even when a penalty is assessed and paid, as many state officials told us, the funds collected do not go to their water enforcement division, but rather to the general fund. Therefore, the incentive to pursue judicial action is greatly reduced. The costs of judicial action are incurred whether enforcement officials win or not, but they do not receive the compensation for these costs even if they win the case. And even if the EPA wins a legal case, appeals can delay the resolution of the case for several years and the penalty is almost certain to be reduced.

In addition to these cost factors, it is nearly impossible to bring a criminal action against violators in the federal courts. Such legal action is permitted in some states, but federal actors must be content to pursue less punitive civil actions against even the most egregious of violators. As many NPDES personnel told us, it is easier for states to litigate under current law than it is for the federal EPA to take legal action. In summary then, the obstacles against the implementation of level 6 and 7 enforcement actions at the federal level are formidable. On purely pragmatic grounds, then, NPDES personnel have largely eschewed these more stringent remedies in favor of approaches that promise a more palpable regulatory result. We should note that they have not abandoned legal remedies entirely. The threat of legal action is still an effective deterrent for many violators. But the obstacles to the legal option are formidable. As a result, NPDES personnel have a much greater propensity to employ administrative remedies even for serious enforcement violations.

Administrative Enforcement Responses

EPA activity is therefore largely constrained within the range of enforcement activities represented by levels 0 to 5. Of these six enforcement levels, the most frequently employed by NPDES personnel is a level 2 action. This consists mainly of warning letters, notices of violations, and a number of state-induced actions. In short, they represent what EPA personnel call informal enforcement actions (versus formal actions). Forty percent of all enforcement actions were conducted at level 2. The second most frequent type of enforcement approach employed by NPDES personnel consisted of the very lowest category of enforcement: level 0. These actions predominantly include cases in which EPA personnel, following an inquiry, determine that no current action is warranted. The category also includes permit modifications and comments. In fact, of all enforcement actions conducted during the period from 1975 through 1988, 70 percent were conducted at the three lowest enforcement levels! The low level of most EPA enforcement is further exemplified by the fact that the mean level of enforcement for all activity from 1975 through 1988 was 2.293. In Table 3.2 we provide the breakdown of all enforcements into two categories, informal and formal actions. The results further underscore the point made in Table 3.1. As can again be seen, more than 70 percent of all enforcement activity can be characterized as low-level informal actions. Only 28.5 percent of all NPDES enforcement occurred within the bounds of what the EPA characterizes as formal activity.

Additional evidence for the low level of NPDES enforcement is provided in Table 3.3. There we provide the mean severity levels for each year; a mean average based on the severity of enforcement actions (categories 0–7) undertaken during each year. Again, the table reveals that the mean severity level for the entire data set was only 2.293; it also shows that the mean severity level did not exceed 3.0 during any given year in the series. The

Table 3.2

Formal and Informal Enforcement Actions Conducted by EPA Officials, 1975–1988

Type of action	Number of actions	Percentage
Formal	7,814	28.5
Informal	19,625	71.5
Total	27,439	100.0

highest mean severity level occurred in 1986 and was only 2.93, suggesting most activity occurred within the informal, versus formal, range. Thus, it is crystal clear that much of what the EPA has called enforcement with regard to surface-water pollution control has occurred at a decidedly low level, no matter how one operationalizes the concept of enforcement.

We have explained why EPA personnel have eschewed level 6 and 7 type actions. But why have EPA personnel been reluctant to employ level 3 and 4, and to a lesser extent level 5 actions? One reason is that the EPA rarely receives a penalty that matches the benefit received by a permittee from violating the law. As Ashworth (1995: 153) wrote,

> Although the U.S. Environmental Protection Agency has policies in place, dating back to 1984, which require all field offices to make certain that the fines they impose match or exceed the benefits companies have received from breaking the law, few appear to do so. Of 685 EPA enforcement actions looked at by the General Accounting Office (GAO) for a 1991 study, data on the financial gain the offending firms reaped from their infractions were reported in only 243 cases—less than 35 percent.

Ashworth (1995: 154) then noted, "Businesses that run afoul of state and local antipollution ordinances do even better than those that face the EPA." In short, the problem is not confined to the national level, but permeates environmental enforcement at all levels. Why? One possibility is that command-and-control regulation does not provide a sufficient penalty to deter violators from breaking the law. Permittees thus have an economic incentive to break the law. Not only do they have a better than average chance of avoiding detection for a violation, given the low level at which most inspections are conducted (see Chapter 2), but even if a violation is detected the chances are they will also still derive an economic benefit from the violation. The incentive for permittees is therefore clear. But what about NPDES enforcement personnel? What are their motives?

Table 3.3

Mean Severity Level of Enforcement Actions by Year, 1980–1988*

Year	Number of actions	Mean severity level	Standard deviation
1980	1,805	1.29	1.24
1981	2,506	1.63	1.12
1982	2,040	1.62	1.40
1983	2,113	2.18	1.82
1984	2,122	2.81	2.02
1985	3,047	2.81	1.80
1986	3,444	2.93	1.95
1987	6,400	2.24	1.93
1988	3,792	2.35	1.93

Overall mean severity level = 2.29
Standard deviation 1.85
*Data for the years 1975–1979 reflect enforcement activities at very low levels and therefore are not presented in the table.

Given the present regulatory structure, NPDES personnel have little incentive to conduct higher-level actions. Why pursue an aggressive pattern of fining permittees if the permittees still have an economic incentive to violate the law? There is no logic to applying penalties under the present regulatory structure. Obviously, the incentive structure could be changed by increasing the size of the fine associated with a higher-level action, such as an administrative order (level 5). This would involve keeping a clear record of the benefits accruing to permittees for each violation of the law. As Ashworth (1995: 153–54) wrote, however, "the GAO found [that] the penalty policy was so poorly enforced that the EPA's internal forms for reporting fines did not even carry the necessary fields to enter the data needed to determine offenders' illegal benefits." As a result of this shortcoming, the EPA cannot adequately measure the relative benefit permittees derive from breaking the law. This also means they cannot reliably match fines to the benefit derived by permittees from violating the law.

As with the assessment of penalties by the courts, officials in many states told us that the fines ultimately collected from violators are invested into the general fund rather than back into the agency's budget. This again means that many NPDES personnel do not have an economic incentive to assess fines, even if they do recoup the benefits of violating the law.

Another problem with the strategy of emphasizing a more aggressive assessment of penalties is that a large percentage of the EPA's actual enforcement role is to serve as an overseer of state environmental enforcement personnel. Most enforcement actually occurs in the states, rather than at the federal level (a topic we return to in more detail in Chapters 6 and 7). Consequently, state officials actually levy the fine. As Ashworth (1995: 154) wrote, "The EPA has the power to levy compensating fines in those cases where state fine structures are found to be 'grossly deficient,' but this so-called overfine power is almost never used. Faced with an almost complete absence of the definition as to what constitutes 'grossly deficient,' EPA overseers are forced to resort to what they call the 'laugh test'; if you mention the amount of the fine and everyone laughs, overfining is probably called for."

Given the definitional problems with the term "grossly deficient," variations in state-level legislation regarding the amount permittees can be fined for various offenses, and the EPA's uncertainty over what actually constitutes an appropriate fine, it is not surprising that the EPA has not relied more frequently on fines to ensure compliance with the Clean Water Act and other environmental legislation. Because fines do not provide an adequate deterrent effect, and because judicial action is no more fruitful an option, it is clear why in general EPA NPDES personnel have relied to the extent they have on lower-level actions. Given the incentive structure created by the existing NPDES program, they have little reason to pursue actions at higher levels, and a concomitantly greater incentive to act at lower levels. At these levels they can negotiate with permittees in an attempt to achieve compliance. Because command-and-control regulation is largely ineffectual and exceedingly difficult to implement, the incentive for NPDES personnel then, at both the state and federal level, is to rely more heavily on lower-level enforcements.

A Pragmatic Approach

To provide a more detailed examination of why most NPDES enforcement has occurred at decidedly low levels of activity, we interviewed a wide variety of agency personnel. The answers we received will no doubt be perceived as controversial, particularly if one sees strict enforcement of the Clean Water Acts as the goal of the NPDES program. We stress, however, that the explanations cited here were provided to us by numerous EPA officials who were queried about our statistical findings. In short, we have tried to keep our own biases out of the explanation.

In our many interviews with EPA water officials one finding was quite apparent. A strict enforcement approach is not the goal of NPDES enforcement personnel! What was clear from an examination of the data thus becomes even clearer in the interviews. We were repeatedly told that the elimination of pollution was the primary goal of NPDES regulations. The intent of the enforcement process, therefore, was not to punish violators, but rather to coax them toward compliance. Most enforcement personnel explicitly informed us that a reliance on higher-level enforcement activity is not the best means of achieving compliance for a variety of reasons. Because strict enforcement involves extreme costs and offers only a limited payoff (as we have already noted in the case of judicial action), EPA personnel argued that on purely pragmatic grounds they had limited their employment of level 6 and 7 enforcement actions to only the most egregious violators; what one top EPA official called "willful violators." Another official, a head of the NPDES office in one of the EPA's ten regional offices, also said that judicial action was not really even an alternative, especially because criminal action did not exist as a realistic alternative ("unless a dead body was present" at the scene of the pollution).

As we noted above, due to these constraints on the use of these judicial enforcement actions, EPA personnel told us they try to work within the framework of agency level actions (levels 0–5). EPA officials have not used these remaining available enforcement mechanisms as a whip to ensure compliance, however, but rather as a means of prodding action. The key to this strategy is that most of the EPA enforcement personnel and higher-level officials we spoke to told us they have a high level of trust in the regulated industry. When we specifically asked individuals which percentage of permitees could be classified as "good apples" and which percentage as "bad apples," the results generally conformed with those already presented by Bardach and Kagan (1982). Most people told us that they believed that 90 to 95 percent of the firms they regulated could be classified as essentially "good apples." We were further told that most permittees genuinely try to obey the law. As the head of an NPDES office in one region told us, "95 percent of permittees are in compliance." But, this official noted, this is only because of the deterrent effect provided by EPA enforcement and the threat of citizen suits. He also added that without the EPA deterrence many permittees would clearly violate the law.

When we asked NPDES officials if there was any pattern to the so-called bad apples, we were told that municipalities tended to be the most serious violators of the Clean Water Acts, not industry or agricultural firms as might have been expected. In fact the characterization by NPDES personnel of municipalities was nothing short of scandalous, suggesting that the real problem nationwide with point-source water pollution is municipalities that believe they can skirt the clean water laws with impunity. Most industrial

enterprises, it was explained to us, have to worry about their public images. A bad environmental record can be bad for business. On the other hand, municipalities do not seem to be as concerned with their image. Municipalities also have other constraints to timely compliance. They cannot pass on the costs of enforcement to consumers and therefore are more reluctant to comply. Also, many municipalities argue that they do not have the necessary financial resources to comply with the clean water laws.

It should be noted that a high level of trust is built into the NPDES enforcement process. As we noted in the last chapter, in terms of compliance-monitoring activity the discharge monitoring reports (DMRs) play a vital role. Essentially, these reports depend on the honesty of permittees to report emerging problems. As we were told over and over again, most reports of problems with NPDES permits come from the permittees themselves. As one official told us, "They will generally tell us if a problem exists." Likewise, research by Downing and Kimball (1982) suggests that most of the compliance with various environmental laws in the United States is voluntary. Again, the key inference is that permittees try to comply with the law.

We note the controversial nature of this finding because the traditional idea of regulatory enforcement is by its very nature perceived as adversarial. As the adherents of a strong, by-the-book approach to regulation have argued, regulation is perceived as an agency vigilantly and dutifully watching over a wily and deceitful industry, which is looking for any opportunity to avoid compliance with costly environmental laws. One of the authors of this study came into this project with this basic idea in mind (we will let the reader enjoy the prospect of guessing which one of us did so), but our many interviews with EPA officials clearly reveal that EPA NPDES enforcement personnel do not share this pejorative view of the regulated industry. They view regulation as a cooperative enterprise that would literally be impossible to manage if the trust factor were vitiated.

This high level of trust between the regulators and the regulated has a direct impact on the methods selected for enforcing the law. Rather than proceed with strict penalties against violators, we were told, if a warning letter or a telephone call will encourage a company to comply with the law, then there is simply no need to move to a higher level of enforcement activity. If, on the other hand, a violator ignores a series of warning letters and other lower-level actions, then EPA personnel feel justified in moving to stricter enforcement mechanisms. Once an administrative order (a level 5 action) has been issued, one of the strongest actions the agency can take without involving the courts, if compliance is signaled,

then the incentive returns to a focus on promoting voluntary compliance. A compliance schedule, meetings with the permittee, or a warning letter can then serve this purpose by underscoring the EPA's intent to continue its pursuit of compliance. If additional such actions are not successful in promoting compliance, then EPA personnel will move to a stricter enforcement approach yet again. Through this nonsystematic process of moving between different severity levels, EPA personnel aspire to achieve compliance in a manner that does not unduly punish those permittees that seek to cooperate.

Beyond the strategic reasons for this flexible approach to enforcement, EPA officials told us that there are financial reasons for this strategy, as well. The agency, it was pointed out again and again, simply does not have the fiscal or personnel resources necessary to implement a strict enforcement approach. The implementation of a strict approach would require a radical increase in the number of enforcement personnel available to the NPDES program. Because this outcome is not likely in a period of tight federal and state budgets, a continuing reliance on a more flexible, negotiated enforcement style is likely to occur.

Bureaucratic Discretion

Clearly, pragmatic enforcement can be criticized on several grounds. First, for those individuals who do not share the same level of trust in NPDES permittees as EPA personnel have demonstrated in their interviews with us, a pragmatic enforcement style will likely prove troubling. We argue, however, that the alternative is to increase agency budgets and to hire sufficient enforcement personnel to make sure that a strict enforcement approach is feasible. Additionally, changes will have to be made that will make the assessment of fines and court penalties more attractive to agency personnel. We will examine the feasibility of adopting these alternatives in the last chapter of this book. Without these types of major fiscal, personnel, and institutional changes, however, a flexible, pragmatic approach will continue, no matter what arguments are advanced against it.

Second, and perhaps even more troubling to many scholars, is the relationship between bureaucratic discretion and pragmatic enforcement. This is a topic that we will return to in greater detail in the following chapters. In this chapter we merely note the obvious. A pragmatic approach, or even a purely negotiated approach to enforcement, will necessarily involve increased levels of bureaucratic discretion. Once we move away from a by-the-book philosophy of regulatory enforcement, increased bureaucratic discretion is inevitable.

Variations in NPDES Enforcement

In a regulatory environment in which agency personnel wield considerable discretion, it would be expected that wide variations would exist in the manner in which the law is enforced. In fact, the discretionary authority that EPA personnel have developed has led to more than simply a reliance on low-level enforcement mechanisms. It has also promoted broad variations in the manner in which the clean water laws have been enforced, both across the EPA's ten regional offices and the fifty states. These variations demonstrate that the EPA has indeed been willing to sacrifice the goal of uniform enforcement and national consistency.

Table 3.4 provides a graphic demonstration of the wide variations in the application of the Clean Water Acts across the EPA's ten regional offices. This is the case both in terms of the total number of enforcement actions undertaken and their mean severity level. The largest number of enforcement actions were conducted in region 2, a total of 13,231, whereas the least number of enforcements undertaken were conducted in region 8, with only 123 total actions! Considerable variations also exist across regions with regard to the mean severity levels. Region 4 was the most aggressive in its enforcement zeal, with a mean severity level of 4.24. This conclusion is surprising inasmuch as one top EPA official commented that region 4 was not strongly committed to enforcement, a conclusion that is not supported by this measure. On the other hand, region 2, which had the highest total of number of enforcement actions, had a mean severity level of only 1.64, which indicates that personnel in that office employed mostly low-level enforcement actions. The region with the lowest mean severity level was region 1 (at only 1.57). These differences, then, are quite extreme; from vigorous enforcement in region 4 to an emphasis on low-level enforcement in region 1.

Table 3.5 provides a similar breakdown of enforcement in each of the fifty states. Again, wide variations exist, both in terms of the total number of enforcement actions and the mean severity levels. The state in which the most enforcement actions were conducted was New Jersey (with 9,076 actions). At the other extreme were North Dakota, which reported no enforcement actions, and both Montana and Wyoming, with only two enforcement actions reported during the entire period from 1975 to 1988! Additionally, only one enforcement action was reported for the territory of American Samoa.

Likewise, there is a broad disparity in the mean severity levels across the fifty states, from a high of 5.80 in Delaware (but with only 5 total enforcement actions) to a low of 1.22 in Maine (with 203 total enforcement

Table 3.4

Mean Severity of Enforcements by Region, 1975–1988

Region	Number of actions	Mean severity level	Standard deviation	Nonprimacy states	Territories
1	1,481	1.57	2.34	3	0
2	13,231	1.64	1.54	0	1
3	366	3.87	1.70	0	0
4	2,321	4.24	1.44	1	0
5	3,215	2.73	2.16	0	0
6	5,984	2.59	1.43	4	0
7	190	4.11	1.33	0	0
8	123	2.58	1.71	1	0
9	141	3.85	1.16	1	4
10	388	3.39	2.02	2	0

States and U.S. Territories by Region:
  1 = Connecticut, Maine,* Massachusetts,* New Hampshire,* Rhode Island, and Vermont
  2 = New York, New Jersey, and Puerto Rico
  3 = Delaware, Maryland, Pennsylvania, Virginia, and West Virginia
  4 = Alabama, Florida,* Georgia, Kentucky, Mississippi, North Carolina, South Carolina, and Tennessee
  5 = Illinois, Indiana, Michigan, Minnesota, Ohio, and Wisconsin
  6 = Arkansas, Louisiana,* New Mexico,* Oklahoma,* and Texas*
  7 = Iowa, Kansas, Missouri, and Nebraska
  8 = Colorado, Montana, South Dakota,* North Dakota, Utah, and Wyoming
  9 = Arizona,* California, Hawaii, Nevada, Guam, Micronesia, Trust Territories, and American Samoa
  10 = Alaska,* Idaho,* Oregon, and Washington

*Indicates that a particular state does not have primacy over its NPDES program.

actions), not counting North Dakota with a severity level of 0, since no enforcement actions were reported. As with the regional data, the data on the states demonstrate that there has been wide discretionary latitude, on the part of EPA personnel, in the actual enforcement of the clean water laws. The stated goal of national consistency has clearly not been achieved.

Primacy

Simply stating that variations exist in the level of EPA enforcement across regions and states is not satisfactory. Throughout the remainder of this book we will be interested in explaining why these variations exist. We therefore ask a fundamental question that we will return to throughout this book: What accounts for variations in NPDES enforcement across the EPA's ten regional offices and the fifty states? The main theme of this book is that EPA personnel have responded pragmatically to the diverse regulatory environment that is characteristic of surface-water problems in America. One key component of that diverse regulatory environment is organizational in nature and relates to the issue of primacy; that is, whether an individual state has primacy over its NPDES program or whether federal EPA officials implement the program. As can be seen in the lower half of Table 3.4, thirty-eight states have primacy over their NPDES programs, whereas the federal EPA has primacy in twelve states (the so-called nonprimacy states). The distinction between a primacy and a nonprimacy state is important. As we will describe in greater detail in Chapter 6, in states with primacy federal personnel largely operate in an oversight capacity. This means that state officials enforce the law, while federal officials ensure that the law is being adequately enforced. There are two possible relationships between federal and state personnel with regard to how they enforce the NPDES program. First, when state officials enforce the law directly, federal personnel may be more likely to conduct lower-level actions, such as issuing warning letters or notices of violation to spur state officials into action. In nonprimacy states federal personnel conduct all actions. Because the data in Tables 3.4 and 3.5 represent enforcement actions conducted by federal-level personnel only, we offer the following hypothesis:

> *Hypothesis 1:* A greater number of enforcement actions will be conducted by federal personnel in nonprimacy states and the magnitude of the mean severity levels will be greater, as well. Likewise, we would expect the number of enforcement actions conducted and the magnitude of the mean severity levels to be greater in regions that have more nonprimacy states.

There is, however, an alternative way of hypothesizing the relationship between primacy and federal enforcement activity. As we will empirically demonstrate in Chapter 6, it is clear that the states do most of the enforcement work in the thirty-eight primacy states, but it is also possible that they pass off the most serious enforcement cases to federal EPA personnel. If this is true, then we would expect to find precisely the opposite relationship from that hypothesized above, at least with regard to the magnitude of the mean severity level. EPA personnel would handle all of the cases in the nonprimacy states, including lower- and higher-level cases. As a result, the number of enforcements conducted by federal EPA personnel would still be expected to be greater in nonprimacy than in primacy states. But the mean severity levels for nonprimacy states would actually be lower because EPA

Table 3.5

Mean Severity of Enforcements by State and Territory, 1975–1988

State	Number of actions	Mean severity level
Alabama	245	4.15
Alaska	207	3.13
Arizona	48	4.15
Arkansas	957	2.77
California	54	3.76
Colorado	42	1.76
Connecticut	110	3.65
Delaware	5	5.80
Florida	300	4.11
Georgia	444	4.36
Hawaii	25	3.72
Idaho	57	3.09
Illinois	1,144	1.73
Indiana	424	4.43
Iowa	31	3.45
Kansas	4	3.75
Kentucky	751	4.52
Louisiana	1,235	2.71
Maine	203	1.22
Maryland	77	4.19
Massachusetts	778	1.33
Michigan	169	4.66
Minnesota	218	3.88
Mississippi	204	3.60
Missouri	149	4.30
Montana	2	3.00
Nebraska	10	3.00
Nevada	4	3.00
New Hampshire	275	1.52
New Jersey	9,076	1.53
New Mexico	144	2.44
New York	2,090	2.08
North Carolina	129	4.47
North Dakota	0	0.00
Ohio	1,172	2.57
Oklahoma	584	2.84
Oregon	12	3.33
Pennsylvania	196	3.72
Rhode Island	104	1.59
South Carolina	49	5.59
South Dakota	29	3.00
Tennessee	199	3.47
Texas	3,064	2.44
Utah	48	2.94
Vermont	11	5.91
Virginia	22	4.55
Washington	113	4.04

(continued)

Table 3.5 *(continued)*

State	Number of Actions	Mean Severity Level
West Virginia	66	3.55
Wisconsin	87	3.05
Wyoming	2	4.00
Guam	2	5.00
Puerto Rico	1,962	1.72
Micronesia	2	5.00
Trust Territories	4	5.00
Virgin Islands	103	1.45
American Samoa	1	5.00

personnel would be conducting many more higher-level actions in the primacy states, the cases passed off to federal personnel by the states. Thus we offer the following rejoinder:

Hypothesis 2: The number of enforcement actions conducted by federal personnel in nonprimacy states will be greater than the number conducted in primacy states, but the magnitude of the mean severity levels will be greater in the primacy states. We likewise expect that the magnitude of the mean severity levels will be greater in regions with more primacy states.

When we compare the two hypotheses, we expect to find the same relationship with regard to the number of enforcement actions conducted. The difference between the two hypotheses relates to the issue of the magnitude of the mean severity level of enforcement. In Hypothesis 1 we expect it to be greater in nonprimacy states. In Hypothesis 2 we expect it to be greater in primacy states.

We turn our attention first to the ten EPA regions. As can be seen in the lower half of Table 3.4, the largest number of nonprimacy states are located in regions 1 and 6. We posited in Hypothesis 1 that the severity levels would be greater in these regions, but the results indicate that they are not. As aforementioned, region 1 has the lowest mean severity level of any of the ten EPA regions, while the mean severity level for region 6 ranks seventh overall. The mean severity level in region 10, which has two nonprimacy states, ranks somewhat higher at fourth overall. Because two of the three regions with the greatest number of nonprimacy states rank at the low end, and the other toward the middle of the scale, it is apparent that the mean severity levels are not greater in regions composed mostly of nonprimacy states. This finding is consistent with Hypothesis 2.

In Table 3.6 we compare the mean severity levels for primacy and non-

Table 3.6

Primacy and Nonprimacy States

Type of state	Enforcements	Mean severity level	Standard deviation
All states:			
Primacy	18,436	2.24	1.89
Nonprimacy	6,929	2.44	1.73
T = 5.36			
Minus New Jersey:			
Primacy	9,210	2.99	2.11
Nonprimacy	6,929	2.44	1.73
T = 18.97			

primacy in the fifty states. As can be seen, the mean severity level for the twelve nonprimacy states was 2.44, while for the thirty-eight primacy states it was 2.24. The difference between the two groups of states is statistically significant, but not really substantively significant; a difference of only .20. These figures suggest that enforcement was comparable in the two types of states and that each clearly emphasized lower-level enforcement actions.

There is one potentially confounding factor in this analysis, however. This relates to the overwhelming number of enforcement actions conducted by federal personnel in the state of New Jersey. New Jersey is a primacy state, yet it accounts for approximately one-third of all of the EPA's regulatory activity. When asked about this point, EPA officials, including a former head of the EPA Water Office, told us that the EPA has had to keep a vigilant eye on New Jersey's state enforcement personnel. Otherwise, it was suggested, they simply will not do their job. Consequently, in terms of the overwhelmingly large number of federal actions conducted, New Jersey is different from other primacy states. This also accounts for the mostly low level of EPA activity in New Jersey, as represented by the mean severity level. EPA officials are not trying to enforce compliance from permittees, but rather are attempting to prompt recalcitrant state officials into action. By sending warning letters and other low-level actions directly to permittees, EPA officials have told us they are attempting to compel state officials to respond. Thus, the case of New Jersey is clearly consistent with the expectations posited in Hypothesis 1. Because, however, the federal response to New Jersey has been so overwhelming, in comparison to the other thirty-seven primacy states, we remove it from the analysis in the second half of Table 3.6. By doing so, we can derive a more accurate picture of how federal EPA surface-water personnel have enforced the law in the other thirty-seven primacy states.

As would be expected, once New Jersey is removed, wider variations are identified between the two groups of states. In nonprimacy states there were an average of 533 enforcement actions per state. In primacy states the EPA conducted only 256 actions on average. Thus, with the removal of New Jersey, the difference in the average number of actions per state jumps from about 35 to 277. This is consistent with both of our hypotheses.

In Hypothesis 1 we posited that the magnitude of the severity levels would be greater in the nonprimacy than in the primacy states. Once we remove New Jersey from the analysis, however, it is apparent that EPA NPDES personnel actually enforced the law at higher mean severity levels in the thirty-seven primacy states than they did in the twelve nonprimacy states. This finding is consistent with Hypothesis 2 and suggests that the primacy states do pass off many of their most serious cases to EPA personnel. The statistical results presented in Table 3.6 also demonstrate that primacy is one reason for the observed variations we have identified in Table 3.5. And even with our rudimentary analysis of the ten EPA regions, it is apparent that primacy is an important factor in determining regional variations, as well. Thus one factor that conditions the level of the NPDES response is primacy. We will therefore return to a more detailed empirical examination of primacy's effects later in this book.

The Permittees

Primacy relates to who has responsibility over the enforcement of the NPDES program. As we have shown, it is an important determinant of variations in the level of the federal NPDES enforcement response. Another possible explanation for variations in enforcements across the EPA's ten regions and the fifty states may be that EPA officials respond in varying degrees to different types of permittees, again both in terms of the number of enforcement actions conducted and in the magnitude of the mean severity levels. In particular, much of the evidence we have presented in this chapter suggests that EPA personnel see municipalities as the greatest threat to clean water. Other scholars also have noted the potential environmental hazards presented by municipalities. As Rosenbaum (1985: 167) noted,

> When the water pollution control amendments were written in 1972, it was obvious that the nations' municipal waste treatment systems had to be substantially improved. Municipal waste water was the largest source of BOD, coliform bacteria, phosphorus, and several other pollutants widely contaminating surface and subsurface waters across the United States. In the early 1970s, more than 21,000 municipal treatment plants were pouring wastes into the nation's waterways, yet only 16 percent were

achieving even secondary treatment levels needed to control the most commonly recognized of these pollutants.

As we already have noted, in our interviews with EPA officials, municipalities were cited most often as the type of permittee most likely to evade compliance with the Clean Water Acts. Interviews with water officials reported by Zachary Smith (1992: 109) also come to a similar conclusion. He wrote, "When asked why their surface water sources were below standards, nineteen state water officials identified municipal waste water as the first reason, and officials representing twenty additional states ranked municipal waste water as the second most important reason. Nonpoint sources of water pollution tied municipal waste water as the primary cause of water pollution." Giving further credence to these findings is a report of the EPA administrator (1991) that concluded that municipalities were the largest producers of point-source water pollution. The Council on Environmental Quality (1993: 227) likewise reported that, with regard to U.S. rivers, municipalities ranked second only to agriculture as a source of pollution. On the other hand, industrial-source pollution ranked sixth following agriculture, municipalities, habitat modification, resource extraction, and storm sewers/runoff. Likewise, in its 1988 report the Fund for Renewable Energy and the Environment (FREE 1988) concluded that industrial facilities have a better compliance record than municipal facilities. A survey conducted by the Association of State and Interstate Water Pollution Control Administrators (ASIWPCA 1984) also concluded that municipalities are a greater threat to the environment than industrial facilities. And as Ringquist (1993: 174) noted, "Industrial facilities have been especially successful in reducing their discharge of pollutants into the nation's waterways" (see also Magat and Viscusi 1990). Ringquist also warned, however, "These decreases are a bit misleading . . . Since the mid-1970s, nearly half of all industrial polluters have stopped discharging their wastes directly into waterways, discharging them instead into municipal wastewater treatment systems" (1993: 174). In short, then, this change in industrial discharge sites has placed a greater burden on municipalities. The results presented in Table 3.7 provide yet additional evidence confirming this opinion. The largest number of enforcements conducted by the EPA were against municipal facilities. Industrial facilities ranked second. An examination of the mean severity level exhibits even further trust in industry. On this measure industry ranked fourth out of the five available categories of permittees with a mean severity level of 2.79. Government facilities ranked at the top at 3.70, municipalities ranked second at 3.12, and sewage treatment plants (which are generally run by municipalities) ranked third with 3.07. Only public utilities ranked lower than industry at 2.73.

Table 3.7

Average Severity of Action by Type of Permittee, June 1988–June 1989

Type of permittee	Number of actions	Mean severity level
Industry	686	2.79
Public utility	64	2.73
Sewage treatment	498	3.07
Municipality	899	3.12
Government facility*	54	3.70

*Includes schools, armed services, and so forth.

One reason for the high ranking on this scale for government facilities may be that until 1992, when legislation provided the states with greater regulatory authority in this area, the Supreme Court had limited "state prosecution and civil penalties" against government facilities (Ringquist 1993: 74). As a result, EPA officials may have by necessity taken on a greater regulatory responsibility for these permittees.

In Table 3.8 we present data for the period from 1989–1992. The data reveal a similar pattern to that presented in Table 3.7. In both primacy and nonprimacy states NPDES officials have dedicated considerably more effort to municipalities than to industry. In nonprimacy states, with regard to minor permittees, the number of actions is nearly two to one in favor of municipalities. With regard to major permittees, municipalities account for 3,093 actions compared to only 1,969 for industry. When we examine primacy states, the results are similar. For minor permittees, municipalities have been subject to 338 enforcement actions, whereas industry has been subject to only 81. Regarding major permittees, municipalities have been subject to 1,002 actions, compared to just 322 for industry. These data confirm the reliability of our interviews with federal EPA officials. They also again provide another explanation for the variations we identified in Tables 3.4 and 3.5.

Our analysis therefore provides some explanations for state and regional variations in EPA enforcement. Only one task remains for us in this chapter. Before Rouse and Wright proceed to a detailed profile and analysis of the people who make up the NPDES program in the next chapter, we first turn to an updated analysis of aggregate data from the NPDES program for the period following from 1988 to July 1994. These aggregate data provide us with a means of determining if NPDES enforcement has continued to rely on lower-level enforcement actions in recent years.

Table 3.8

Type of Violations, 1989–1992

Type of permittee	Number of actions
Nonprimacy states: Minor permits	
Industry	618
Municipality	1,119
Federal	2
Small business	2
Nonprimacy states: Major permits	
Industry	1,969
Municipality	3,093
Federal	24
Primacy states: Minor permits	
Industry	81
Municipality	338
Primacy states: Major permits	
Industry	322
Municipality	1,002
Federal	17
Small business	2

An Update

In Table 3.9 we present the results of the aggregate data from January 1986 through July 1994. As can be seen, there is some minor overlap in the time periods between the data presented in Table 3.1, which included the years 1975–1988, and this second data set. Despite this time overlap we can still compare the two data sets to see whether the nature of the EPA enforcement response has changed over time. The more recent data set includes most of the categories of actions included in our original data set. With these data, there was less of a reliance on the part of EPA NPDES personnel with level 0 actions, the lowest level of response. As we move toward the end of the Reagan presidency, and on into the Bush and Clinton administrations, this number declines from 21.6 percent (see Table 3.1) to just 8 percent. The number of level 1 actions also declines somewhat from 8.3 percent to 5 percent. The tendency toward conducting most actions at the lowest levels continues, however. Level 2 actions increased from 40.2 percent for 1975–1988 to 55 percent in the later period. Consequently, 68 percent of all actions were still conducted at the three lowest levels, this compared to 70 percent for the years 1975–1988.

Table 3.9

**Types and Frequencies of Enforcement Actions Conducted by EPA
Officials, January 1988–July 1994**

Action	Frequencies	Percentage
0	5,730	8
1	3,787	5
2	39,213	55
3	4,177	6
4	412	1
5	14,779	21
6	3,299	5
7	462	1

When we move to higher-level actions there has been a slight decrease in
level 3 responses (from 8 to 6 percent), an increase in level 5 responses
(from 14.1 to 21 percent), a slight decline in level 6 responses (from 6.9 to 5
percent), and a slight increase in level 7 responses (from 0.4 to 1 percent).
Consequently, although there is some evidence of variations within response levels, the overall picture emerging from our more recent data set is
the same as that for the earlier period. Overall, we can conclude that
NPDES officials have not responded much differently, even during the
Bush and Clinton administrations, than they did during the Reagan years, at
least with regard to the preferred level of enforcement activity. In this
regard, most enforcement action continues to be conducted at the very
lowest levels. Although there has been an increase in level 5 and 7 actions,
these changes do not reflect a fundamental alteration in the regulatory enforcement philosophy of NPDES personnel. In fact, the data from Table 3.9
suggest that EPA NPDES personnel continue to employ a pragmatic enforcement approach.

Conclusions

In this chapter we introduced the concept of pragmatic enforcement. The
key to this concept is the idea that agency officials have not adopted an
ideological approach to enforcement, but rather adopt pragmatic strategies
to navigate through the various obstacles that exist to a stricter enforcement approach. In this chapter we delineated several such obstacles to a
strict enforcement approach, as they relate to the EPA's NPDES program.
For example, both the cost of legal action and the rules of evidence greatly
limit the federal courts as a feasible venue for a great deal of NPDES
activity. Likewise, the lack of sufficient resources has forced EPA enforce-

ment personnel to rely more heavily on lower-level enforcement actions, rather than a strict or hierarchical approach (see Melnick 1983; Yandle 1989). Our findings are therefore consistent with those of Gary Bryner (1987: 6), who wrote, "In virtually every case the scope of agency responsibilities and authority greatly exceeds the resources provided. Congress regularly only provides a fraction of the resources required to accomplish the regulatory tasks delegated to regulatory agencies. As a result, administrative agencies are given little guidance in their enabling statutes concerning how they should shape their regulatory agenda, set priorities and allocate scarce resources." This remark is certainly relevant to the situation of the EPA NPDES program. In addition to concerns over resources and agency responsibilities, most EPA officials we interviewed demonstrated a high-level of trust in the permittees they deal with on a regular basis, with the notable exception of municipalities. EPA officials informed us they believe the overwhelming majority of permittees will voluntarily comply with the law. Our analysis of EPA enforcement data then provided empirical support for this finding.

Most EPA officials also told us their ultimate goal is not strict enforcement of the law, but rather compliance with the law. As many EPA officials argued, so long as permittees comply with the law, the goal of the Clean Water Acts is being achieved. Therefore, whatever method brings about compliance is acceptable. If compliance can be achieved without resort to higher-level actions, then so much the better.

Given these views, it is not surprising that EPA NPDES personnel have adopted a pragmatic enforcement approach. This may, however, be disturbing, on a normative level, to many environmentalists and academics. Should mere pragmatic concerns dictate how a law will be implemented? The near unanimous response we got from NPDES personnel to this question, from all levels of the agency, and even from state level officials, was that if you want stricter enforcement you will have to provide us with the necessary resources to do the job. This means much larger budgets and many, many more enforcement personnel. In a time of federal and state budgetary retrenchment, this is not a likely alternative. In short, whether we like it or not on a normative level, pragmatic enforcement appears to be here to stay.

For us, the most troubling outcome of pragmatic enforcement is the observed variations across both regions and states. Therefore, in the chapters to follow we will combine the results of closed and open-ended interviews with EPA and state-level enforcement personnel, along with an empirical analysis of additional enforcement data, to empirically examine the reasons for these variations in enforcement practices. We will argue that variations in enforcements can predominantly be traced to variations in the regulatory environment that EPA officials deal with on a daily basis. As we argued earlier in this chapter, that regulatory environment is much more diverse than the one confronted by enforcement personnel working for the Nuclear Regulatory Commission. Over the next several chapters our goal will therefore be to show how variations in the surface-water regulatory environment nationwide have encouraged pragmatic solutions to water pollution problems. In so doing, our objective will not be to advocate pragmatic enforcement as a solution to regulatory problems, but rather to provide a sounder context under which its existence can be understood.

4

Bureaucrats and Attitudes: The Seeds of Discretion

Amelia Rouse and Robert Wright

Inherent in the idea of pragmatic enforcement is the notion of *bureaucratic discretion*—that individual bureaucrats choose among various enforcement options largely in response to the diversity of the regulatory environment. Bureaucratic discretion has been empirically tested in the literature on street-level bureaucrats (Lipsky 1971; Yin and Yates 1975; Worden 1984) which has described many manifestations of individual discretion within bureaucracies. This literature has also examined attributes that act as determinants of individuals behavior, such as race, class, and perceptions of clients. These studies are found predominantly in the literature of sociology, public administration, and urban studies. In contrast, relatively little attention has been paid to these individual-level concerns by political scientists (though see Meier, Stewart, and England 1991). This chapter examines the personal characteristics of bureaucrats in the Environmental Protection Agency's National Pollutant Discharge Elimination System as a first step toward discovering whether these traits affect their exercise of discretion when enforcing environmental regulations.

In addition to personal attributes and attitudes, there are political factors that might influence the behavior of individuals. As Wilson (1989: 13) wrote, "The freedom of action of bureaucrats is importantly constrained, and sometimes wholly determined, by the decisions of their political superiors." This is borne out in the literature about political control of the bureaucracy where it is shown that appointment decisions made by Congress and the president are influential in directing agency behavior, though this influence is not always in the anticipated direction (Wood 1988; see also Chapter 5 of this volume). Waterman, Rouse, and Wright (1994) found that NPDES personnel attribute substantial influence over their actions to political actors such as federal courts, Congress, and interest groups.

Of course, individuals' attributes are only one source of possible influence on agents' perceptions and exercise of discretion. The behavior of an individual in any organization is constrained by rules and norms of that organization. Standard operating procedures (SOPs) and other rules are in place to guide the bureaucrat in decision making. There is oversight by direct and indirect superiors, feedback from supervisors and coworkers, and there are incentives and sanctions in place to make sure the rules are followed (see Wilson 1989). The institutional decision-making context can be categorized by the amount of expertise and information available, the tractability of the issue, or by its place in the outside political sphere (Gormley 1987). This chapter does not address empirically the organizational constraints imposed on individual behavior in the EPA NPDES program; Hunter and Waterman turn to an analysis of that point in Chapters 6 and 7. We do, however, examine the individual attributes associated with discretion.

It stands to reason that in order to understand the outputs derived from pragmatic enforcement, that is, terms of compliance negotiated by bureaucrats with discretion in their enforcement behavior, we need to understand what variables influence their perception about the system in which they work, and about how their discretion can be used. To begin an investigation of these questions, we conducted a survey of environmental-enforcement bureaucrats.

Research Design

The respondents to this survey were seventy-two employees from eight of the EPA's ten regional offices who are responsible for enforcing the NPDES program.[1] The survey was composed of close-ended, multiple-choice questions, and limited-option, priority-ranking questions. In addition, a few open-ended questions were included when it seemed more appropriate to the subject matter. Respondents were asked questions to provide standard demographic information, and were asked questions about their political ideologies, their views of several environmental problems, and their perceptions of discretion involved with their job responsibilities.

The survey was administered through a mail questionnaire. This method has the advantages of eliminating interviewer bias inherent in face-to-face or telephone interviewing; guaranteeing that all members of our sample had an equal opportunity to be contacted; and providing the confidentiality necessary for agency personnel to answer questions of a potentially sensitive nature. To secure as high a response rate as possible we used the total design method (Dillman 1978), which consists of three steps. First, we sent an initial identifying letter in which we identified ourselves and briefly described the nature of the survey. This letter was sent to all the members of our target group. A week later a copy of the questionnaire with a cover letter and a self-addressed stamped envelope (SASE) was mailed. Three weeks after that a second copy of the survey was sent to those people who had not yet responded, along with another brief introductory letter and another SASE.[2] In this manner, seventy-two surveys were conducted from May 17 to September 30, 1994, making the response rate 37.8 percent.

This response rate suggests that caution be used when generalizing from the results of the study. Still, this research design is an improvement over the methods used by most scholars of the bureaucracy. In particular, this improvement is due to the use of the total design method of data collection, a close-ended survey, and the targeting of all EPA NPDES compliance and enforcement personnel.

Characteristics of NPDES Personnel

Who are the people who enforce the National Pollutant Discharge Elimination System's regulations? Does enforcement vary with the characteristics of the enforcers? If it does, then who these people are becomes a very important issue indeed. Overall, our sample is a highly educated group: fifty-three said they had an undergraduate degree and eighteen said they had at least one postgraduate degree. Nine of the inspectors declined to answer the education question and seven specified that they had "none" when asked to list the degrees they had received. Table 4.1 shows the frequency distribution of the types of degrees held by our respondents and of the relative fields in which they were awarded.

Almost 53 percent of the baccalaureate degrees (28 of 53) are in an engineering field, with Chemical and Civil Engineering each accounting for 19 percent of these. Nine percent of the undergraduate degrees are in biology, and seventeen percent are in other fields of the physical sciences. Degrees in the humanities or social studies (both included in the "other" category) account for 11 percent of the total. Altogether, 89 percent of the undergraduate degrees held by these NPDES personnel are in engineering or the physical sciences.

Of the enforcement personnel who had completed postgraduate educational work, the predominance of masters of sciences in engineering fields other than chemical or civil engineering was particularly noticeable. Chemical and civil engineering seemed to be popular undergraduate degrees, but there is only one M.S. in each of those fields. Sixty-seven percent (twelve

Table 4.1

Degrees and Fields of Study

	B.A.	B.S.	M.S.	Other	Total
Biology	3	7	0	0	10
Chemistry	1	3	0	0	4
Chemical engineering	0	10	1	0	11
Civil engineering	1	9	1	0	11
Environmental engineering	0	3	6	0	9
Other engineering	0	5	4	0	9
Other physical sciences	1	4	5	0	10
Other fields	5	1	1	5	12
Total degrees	11	42	18	5	76

N = 55

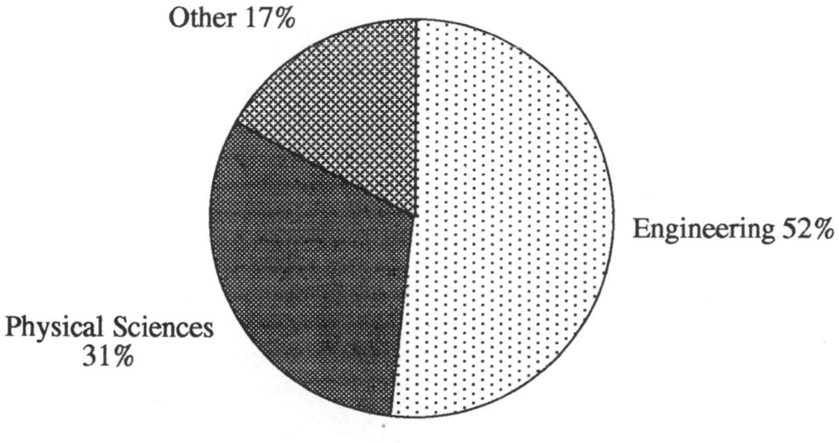

Figure 4.1. **Distribution of Degrees by Field**

of eighteen) of the postgraduate degrees held by our sample of NPDES respondents are in an engineering area, six of those in environmental engineering. The distribution of fields of study is slightly different between undergraduate and graduate level degrees, but similar in that both degree levels were dominated by engineering and physical-science specialists. Not only are the members of this group of enforcement personnel highly educated in general, but the people in these positions also tend to be trained in fields with considerable relevance to the demands of their jobs (see Figure 4.1).

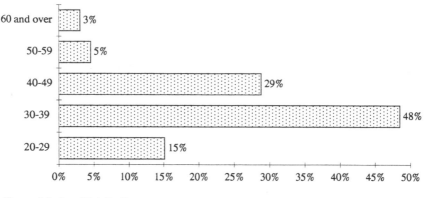

Figure 4.2. **Age Distribution**

In general, fields requiring more technical knowledge and expertise tend to be dominated by men. In light of the highly scientific and technical nature of the education for this group, one might suppose that the NPDES enforcement personnel would fit this pattern. Perhaps surprisingly, the ratio of women to men was nearly 1:1. Of those who indicated their sex, 47 percent (thirty-two) were women and 53 percent (thirty-six) were men; there were nearly equal numbers of women and men at each grade level. The sample frame for this study included only nonclerical enforcement and compliance personnel; therefore this parity is not a function of the sample being skewed by the inclusion of a predominantly woman-dominated job category.

We also asked the respondents their ages and whether they had children. Most of the respondents who provided information on their ages were in their thirties (see Figure 4.2). The median age was thirty-seven. Fifty-seven percent of our respondents indicated that they had children.

Another variable that is typically associated with attitudes is income. Given the nature of our sample, we expected the range of incomes for our respondents to be fairly narrow. In the civil service one's salary is associated with a GS-level. The GS-level ranks of the respondents were more varied than we had anticipated. The respondents' grade levels ranged from GS-4 to GS-14, however the majority (62 percent) of those who indicated their rank were GS-12s. In order to set a more accurate picture of the affluence of our respondents, we asked them to indicate their annual household incomes. Given that most of our respondents were all the same GS-level, annual household income also provides us with a wider range of incomes than we would have received if using individuals' salaries. The median household income for our respondents was between $60,000 and

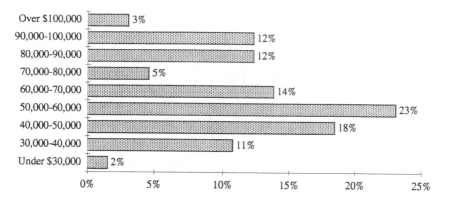

Figure 4.3. **Distribution of Household Income**

$70,000. The modal income, however, fell between $50,000 and $60,000. The distribution of incomes is shown in Figure 4.3.

Political Attitudes

We can also classify our respondents according to their beliefs, attitudes, and behaviors related to politics. In particular, certain assumptions about bureaucrats' political attitudes are common in general discourse. Among these, for example, are that bureaucrats are politically "liberal" and are predominantly Democrats. In order to investigate these questions, the bureaucrats were asked, "With which political party do you identify?" It is interesting to note that 22 percent (sixteen) of our respondents declined to answer this question at all (see Figure 4.4). This may reflect reluctance on the part of federal civil-service bureaucrats to seem overtly political, given that a requirement of their employment is that they limit personal political involvement.

Thirty percent (seventeen) of those who answered the party identification question stated that they did not identify with any political party. Of the twenty-nine who did indicate a party preference, almost three times as many said they were Democrats (twenty-eight) as Republicans (ten).[3] The fact that just under half (47 percent) of the entire sample of NPDES respondents did not indicate that they had an affinity for any political party does not mean that the group, as a whole, is disaffected from the political system. Only one respondent indicated that he or she was not registered to vote. Ninety-six percent of our enforcement personnel said that they had voted in the 1992 presidential election, and 80 percent said they had voted in their state's last gubernatorial race (see Figure 4.5). This reflects a far greater

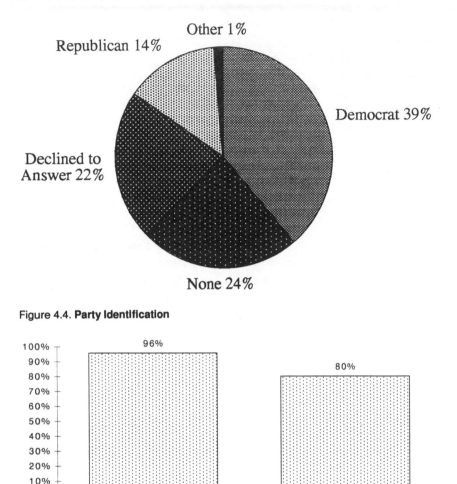

Figure 4.4. **Party Identification**

Figure 4.5. **Political Participation: Voting**

degree of voting participation than is characteristic of the general population. Only 55.9 percent of voters over eighteen years old, for example, voted in the 1992 presidential election.[4] When asked about the winner of that election, Bill Clinton, two-thirds (67 percent) of our respondents who rated the president's job performance said they approved. But just over half (55 percent) of those who rated Clinton's performance in regard to environmental issues approved.

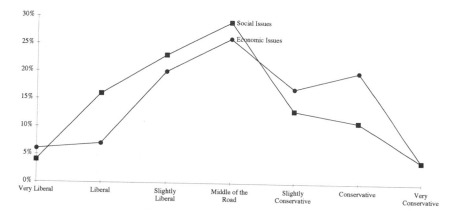

Figure 4.6. **Comparison of Self-placement on Ideology Scale for Social and Economic Issues**

To discover more about the NPDES enforcers' general political beliefs, we asked them to place their attitudes about social and economic issues on a seven-point scale of ideology ranging from very liberal to very conservative; these ideological placements represented each individuals' conceptions of the terms "liberal," "conservative," "social issues," and "economic issues;" the terms were not identified for the respondents. In regard to both social and economic issues, a plurality of respondents (28 percent and 26 percent respectively) defined themselves as "middle of the road." As displayed in Figure 4.6, respondents tended to have slightly more liberal leanings toward social issues and slightly more conservative leanings toward economic issues.

Environmental Attitudes

Because our respondents are charged specifically with enforcing environmental laws, it stands to reason that their attitudes about environmental issues might influence their enforcement style. We asked our respondents several questions about their attitudes toward and perceptions of environmental issues. A logical starting point was to find out how severe they thought environmental problems were at present. For this purpose we asked them to what extent they agreed or disagreed with the statement: "The environment can be made clean and safe without making drastic changes to our lifestyle" (see Figure 4.7). We would assume that the more serious respondents perceive problems facing the environment the more likely they would be to say lifestyles needed drastic modification. A majority of our

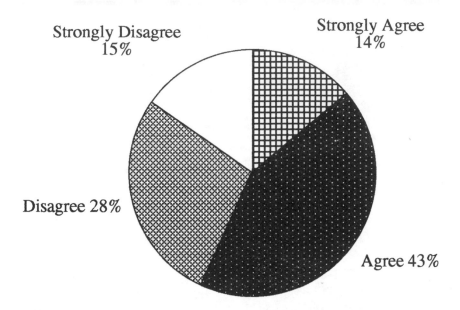

Strongly Disagree
15%

Strongly Agree
14%

Disagree 28%

Agree 43%

Figure 4.7. **"The environment can be made clean and safe without making drastic changes to our lifestyles."**

respondents (57 percent) agreed with the statement that drastic changes in lifestyle were *not* necessary to make the environment clean and safe. Those who indicated a strong reaction to this statement, however, were nearly equally divided between strong agreement (14 percent) and *strong* disagreement (15 percent).

Personal behavior might also be a good indicator of beliefs in regard to the environment. Eighty-three percent of our respondents indicated that they would be willing to keep their home thermostats at 65 degrees Fahrenheit during the winter. Nearly all (95 percent) indicated that they would be willing to take alternative transportation to work if it was made available. In fact, almost 78 percent said they already commuted to work by means other than driving their own cars; over half of our NPDES respondents indicated that they walked, bicycled, or took public transportation to work; and almost 25 percent carpooled.

Another factor we wanted to examine was the *salience* of environmental issues in the opinions of these bureaucrats. How did the environment weigh in against other concerns? When enforcers were asked what they thought was the single most important issue facing America today, only 10 percent indicated the environment (see Figure 4.8). This ranked environmental is-

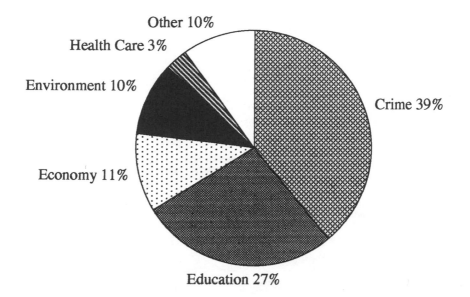

Figure 4.8. **Most Pressing Issue Facing the United States Today**

sues in a tie for fourth place, well behind crime (first) and education (second) as national concerns, and slightly behind the economy (third). If it is reasonable to expect that environmental issues would have high salience for NPDES personnel, then this result is somewhat surprising. Certainly it does not lead to the conclusion that these bureaucrats are environmental zealots. In addition, 10 percent of our respondents eschewed our list and offered their own most important issues, which included "moral decay," "population problems," and "political corruption." These are represented in the graph by the "other" category. From the same list of issues we then asked our respondents to rank order the second most important through the sixth most important issues. Figure 4.9 shows that the environment was ranked as either the third or fourth most pressing issue facing America by over half of the NPDES personnel who responded to this question.

Enforcement personnel were also asked which area of environmental law enforcement they thought deserved the most attention in the United States. The greatest number (24 percent) said that water pollution should be the primary target of environmental enforcement. Because all of these officials worked in surface-water pollution control, it is interesting that 76 percent of our respondents said that something other than water pollution should be the top priority: 17 percent chose air pollution, and 16 percent

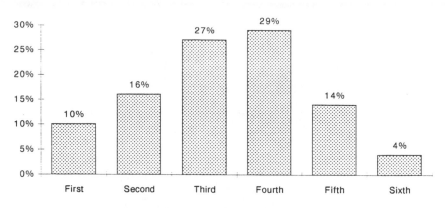

Figure 4.9. **Placement of "the Environment" in Issue Ranking**

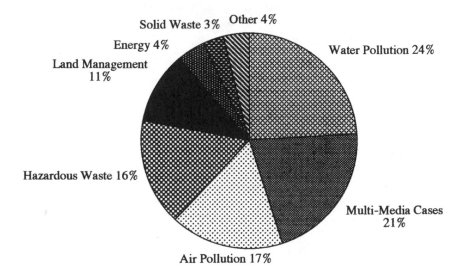

Figure 4.10. **Top Priority for Environmental Enforcement**

hazardous-waste disposal. Twenty-one percent of our respondents said multimedia cases should be the top priority of environmental enforcement. The complete response set is shown in Figure 4.10.

All in all, these results suggest that the NPDES personnel charged with administering the law are by no means "fanatics" about environmental problems generally, nor do they have a particularly biased assessment of the severity of water pollution problems as compared to other environmental issues.

Job Descriptions

Basic demographic information and political and environmental attitudes of our respondents gave us substantial information about the characteristics of the bureaucrats themselves. Also important, though, to possible bureaucratic discretion is what job the respondent holds. We examined several characteristics associated with the positions they occupy at the EPA. Most of our respondents have the title of environmental engineer (40 percent), environmental scientist (21 percent), or environmental specialist (20 percent). Five division chiefs were included in this sample, which might account for the higher-level GS ratings delineated in the previous section. On average, these enforcement personnel have worked for the EPA for 9.4 years, but most of them had been at the EPA for five or fewer years. In addition, nearly 40 percent (twenty-eight) of our respondents have, at one time, worked for a federal agency other than the EPA.

Now that we understand a little more about who the NPDES enforcement personnel are, let us look at their job responsibilities and their attitudes about various aspects of the atmosphere in which they operate as NPDES enforcers. EPA regions are varied in size and organized differently from each other. The maximum number of states included in any region is eight. Across the regional offices the mean number of states that each enforcement person primarily deals with is 2.5. Within their regions, EPA employees deal with as many as three hundred permittees or as few as two. The average number of permittees dealt with by each person is 52.8, the median is 30. To determine what kind of permittees our respondents handled, we offered them a list of three types of permittees and asked, "What type of permittee do you personally deal with most often?" Respondents most frequently chose a category not offered in our original list—"several of the above" (25 or 36 percent) (see Figure 4.11), but 34 percent said they dealt primarily with sewage-treatment facilities and 27 percent stated industrial permittees were their primary clientele.

What, exactly, do these enforcement people do in the course of their jobs? There are several actions that an NPDES enforcer might undertake in the course of his or her duties. Inspections and permit reviews are conducted with some regularity. Possible correctional actions include writing warning letters, notices of violation, and administrative orders. Our average respondent is responsible for 3.4 of these different tasks. Half as many people do only one task as do all five. This suggests that there are very few specialists among the respondents and that most of them deal with a large portion of the NPDES enforcement process.

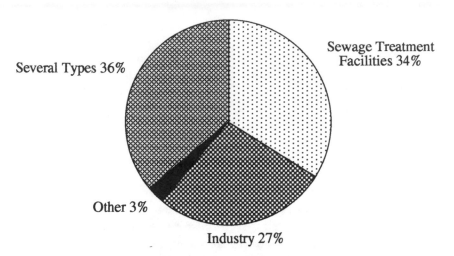

Several Types 36%

Sewage Treatment
Facilities 34%

Other 3%

Industry 27%

Figure 4.11. **Type of Permittee for Whom Respondents Are Responsible**

Table 4.2

Enforcement Activities (per respondent per month)

Variable	Mean # performed	Standard deviation	Modal # (%)	% of performers (N)
Warning letters	4.2	5.9	1.0 (30)	68 (48)
Notices of violation	2.8	2.9	0.0 (23)	57 (41)
Administrative orders	1.2	2.3	0.5 (15)	90 (65)
Inspections	2.1	2.4	1.0 (51)	60 (43)
Permits reviewed	6.3	8.8	1.0 (32)	56 (40)

As shown in Table 4.2, nine out of ten NPDES employees were responsible for recommending or sending administrative orders. The next most widely dispersed responsibilities were sending warning letters (which almost seven of ten do), and conducting inspections (six of ten). Slightly more than half of the respondents (57 percent) send notices of violation and about the same number review permits (56 percent).

Table 4.3

Frequency Distributions: Perceptions of Discretion in Agents' Tasks
(in percent)

Variable	None	Very little	Some	A great deal	Total	N
Inspections	2.3 (N = 1)	9.3 (N = 4)	46.5 (N = 20)	39.5 (N = 17)	2.3 (N = 1)	100 (43)
Warning letters	6.4 (N = 3)	6.4 (N = 3)	27.7 (N = 13)	44.7 (N = 21)	14.9 (N = 7)	100 (47)
Notices of violation	7.5 (N = 3)	10.0 (N = 4)	40.0 (N = 16)	32.5 (N = 13)	10.0 (N = 4)	100 (40)
Administrative orders	1.5 (N = 1)	6.2 (N = 4)	43.1 (N = 28)	43.1 (N = 28)	6.2 (N = 4)	100 (65)

Perceptions of Discretion

In addition to identifying the variety of tasks each of our respondents performed, we wanted to know how much discretion they perceived themselves as having with regard to each task they perform. Respondents were asked to indicate whether they thought they had no discretion, very little, some, a great deal, or total discretion in carrying out these duties. The results are presented in Table 4.3. The discretion associated with permit reviews was measured with a different scale than the other tasks and is displayed in Table 4.4.

For each type of task, the majority of respondents see themselves as having some or a great deal of discretion. The activity in which the greatest number of enforcers stated they had "total" discretion was the issuance of warning letters (15 percent). Issuing notice of violation is the task over which the largest number of respondents said they had no discretion (10 percent). The line graph in Figure 4.12 allows us to compare the amount of perceived discretion across all four tasks.

NPDES covers over sixty thousand specific conditional authorizations to discharge into surface waters in the United States. Businesses and government entities are required to have a permit to commence and continue to discharge each of the controlled pollutants. The permitting process involves review by federal enforcement personnel, even in primacy states (where they act more in a supervisory capacity), and review by the district engineer of the U.S. Army Corps of Engineers, as well as by other state and local

Table 4.4

Frequency Distributions: Perceptions of Discretion of Change Made or Recommended in Permits (in percent)

	Minor adjustment	2	3	4	Fundamental changes	N
Permits reviewed	40.0 (N = 16)	32.5 (N = 13)	20.0 (N = 8)	7.5 (N = 3)	0.0 (N = 0)	100 40

authorities. Permit reviews are mandated by the Clean Water Act and are more circumscribed by administrative guidelines than are the issuance of warning letters, notices of violation, or administrative orders.

The measurement of discretion used for the review of permits differed from that used for the other tasks. The scale used for the other four activities measured perceptions of discretion whereas the measurement for the permit review variable focused on the exercise of discretion. Discretion as it pertains to permit reviews is defined as the extent to which reviewers changed or recommended changes in permits they processed. We asked: "On a scale from 1 to 5 where 1 is minor adjustments and 5 is fundamental changes, in general, how would you characterize the changes you make or recommend in the permits you review?" Of the respondents who review permits, few are likely to make or recommend extensive changes in the permits they review (see Table 4.4). A plurality (40 percent) indicated that they make or recommend minor adjustments to permits.

The essence of a pragmatic enforcement style is that there are concerns other than the letter of the law that are considered when enforcing the NPDES regulations. Local economies can be affected by environmental laws. With this in mind, we asked respondents to indicate to what extent they considered the state of the local economy when enforcing the law. As presented in Figure 4.13, almost half (49 percent) of those who answered this question said they give "some" consideration to the state of the local economy; 17 percent said they did not consider it at all. On the whole, 73 percent of these NPDES enforcers reported that they took into account extenuating circumstances when enforcing the law. This indicates that although NPDES regulations do not always explicitly provide for extenuating circumstances, like economic conditions, by far most enforcers both perceive and act upon an amount of personal discretion when performing their duties.

In addition to the internal considerations and foibles these enforcement individuals bring to their implementation of the law, we were interested to

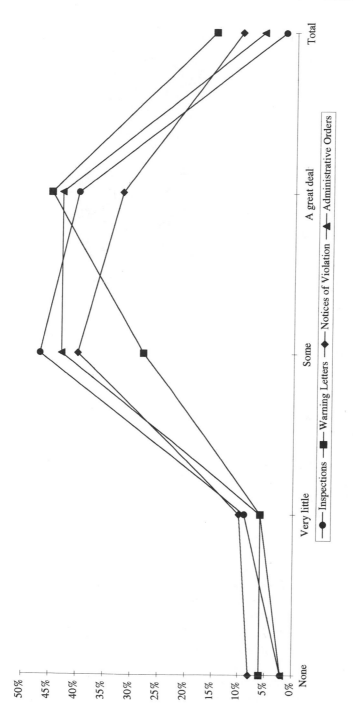

Figure 4.12. Perceptions of Discretion in Agents' Tasks

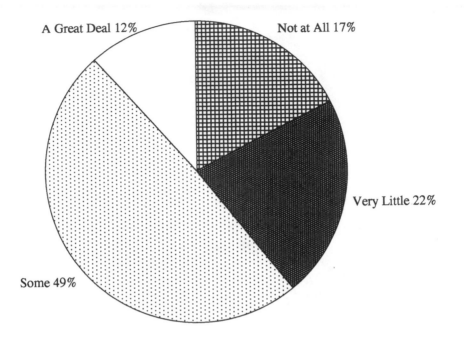

Figure 4.13. **"To what extent do you consider the state of the local economy when enforcing the law?"**

see if they perceived any external obstructions to their enforcement of the law. Respondents were asked to rank five different potential obstacles to their enforcement of the NPDES laws. The most frequently mentioned problems were insufficient allocation of resources (47 percent) and bureaucratic inefficiency (25 percent). Although such problems do not indicate discretion by individuals, they do have pertinence to the concept of a pragmatic enforcement style. Circumstances have consequences for how personnel enforce the law.

Demographic Summary

When we assemble the information that we have acquired so far, we can begin to form a generalized picture of the bureaucrats who enforce the Clean Water regulations. Somewhat to our surprise, the group includes nearly as many women as men. They are highly educated, many at the postgraduate level, and tend by training to be engineers or physical scientists of some type. The average enforcer is in his or her thirties, is a GS–12 with a little over nine years experience at the EPA, and enjoys an annual household income of $60,000 to $70,000.

Politically, the most experienced attribute of the NPDES enforcement personnel is their extremely high rate of participation in elections at both the presidential and the gubernatorial levels. By and large they are not very partisan. They are about as likely as not to identify with any political party. Those who do are about three times as likely to be Democrats as Republicans. They tend to be ideologically slightly conservative about economic issues and slightly liberal about social issues. In regard to the environment, the majority of NPDES respondents believe that something other than water pollution should be the top priority of environmental enforcement. When the environment is compared to other issues, most respondents do not think that it is as pressing an issue as crime or education. Obviously, then, the NPDES enforcement staff is not characterized by political or environmental radicalism.

Finally, we believe the attributes of bureaucrats presented here are important to consider as a first step toward identifying the characteristics that help govern individuals' discretionary behavior. According to a pragmatic enforcement model, who enforces the law should be of great importance; in other words, unlike the principal-agent model, it does not assume that all bureaucrats are driven by the same motivations. In this case, the commonly held perception that bureaucrats, especially those in technical and scientific areas, are male and politically liberal, has been shown to be erroneous. Obviously individuals' behavior cannot be attributed to characteristics the individuals in question do not possess. The determination of what characteristics affect perceptions of discretion and individual behavior, and to what degree they do so, is the subject of the next section of this chapter.

Determinants of Perceptions of Discretion

As discussed above, the pragmatic enforcement model presupposes that bureaucratic discretion exists, that is, the freedom of individuals to make choices among various enforcement options. Our NPDES sample offers sufficient variation in demographic characteristics and political environmental attitudes to examine whether the perceptions of discretion and exercise of discretion within this group are, in part, shaped by these types of variables. In this section we will identify the factors that effect the perceptions of discretion and exercise of discretion among our NPDES respondents.

Our survey asked respondents to rate, on a scale of 1 to 5, how much discretion they had in issuing administrative orders (AOs). It must be remembered that their responses reflect their perceptions of discretion, not any measure of how much discretion they might in fact have according to some objective criteria. AOs are classified as formal actions but there are few procedural dictates governing AOs. As discussed above, respondents were more likely to report having "some" or a "great deal" of discretion in regard to AOs (83 percent; see Table 4.3).

In the following analysis, we use ordinary least squares (OLS) regression to test the basic models for the influence of various independent variables upon perceptions of discretion.[5] Political-science literature, to date, offers little theoretical guidance for the construction of models using perceptual dependent variables. Work in the field of psychology suggests that general personal characteristics affect how people perceive their environments. Our survey included questions about age, gender, and parental status. Variables commonly considered by political scientists in their exploration of political attitudes were also included in our analysis. These variables include education, political ideology, party identification, political participation, attitudes toward the environment, and perceptions of the influence of various political actors and institutions (for a more detailed analysis of this see Waterman, Rouse, and Wright 1994).

Administrative Orders

Our original model explaining the perceptions of discretion in the issuance of administrative orders included all the dependent variables mentioned above. In the interest of clarity, only the variables with statistically significant coefficients are presented in Table 4.5. Because we are interested in the relative impact of each of the independent variables within our model, the discussion of our findings will be limited to their standardized coefficients.

In this model of the perceptions of discretion involved in the issuance of administrative orders the strongest relationship is the level of perceived influence associated with state legislatures (std. coeff., −.389). This is the only statistically significant exogenous political variable in the model and it is associated with perceptions of decreased discretion—for example, the more influence respondents attribute to the state legislatures, the less discretion they perceive themselves as having.

The other three variables in the model represent personal characteristics—age, parenthood, and self-placement on the ideology scale. It is difficult to predict the directional effect of age on perceptions of discretion. In this case, age (std. coeff., .249) is positively associated with perceptions of increased discretion for this task. Having children (std. coeff., .219) is positively associated with increased perceptions of discretion in the issuance of AOs, which means that being a parent tends to increase perceptions of discretion. Why this would be so is not immediately clear. It is possible that these findings reflect the natural process of maturation: as people get older

Table 4.5

Determinants of Perceptions of Discretion for Administrative Orders

Variable	Coefficient	Standard error	Standard coefficient	t–value
State legislatures	−.325	.089	−.389	−3.666
Age	.023	.010	.249	2.250
Have child(ren)*	.355	.172	.219	2.057
Ideology	.152	.059	.260	2.562
Adjusted R–square	.425			

*Yes = 1 for this dummy variable.

and acquire additional responsibilities, they somehow come to see themselves as having greater discretion and are less likely to perceive themselves as going strictly by the book.

Increasing conservative ideological self-identification is also associated with perceptions of increased discretion for this enforcement activity (std. coeff., −.260). There could be any number of explanations for this. Conservatives might be more likely than liberals, for example, to adopt a pragmatic enforcement style, believing that the strict enforcement of environmental regulations is "unreasonable" and that these regulations should be better tailored to individual cases. As Hunter and Waterman noted in the Introduction to this book, liberals are more likely to favor the strict enforcement model, whereas conservatives are more likely to favor the negotiated approach. Our findings, with respect to EPA personnel, appear to support that conclusion.

The model in Table 4.5 has an adjusted R-square of .425, meaning that almost 43 percent of the variance in perceptions of discretion for this task can be accounted for by two demographic variables (age and parenthood), respondents' self-placement on a standard liberal/conservative scale, and the perceived influence of the state legislatures in the respondents' regions or states. The one variable that decreased the level of perceptions of discretion associated with the issuance of administrative orders was the perceived influence of state legislatures.

Permit Reviews

In Table 4.6 we examine the factors related to the extent to which NPDES personnel make adjustments in the permits they review.[6] As is evident in Table 4.6, the enforcement personnel's view of the Clinton administration's

Table 4.6

Determinants of Exercise of Discretion for Permit Reviews

Variable	Coefficient	Standard error	Standard coefficient	t–value
Presidential budget recommendations	−.572	.210	−.408	−2.720
Believe Clinton supports environmental regulation	−.564	.248	−.338	−2.273
Several types of permittees	.607	.285	.313	2.126
Adjusted R–square	.232			

support for environmental regulation (std. coeff., −.338) and whether they think the Clinton administration is influenced by the agency's current enforcement behavior when making budget recommendations for the EPA (std. coeff., −.408) is related to the extent to which NPDES personnel make changes in the permits they review. If respondents see the budget recommendations of the Clinton administration as reflective of their own enforcement activity, they tend to characterize the changes they made to the permits they reviewed as more fundamental (as opposed to minor changes). This could be seen as an exercise of discretion. However, believing that the Clinton administration's attitude toward environmental regulation is actively supportive is associated with a decrease in the discretion exercised in the permit reviews; that is, it is more conducive to making only minor adjustments. These contradictory influences are interesting and would seem to suggest that the president's cues to his agents (EPA enforcement personnel) might work at cross purposes. Unfortunately, we can only speculate as to why budget-related factors would stimulate greater discretion and why the Clinton administration's support for regulation would lead to a reduction in discretionary activity.

The third statistically significant variable in this model is a dummy for whether the respondents worked with only one type of permittee (e.g., only public utilities) or with several types of permittees (e.g., public utilities, private businesses, and government facilities). Responsibility for a variety of permittees is associated with an increased exercise of discretion (more fundamental changes) over the permit reviewed (std. coeff., .607). There are several possible explanations for this result. One might be that people who work with one type of permittee may be more likely to be "captured" by that permittee—enforcement personnel might have more input into the original permit and would therefore be less likely to make major permit revisions. Another explanation might be that an enforcement person would be able to be more familiar with individual permittees if he or she only works with a few clients. The adjusted R-squared (.232) suggests that these three variables account for nearly a quarter of the variance for the discretion exercised in the permit review process.

Conclusion

As we have seen, the bureaucrats who enforce the NPDES regulations are, on average, highly educated and no more likely to be men than women. Politically they are not particularly partisan or ideological, though they are more likely to be Democrats than Republicans. They also report a higher level of participation in elections than does the general public. Their impressions of the salience of environmental issues in general and water issues in particular would not earn them the label of "rabid environmentalists." In short, given the "middle of the road" and nonzealous environmental nature of our NPDES respondents, it is not surprising that they would employ a pragmatic enforcement style.

Perhaps even more interesting is our finding that if the erroneous picture of EPA bureaucrats as liberal, male, radical environmentalists were accurate, it would make little difference in the way environmental laws are actually enforced. Given the characteristics we examined, our study suggests that there is a minimal connection between perceptions of discretion and personal characteristics and none at all between these characteristics and the exercise of discretion.

The authors of the next chapter turn their attention to an analysis of aggregate data on NPDES enforcement activity. In so doing they provide yet another means of operationalizing and analyzing the propensity of EPA personnel to exercise bureaucratic discretion. They also present a test of three theories of the possible relationship between hierarchy and bureaucratic discretion. In Chapters 7 and 8, Hunter and Waterman then provide an examination of the determinants of bureaucratic discretion.

Notes

1. Personnel in regionally specific programs, for example, ocean dumping, were not included.

2. The calculation for the percentage increase in response rate generated by the nth wave of a survey suggested that a third wave of the survey would have generated a 1.3 percent increase (approximately) in the response rate. Therefore, a third wave was not sent.

3. One person indicated "other."

4. Thomas, et al. (1994: 85).

5. For this analysis we are violating an assumption of OLS by treating ordinal data as if it were interval data. Though this is a common practice in political science, it is

important to be aware of the potential biases a violation of this assumption can introduce. We have no reason to expect, however, that this potential would alter the general conclusions made here.

6. Although the assumptions of the intervalness of a four- or five-category ordinal variable may give some researchers pause, we verified the results of the OLS analysis with an ordered probit analysis.

5

Bureaucratic Discretion and Hierarchical Political Control

Susan Hunter, Richard W. Waterman, and Robert Wright

In Chapter 3 we argued that EPA NPDES personnel employ a pragmatic enforcement approach to enforce surface-water pollution control legislation because a strict by-the-book approach is not feasible. This is because of the diverse nature of the existing regulatory environment. As Rosenbaum (1985: 156) wrote, the 1972 Federal Water Pollution Control Act delegated "enormous administrative discretion . . . to the EPA in prescribing the multitude of technologies that must be used by effluent dischargers to meet the many different standards established by the law." Likewise, we have argued that the provisions of the 1972 act, and the EMS manual establishing the operating procedures for the NPDES program, have delegated considerable discretion to NPDES personnel.

In Chapter 4 Rouse and Wright provided empirical evidence demonstrating that NPDES personnel perceive themselves as possessing considerable discretion in the performance of their jobs. They also provided an empirical analysis of the determinants of that discretion. The existence of bureaucratic discretion raises other issues which we have yet to address, however. In particular, is the bureaucratic discretion that Rouse and Wright empirically identified consistent or inconsistent with hierarchical political control of the bureaucracy by the so-called principals of the principal-agent model? On this point, Landis, Roberts, and Thomas (1994:6) wrote, "Agencies like EPA exercise much discretion in choosing which master to serve, and for what purposes. Constitutional law leaves their relationship to Congress and the President ambiguous. Statutes do not and cannot fully guide their behavior. Thus they possess substantial power that needs to be understood, managed, and used to advance democratic purposes."

If the behavior of NPDES personnel is not guided by any principles of political hierarchy or overhead democracy and if existing laws necessarily provide bureaucrats with wide discretionary authority when they enforce the law, then democratic accountability may be at risk. A wide variety of scholars over the past few decades have advanced this particular thesis. In this chapter, however, we will approach the issue of bureaucratic discretion from a different direction. We will present evidence suggesting that bureaucratic discretion and hierarchical political control actually coexist. We will then argue normatively that the two should coexist; that is, that bureaucratic discretion is a necessary component of enforcement in agencies such as the EPA, where the regulatory environment is diverse and procedures and laws are necessarily imprecise.

Pragmatic Enforcement and Bureaucratic Discretion

Because it involves a choice by agency personnel of which regulatory approach is appropriate under different circumstances, the pragmatic enforcement approach, by its very nature, means that agency personnel will employ considerable bureaucratic discretion when they enforce the law. It is therefore imperative that we analyze in some detail the relationship between the concepts of pragmatic enforcement and bureaucratic discretion. Scholars (e.g., Lowi 1979) have long argued that bureaucratic discretion or "policy without law" is most likely to occur in those agencies that are not guided by strict legislative provisions or clear procedures, rules, and regulations. Likewise, we argue that pragmatic enforcement will occur when existing legislative provisions and the resulting administrative procedures create unrealistic demands on agency personnel. An example of this is when full and proper implementation of the law is simply not feasible because a sufficient number of agency personnel are not present to enforce the law in the prescribed manner. Another example is when the necessary fiscal resources are not available to support strict enforcement of the law. Under these circumstances, agency personnel will either find alternative solutions to enforcement problems or leave the law largely unenforced. According to Gary Bryner (1987: 207), this description is commensurate with prevailing conditions at the EPA:

> The EPA's statutes are much more detailed than those of their sister agencies, but with only a few exceptions, such as those for automobile emissions under the Clean Air Act, the agency is given little guidance about the substance of regulations. . . . The statutory responsibilities dwarf the resources given, and give little guidance for how they should be allocated. EPA statutes include lengthy lists of actions to take and deadlines to achieve that the agency

cannot even begin to accomplish. This does little to set priorities or give direction: if everything is a priority then nothing is.

From Bryner's description, it appears the EPA would to be conducive to both pragmatic enforcement and the employment of a large degree of bureaucratic discretion on several dimensions (e.g., inadequate legislative guidance, lack of sufficient agency personnel, and lack of adequate fiscal resources). As we argued in Chapter 3, the nature of the regulatory environment also has much to do with the likelihood that agency personnel will adopt a pragmatic enforcement approach; that is, the broad diversity of surface-water pollution control issues is clearly one factor related to the adoption of a pragmatic enforcement approach. Likewise, on this dimension surface-water pollution control appears to favor the employment of broad bureaucratic discretion. As of 1976 "about 42,000 industrial facilities" discharged "their wastes into the nearest ditch, creek, river, lake, or estuary" (Conservation Foundation 1976: 5). This large number of dischargers created immediate problems for EPA personnel. As the Conservation Foundation reported, "Many [industrial facilities] discharge from not one but several sources, sometimes from pipes buried underground. Just finding and listing all these discharge points is an administrative problem of immense proportions. Add to this the vast number of car washes, service stations, laundromats, and other small commercial establishments which often dump into a small urban drainageway behind their property" (ibid.).

In summary, for the NPDES "regulatory program . . . to be successful" the Conservation Foundation recommended that it "must establish controls on industrial facilities as simple as a beet sugar refinery in Idaho and as complex as a petrochemical refinery in Louisiana" (ibid.). The challenge to strict enforcement of the law, then, is that a wide array of dischargers are involved in activities related to surface-water pollution, as well as an incredibly diverse set of dischargers. Add to this the complicated array of possible point and nonpoint pollutant sources, as discussed in Chapter 1, and it is clear that the regulatory environment alone ensures that enforcing the Clean Water Acts will be a monumental undertaking for agency personnel. Even under the best of circumstances, then, NPDES personnel would have great difficulty anticipating in advance each possible enforcement problem. Given the lofty goals and inadequate direction provided by the 1972 Clean Water Act and subsequent legislation, combined with a lack of sufficient enforcement personnel and fiscal resources, it is therefore not surprising at all that the NPDES program has been characterized by a pragmatic enforcement approach and broad employment of bureaucratic discretion.

In fact it can be argued that given existing circumstances, NPDES personnel have done a remarkable job of finding solutions to a wide variety of unanticipated, complicated, and in some cases near intractable problems.

The problem with the above discussion, as far as it relates to bureaucratic theory, is that enforcement personnel apparently must possess and employ considerable discretion in order to decide which enforcement response will best address a particular situation. This means that the development and use of bureaucratic discretion is an inevitable by-product of the pragmatic enforcement approach and the diversity of the regulatory environment characteristic of surface-water pollution problems. Most bureaucratic scholars perceive discretion as an essential problem to be eliminated, however, rather than a predisposition to be encouraged. Many scholars, for example, have been particularly critical of Congress for delegating broad authority to the bureaucracy in the first place. For example, Sharfman (1931–37), in his four-volume study of the Interstate Commerce Commission, contended that Congress delegates too much authority to the bureaucracy. Later, George Calloway (1946: 242) wrote, "Congressmen generally recognize the need for delegating legislative power as a means of reducing their workload and of taking care of technical matters beyond the competence of Congress. But they believe that the great growth of administrative lawmaking has become a menace to the constitutional function of Congress as the legislative branch of the national government."

Perhaps the best known critic of congressional delegation of authority to the bureaucracy has been Theodore Lowi (1979: 274) who argued,

> The federal government literally grew by delegation. Although Congress continued to possess the lawmaking authority, it delegated that authority increasingly in statute after statute to an agency in the Executive Branch or to the president, who had the power to subdelegate to an agency. At first this delegation was rationalized as merely "filling in the details" of congressional intent and therefore consistent with even the most orthodox definition of the separation of powers. But ultimately delegation was recognized for what it really was—administrative legislation.

Lowi also argued that congressional transfers of authority to the bureaucracy have imperiled the democratic process, inasmuch as bureaucrats are neither accountable to elected officials nor, by mere extrapolation, to the public that elects them. In fact much of the argument against bureaucratic discretion is based on the premise that elected politicians, the so-called principals of the principal-agent model, do not have the ability to control their bureaucratic agents, such as the enforcement personnel of the EPA NPDES program. For example, Ripley and Franklin (1986: 41) wrote,

"governmental bureaucracies are not fully controlled by any superior."
They continued, "They have some accountability to Congress and the president, but it is not final." Likewise, Dodd and Schott (1979: 173) wrote,
"The highly dispersed nature of oversight responsibility, the lack of strong
central oversight committees, and the natural conflict among committees all
undermine severely the ability of Congress to conduct serious, rational
control of administration." Lowi (1979: 307) even went so far as to argue,
"Little in the political science literature is clearer than the analysis of Congress showing the shortcomings of efforts to gain administrative accountability through legislative oversight and through the development of
legislative intent." Many other scholars have expressed agreement with this
viewpoint or have argued that Congress has a limited ability to control
executive branch agencies (e.g., Landis 1939; Scher 1960; Wildavsky 1964;
Fenno 1966; McConnell 1966; Redford 1969; Bibby and Davidson 1972;
Ogul 1976, 1981; Stone 1977; Sundquist 1981).

Presidential scholars and others writing about the presidency have also
asserted that the chief executive makes little effort to control the bureaucracy. For example, Noll (1971: 36) wrote, "Although the president could
exercise authority . . . there is little evidence that he or his administration
makes much of an attempt to do so." Likewise, Katzman (1980a: 182; see
also 1980b) wrote, "A chief executive simply does not have the time to
immerse himself in the appointment process." Such eminent scholars as
Rossiter (1956), Fenno (1959), Koenig (1975), and Cronin (1980) also advanced similar arguments about the limited capability of the presidency to
control the bureaucracy, while Heclo (1977) and Kaufman (1981) argued
that presidential appointees exert little influence over the bureaucracy. Not
all scholars agreed with this thesis, however. Meier (1979), for example,
argued that presidents had sufficient resources to influence the bureaucracy.
Still, most scholars believed that presidents neither were capable of, nor had
sufficient interest in, controlling the bureaucracy.

Additionally, bureaucratic scholars argued that the courts played a passive role in oversight of the bureaucracy. Woll (1963: 109–10) wrote, the
"courts have retreated from exercising meaningful oversight" of the bureaucracy. Lowi (1979) lambasted the court's deferential attitude toward the
bureaucracy, while recommending that the judiciary play a more vigilant
oversight function, returning to the spirit of the *Scheter* case.

Much of the legitimacy of the criticism of bureaucratic discretion is thus
dependent on the assumption that elected principals are essentially passive
participants in the bureaucratic process. Yet considerable research in recent
years has challenged this premise. Nathan (1983), Waterman (1989), and
Aberback (1990), for example, argued that presidents and Congress play an

active role in the oversight of the bureaucracy, and Melnick (1983) documented the much more active role the courts play in the enforcement of environmental legislation. Likewise, a number of empirical studies concluded that such diverse political principals as the president, the Congress, and the courts have played an active and successful role in overseeing the bureaucracy (see for example, Randall 1979; Stewart and Cromartie 1982; Moe 1982, 1985; Weingast and Moran 1983; Weingast 1981, 1984; Cohen 1985; Yantek and Gantrell 1988; Wood 1988, 1990; Hansen 1990; Hedge and Jallow 1990; Wood and Waterman 1991, 1993, 1994; Waterman and Wood 1991, 1993; Wood and Anderson 1993; Krause 1994). These empirical studies raise serious doubts about the major premise employed by critics of bureaucratic discretion; that is, they demonstrate hierarchical control of the bureaucracy does exist. They do not, however, tell us what happens to bureaucratic discretion when hierarchical political actors control the bureaucracy.

A few scholars have addressed this point. For example, Wooley (1993: 109) wrote that even when hierarchical actors attempt to control the bureaucracy, "there will always be some range of regulatory discretion." He even discussed the conditions under which bureaucratic discretion could be expected to increase or decrease. Specifically referring to the assumptions of the congressional dominance model of political control, Wooley continued (ibid.), "Regulatory discretion increases as ideological distance increases between gatekeeper [congressional] committees and/or as distance increases between those committees and floor medians."

Likewise, in an analysis of the EPA Water Office, Ringquist (1995a: 360) wrote, "EPA was responsive not only to the wishes of a popularly elected president and Congress, but also to the values of clientele groups and public opinion." At the same time, Ringquist concluded that EPA personnel employed bureaucratic discretion in the performance of their job. On this point he added normatively, "Public bureaucracies play a legitimate role in American government not simply by responding to political directives, but also by using their expertise to craft policy solutions, by being faithful to legislative intent and statutory requirements." He then added, "Governance would be almost impossible if agencies did not sometimes act on these larger perspectives of responsiveness and legitimacy."

Although they have not examined the relationship between hierarchical control and discretion, other scholars have likewise defended the utility of bureaucratic discretion. For example, Francis Rourke (1984: 37), while also expressing some concerns about widespread discretion, wrote, "Without administrative discretion, effective government would be impossible in the infinitely varied and rapidly changing environment of twentieth century society." Likewise, such diverse scholars as Joseph Harris (1965), Kenneth

Davis (1969a, 1969b), Anthony Downs (1967), Gary Bryner (1987), and Kiewiet and McCubbins (1991) have defended the role that bureaucratic discretion plays in a modern society.

Some scholars (e.g., Wooley 1993; Ringquist 1995) examined bureaucratic discretion from the relationship of a principal-agent model, but most research to date on the subject comes from analyses of so-called street-level bureaucrats (see Lipsky 1980). But this is not the only means of conceptualizing bureaucratic discretion. As Ringquist (1995a: 339) wrote, "Discretion can also be exercised by mid-level civil servants (determining acceptable civil penalties, determining research designs), upper-level civil servants (setting agricultural-loan interest rates, approving operating licenses), and political appointees (accepting final administrative rules, setting the discount rate)." In fact a number of studies have suggested that bureaucratic discretion plays an important role in a variety of regulatory agencies. For example, Handler (1986) found that some level of bureaucratic discretion inevitably results from regulatory enforcement. Hutter (1989) found that discretion is related to the size of a regulator's caseload. Hedge, Menzel, and Williams (1988) found that more experienced inspectors for the Office of Surface Mining and Reclamation, and inspectors with more critical views of the regulated industry, issued more notices of violation. Scholz and Wei (1986) found that compliance-monitoring personnel employ considerable discretion. And, of course, Rouse and Wright (in Chapter 4 of this volume) found that NPDES personnel perceive themselves as possessing and exerting a considerable degree of bureaucratic discretion. As a whole, then, these studies suggest that bureaucratic discretion is related to the personal characteristics of enforcement personnel and their jobs.

Our goal is to build on the prior research of scholars such as Wooley and Ringquist, as well as the work of the various scholars who have suggested that discretion is related to a regulator's job characteristics. In the section to follow we will introduce three competing theories postulating a relationship between discretion and hierarchical control of the bureaucracy. Then we will analyze NPDES enforcement data from each of the EPA's ten regional offices to examine empirically the relationship between discretion and hierarchical control. In so doing our goal is to develop more dynamic theories of the interrelationships between principals and agents in the bureaucratic process.

Political Control and Bureaucratic Discretion

There are at least three possible relationships between hierarchical political control and bureaucratic discretion. First, as many scholars have argued, discretion could promote a bureaucracy that is unaccountable to elected superordinates. Under these circumstances we would expect evidence of both bureaucratic discretion and a lack of bureaucratic responsiveness to the goals/preferences of elected officials. This is the traditional argument advanced by such scholars as Lowi (1979). A second possibility is that political hierarchy could diminish attempts at bureaucratic discretion. In other words, political control from the top down could mitigate against bureaucratic initiatives from the bottom up. In this case we would expect to see clear evidence of political control by elected officials, but only limited or no evidence of discretion by bureaucratic agents. A third possibility, suggested by the research of Wooley (1993) and Ringquist (1995), is that both top-down and bottom-up effects could coexist simultaneously. In this case, elected officials would exert control from the top, thus constraining bureaucratic activities within a certain permissible range of action. Bureaucrats, however, would still be free to exert some level of discretion in carrying out the law. Under this scenario, we would expect to find clear evidence of both hierarchical control and bureaucratic discretion. We will refer to the first theory as the dominant bureaucracy model, the second as the obsequious bureaucracy model, and the third as the interactive bureaucracy model.

To test these three models we will use a variant of the methodological approach employed by Wood and Waterman (1993, 1994) in their analysis of the enforcement activity of four EPA divisions. Our analysis will examine only one division, the EPA Water Office, but will retain the multispatial approach of Wood and Waterman's analysis by examining the EPA's ten regional offices. We have chosen regions, rather than divisions, because our primary interest in this book is the enforcement of the NPDES program. But also, as we have been repeatedly told in interviews with top EPA personnel, each regional office tends to have its own regulatory philosophy. As a former head of the EPA Water Office told us, perhaps the biggest problem he faced was trying to get the ten regional offices to enforce the law in a uniform manner. He told us that some regional offices, in different areas of the country, tended to enforce the law less aggressively than the federal EPA in Washington desired. In particular, he said that the western states, which comprise regions 8, 9, and 10, tend to adopt the more populist, antigovernment, antiregulatory views of the "Sagebrush Rebellion" and thus are less likely to aggressively enforce the law. These regional offices are also more likely to be concerned with issues of water quantity than water quality (see Ingram 1990; Ostrom 1990; Munro 1993). On the other hand, bureaucrats in eastern states were generally perceived by the EPA hierarchy as being more likely to enforce the law aggressively than the regional offices in the Midwest (regions 5 and 7) or the West. We should note that the impressions of the former head of the EPA Water Office, which were expressed to us with considerable emotional force, were later reinforced by other agency personnel, especially in interviews with many officials at the regional and state level. Regarding these differences in the ten EPA regions, Evan Ringquist (1993: 37–38) wrote, "Regional offices and regional personnel are more apt to reflect the different political cultures and varying demands for environmental regulation across the country, and this means that regional offices can be more representative of subnational interests and more responsive to subnational needs. This system of regional offices can also lead to significant variations in enforcement, however."

Regional variations are important in terms of their substantive effects on EPA enforcement policy. As noted, they demonstrate a central concern of the EPA hierarchy. Several top officials we talked to were deeply concerned that regional variations in enforcement exist. They noted that they have employed considerable and diverse resources in an attempt to eliminate these differences. Representatives of the EPA hierarchy told us that they have attempted to constrain the level of discretion in the regional offices so that policy can be more consistent with the goals of the EPA's Washington office and with the policy preferences of the EPA administrator. In short, major efforts have been made to control perceived discretion on the part of regional personnel.

Although some variations in regional enforcement patterns can be explained in terms of the size of the regions or the number of permits issued (see Shover, Clelland, and Lynxwiler's 1986 study of the Office of Surface Mining and Reclamation), they also are due to the regulatory philosophy that pervades the regional offices and each geographical region, as well as the different economic, political, and other factors each regional office must respond to. On this basis, we have employed dummy variables representing the ten regional offices as a surrogate measure for bureaucratic discretion. In so doing we note the imperfection of this measure. Clearly a more direct measure of bureaucratic discretion would be more attractive, a point we will return to later in the book, especially in Chapter 7. Still, these differences in regional offices can be documented and are perceived by top officials within the EPA itself as a palpable outcome of bureaucratic discretion. With regard to the ten regional offices, we also can control for various hierarchical measures of political control, which, theoretically speaking, should effectively mitigate against differences in the way the NPDES program is enforced across the ten regional offices.

Our examination of the mean severity of NPDES enforcement actions (Table 3.4) provided evidence of considerable variations across the EPA's ten regional offices. We demonstrated that the most active regions, in terms of the total number of enforcement actions conducted, were regions 1, 2, 4, 5, and 6, whereas the ones with the highest mean severity levels were regions 3, 4, 7, 9, and 10. A cross comparison of the two results indicated that only region 4 scored high in both categories, suggesting that most regions that scored high on the mean severity level were also the ones least likely to conduct a larger number of enforcement actions. As we noted in Chapter 3, some of this variation is obviously related to primacy. More enforcement actions are conducted by federal personnel in nonprimacy states, but higher-level mean severity levels are identified in primacy states, because states with primacy pass off many of their higher level cases to federal EPA personnel. Thus, in examining the results of the models to be presented in this chapter we need to keep primacy in mind.

Table 5.1 provides additional evidence regarding regional variations in enforcement. In this table we provide a list of the most frequently conducted actions by each regional office from 1975 through 1988. As we would expect from the results presented in Table 3.4, with the exception of region 4, those regions that conducted the most enforcement actions were also those that conducted the most actions at the very lowest levels. The most frequent action conducted in region 1, for example, was a "comment." Lagging far behind, the second most frequent action conducted was an administrative order, a level five action. In region 2 the two most frequent actions undertaken were warning letters and a determination that no action was warranted, while higher-level administrative orders and consent decrees lagged far behind. Similar patterns can be seen in regions 5 and 6. Of those regions that conducted far fewer overall actions, all but region 8 most frequently conducted administrative orders or, in the case of region 7, an MCP-Schedule AO-EO. These figures again show that important regional variations exist. Are these variations related to primacy? As we noted earlier in Chapter 3 (see the bottom half of Table 3.4), the three regions with the most nonprimacy states are regions 1, 6, and 10. As would be expected from the discussion in Chapter 3, the findings in regions 1 and 6 are consistent with expectations. The number of enforcement actions is high, especially in region 6, and the level of activity is low, with, respectively, comments and warning letters being the predominant enforcement response. On the other hand, region 10, with fewer nonprimacy states, differs from the above demonstrated pattern. Far fewer total enforcement actions were conducted, although they were conducted at higher levels; administrative orders represented the predominant type of action taken. Thus, as was the case in Chapter 3, the evidence on the whole suggests that primacy is an important determinant of regional variations in enforcement behavior.

Table 5.1

Most Frequent Actions for Each Region, 1975–1988

	Type of action	Actions	Percentage	Total/Acts
Region 1:	Comment	706	47.7	1,481
	Administrative order	193	13.0	
	No action warranted	109	7.4	
Region 2:	Warning letters	6,545	51.2	12,631
	No action warranted	2,812	22.3	
	Administrative order	457	3.6	
	Consent decree	397	3.1	
Region 3:	Administrative order	139	38.0	366
	MCP schedule AO-EO	113	30.9	
Region 4:	Administrative order	1,137	49.0	2,321
	MCP schedule AO-EO	610	26.3	
Region 5:	Warning letters	546	17.0	3,215
	Notices of violation	477	14.8	
	Administrative orders	326	10.1	
	Comment	265	8.2	
	Phone call	247	7.7	
Region 6:	Warning letters	3,233	54.0	5,984
	Administrative orders	991	16.6	
	Administrative action pending	467	7.8	
Region 7:	MCP schedule AO-EO	63	32.2	190
	MCP required AO-EO	36	18.9	
	Administrative order	32	16.8	
	Review by state attorney general	25	13.2	
Region 8:	Phone call	44	36.1	123
	MCP schedule AO-EO	24	19.7	
	Administrative order	21	17.2	
Region 9:	Administrative order	69	48.9	141
	MCP schedule AO-EO	44	31.2	
Region 10:	Administrative order	168	43.3	388
	Section 308 letter	45	11.6	

Table 5.1 suggests that variations occur. To help us explain these variations we analyze two types of actions for our dependent variables. The first is a measure of inspections or compliance-monitoring activity. We cannot simply examine the number of inspections conducted in each region because there are important variations in the number of NPDES permittees

operating in each region; for one, the size of each region is different. We therefore have calculated the dependent variable as the number of inspections conducted divided by the number of permittees for each region. This gives us a percentage relationship of inspections to permittees and controls for variations in the different sizes of the tasks performed by personnel from the ten regional offices. For our second dependent variable we examine the number of referrals for judicial action to the Justice Department from each regional office. The data are compiled on a quarterly basis from the first quarter of 1979 through the second quarter of 1988. This approach ensures that we will be comparing the same enforcement mechanisms over time, for each regional office.

Our surrogate measure of bureaucratic discretion is the variation in enforcement activity conducted across each of the EPA's ten regional offices. This is operationalized as a dummy variable for each region. As noted above, we understand that this is a very rough measure of bureaucratic discretion. Essentially what it allows us to do is to determine if variations in regional enforcement exist once we control for hierarchical political factors, a major concern of the EPA hierarchy. It does not, however, allow us to explain why any remaining variations exist once we controlled for hierarchy. Why, then, have we adopted this measure of bureaucratic discretion? First, the methods (pooled time-series analysis) employed in this chapter greatly constrain our ability to more dynamically measure the concept of bureaucratic discretion. The analysis to be presented is time serial, and dynamic measures that vary over time are unfortunately not available for many of the factors that we argue (in Chapter 7) are related to the diversity of the regulatory environment, the factors we believe bureaucrats respond to. As a result, we are limited in terms of the nonhierarchical measures we can employ. We have, however, included two such measures in the analysis. We include a measure of the unemployment rate, which represents one surrogate for bureaucratic responsiveness to the state of the economy. We also include a measure of media interest in water-related issues. Second, although we do not include other measures representing the diversity of the regulatory environment (e.g., variables related to population stratification, water usage, water quantity, and water quality) in this chapter, we do examine them in considerable empirical detail in Chapter 7. At that point, then, we will be able to present a richer definition of what we believe bureaucratic discretion actually entails. Thus, the results presented in this chapter should be considered as one piece in a broader puzzle, rather than as a full and satisfactory solution to the puzzle. Finally, the method of operationalization that we employ allows us to test the three theoretical relationships that we have hypothesized between discretion and hierarchical control. Significant coefficients for the dummy variables tell us whether regional variations exist—our surrogate for bureaucratic discretion. The coefficients for the hierarchical political control factors then tell us whether bureaucratic discretion is constrained or unconstrained.

We employ several measures to represent hierarchical control of the bureaucracy. As a measure of the EPA's resources, and as a measure of congressional and presidential support over time for the agency, we employ the annual budget for each regional office. We expect that the budget will be positively associated with enforcement actions (e.g., increases in the budget will promote greater enforcement activity). The budget reflects the changing policy preferences of both presidents and Congress, inasmuch as it is a shared power of the executive and legislative branches. Often, however, it does not reflect the policy preferences of both constitutional actors simultaneously. For example, in the case of environmental policy, the budget best represented the interests of the executive branch during the period from 1979 to 1980, when Jimmy Carter was president, and during the first two years of the Reagan administration (1981–82), when severe reductions in the EPA agency budget were enacted (see Wood 1988; Waterman and Wood 1993; Waterman 1989). The preferences of Congress were best represented during the period from 1979 to 1980, when Democrats controlled both Congress and the White House, and from 1983 to 1988, when Congress reasserted its predominance over the environmental budget. Thus, when examining the budget mechanism, we must be careful to realize that it represents the influence of different political principals at different periods of time.

Likewise, with regard to the issue of water pollution control, the appointment power reflected varying degrees of presidential and congressional influence over time. To measure appointments we employ dummy variables for three presidential appointments (Anne Gorsuch Burford, William Ruckelshaus, and Lee Thomas; zero prior to the appointment and one thereafter). Each official was appointed to the position of EPA administrator by Ronald Reagan. Despite Reagan's low level of support for environmental matters, we expect to find different relationships associated with each of the three appointees. We expect to identify a decline in enforcements associated with Burford's appointment, because her tenure was associated with virulent opposition to vigorous enforcement of environmental legislation (see Wood 1988; Waterman and Wood 1993; Waterman 1989). We expect to find increases in enforcement associated with the Ruckelshaus appointment, inasmuch as it followed shortly after Congress held Anne Burford in contempt of the House of Representatives, and therefore represented the return of a more moderate, pro-environmental administration of the EPA. As for the Thomas appointment, we expect to identify no change in enforcement, because his tenure represented a continuation of the policies of William Ruckelshaus. A significant coefficient for the appointment of Anne Burford, therefore, would be evidence of presidential influence, whereas statistical support for either Ruckelshaus or Thomas would be evidence of a more assertive congressional role in NPDES enforcement.

We examined the role of EPA administrators, but we did not incorporate the appointment of regional administrators in the model. Although interviews with EPA officials, as well as a recent study by Waterman, Rouse, and Wright (1994), identified the important role they play in the enforcement process, we found that most new regional administrators were appointed at approximately the same time as the president appointed a new EPA administrator. This was particularly true in the case of Lee Thomas. The correspondence between the two types of appointees is due to the method of selection for regional administrators. They are officially chosen by the EPA administrator, who represents the president, although the actual choice is also based on senatorial courtesy. Although regional administrators may be more likely to reflect local concerns than the EPA administrator, because of problems of severe multicollinearity, we could not include both sets of actors in the model. We incorporated the three EPA administrators in our model because prior studies (e.g., Wood and Waterman 1991, 1993, 1994; Waterman, Rouse, and Wright 1994) have identified the important role they play in the enforcement process.

Both the budget and appointments, then, reflect shared presidential and congressional influence, although the policy preferences of the two constitutional actors may and often does diverge over time. For a more direct operationalization of congressional influence we employed the measure of committee environmental support established by Wood and Waterman (1993, 1994). Variables representing the House and the Senate were created by measuring the frequency and substance of congressional hearings. As Wood and Waterman (1994: 87–88) wrote,

> We measured the frequency of congressional hearings as the number of hearing days on each program during each quarterly time period by the primary oversight committees [related to water pollution issues]. We measured the substance of those hearings as the average score for each committee in each year on the League of Conservation Voters (LCV) rating. The LCV scores were then standardized to the center rating (50) to form a scale, with positive numbers indicating above-average LCV ratings, zero indicating intermediate ratings, and negative numbers indicating below-average LCV ratings. Committee environmentalism was then measured as the product of the number of days of oversight hearings per quarter and the standardized LCV score for each committee.

For a direct measure of presidential influence we included a measure of presidential interest in water pollution issues. This was represented by the number and tone of presidential statements delivered per quarter on issues related to water pollution. These statements were coded from the *Public Papers of the President* and reflect both the number of statements made and the tone of the presidential statements over time. We use the method employed by Wood and Waterman (1993, 1994), which codes statements according to whether their content is pro-environmental, neutral, or anti-environmental. Our expectation here is that because most of the statements were issued by Ronald Reagan, an openly anti-environmental president, there should be a negative relationship between statements issued and enforcements undertaken.

Along with the Congress and the president, we also include two measures of judicial influence. We include a measure of the dollar amount (measured in millions of dollars) assessed each quarter for penalties levied against water pollution violators. We also use a measure of the penalty assessments from the federal courts assessed within each individual region during each quarter. For both of these measures we anticipate that a positive relationship will exist; that is, increases in penalties assessed will promote increased enforcement activity.

These variables examine the influence of the three constitutional branches of government. We also include two measures for potential nongovernmental influences. Elliott, Regens, and Seldon (1995: 50) found that "media concern is a critical factor in motivating [public] concern for environmental matters." It is also possible, as Wood and Waterman (1993, 1994) found, that the media may exert an influence on enforcement personnel. For these reasons, we provide a measure of media influence by including a variable representing the number of news stories on water-related issues reported, per quarter, by the *Reader's Guide to Periodical Literature*. This measure is based on the hypothesis that the more attention (e.g., the more articles published) the media pays to environmental matters, the more active NPDES personnel will be in enforcing the law. Because the level of regulatory enforcement may also be related to each region's economic environment, we also examine the relationship between the unemployment rate and enforcement activity. We anticipate that increases in unemployment should be associated with decreases in enforcement activity. Finally, we control for seasonal variations in enforcements over time (i.e., the number of inspections is likely to decline in winter months due to poor weather conditions).

To analyze the data we have employed a time serial pooled regression analysis. Because of concerns over autocorrelation, we employed a generalized least squares (GLS) analysis. Because a GLS pooled model can correct for presumed cross-sectional unit effects (see Stimson 1985), we employed an ARMA-GLS pooled regression model. An ARMA model allows us to model each of the ten cross-sections (i.e., the ten regional offices). We have modeled the cross-sections as a first-order, moving-average process.

Following Wood and Waterman's (1993, 1994) example, we also examine various types of political stimuli exerted by the hierarchical political actors. We do this in two primary ways. First, as with most of the past principal-agent literature, we determine if there is an immediate or discrete impact between the dependent and independent variables associated with hierarchical political control. As Wood and Waterman (1994: 81) noted, the variables in the analysis represent event processes, which "are just time-ordered variables containing the set of all discrete events in an episodic sequence." Because, however, changes that result "from an event process stimulus . . . may be more difficult to observe since they occur gradually rather abruptly," we also operationalize most of the variables (excluding the dummies for bureaucratic discretion and the appointees, as well as the budget) in a second manner: as tonal stimuli. Rather than exhibiting a direct and immediate impact, a tonal stimulus is hypothesized to develop gradually over time. As Wood and Waterman (ibid.) wrote, "They consist of accumulations of events that affect the character of relations between political actors." The idea here is that we should not necessarily anticipate an immediate or discrete response to hierarchical cues for action. Rather, responses may derive from the accumulated effect of a particular signal being exerted on bureaucratic agents over time. A tonal stimulus is operationalized as a moving average (composed of four time periods) over time.

Our Results

In Table 5.2 we examine the relationship between bureaucratic discretion and political hierarchy. We use the number of inspections divided by the number of permittees for each region, calculated on a quarterly basis, as the dependent variable. The results demonstrate that even after we control for a variety of hierarchical factors, wide regional variations can be identified in the manner in which the Clean Water Acts have been enforced. Furthermore, these variations are not consistent with the past EPA Water Administrator's expectations or with those of other officials we spoke to at the EPA. The head of the Water Office, for example, told us that enforcement activity would be weakest in regions representing the Western states. We do find evidence of variations in two of the three Western regional

Table 5.2

Pooled Regression of Inspections in Ten EPA Regions, 1979–1988

	Inspections per region /Permits per region	
Constant	−0.07** (0.01)	t = 6.90
Budget for each regional office	0.01** (0.00)	t = 13.84
House committee hearings	0.02** (0.01)	t = 2.45
House committee hearings: Moving average	0.01** (0.00)	t = 1.99
Senate committee hearings	−0.01** (0.00)	t = 2.27
Ruckelshaus appointment	0.02** (0.01)	t = 2.61
Court penalties assessed: Moving average	0.02** (0.004)	t = 4.45
Region 1	0.14** (0.02)	t = 8.44
Region 2	0.08** (0.01)	t = 6.16
Region 3	−0.04** (0.01)	t = 4.41
Region 5	−0.07** (0.01)	t = 7.00
Region 6	−0.03** (0.01)	t = 3.51
Region 8	0.11** (0.01)	t = 15.06
Region 9	0.03** (0.01)	t = 3.50

GLS adjusted R^2 = .67
N = 380
The statistics represent the regression coefficient over its standard error.
**Indicates significance at the 0.05 level.

offices (regions 8 and 9), but the positive coefficients for these dummy variables suggest that more inspections were conducted in these regions on average. We also find positive coefficients for regions 1 (the New England states, half of which are nonprimacy states) and region 2 (representing New York and New Jersey). On the other hand, the coefficients for region 3 (the North Atlantic states), region 5 (representing Midwestern states), and region 6 (which is primarily composed of nonprimacy states from the deep South and the Southwest) are negative, suggesting fewer inspections were conducted in these regions on average. In short, then, of the ten EPA regions, seven exhibited coefficients that are statistically significant. Given our prior discussion of regional variations in NPDES enforcement, this is not a particularly surprising finding. It is, however, a finding that is not consistent with the obsequious bureaucracy model of bureaucratic discretion. According to that theory, once we control for hierarchical political factors, we should find no evidence of regional variations or bureaucratic discretion. Consequently, the next question is whether bureaucratic discretion undermines hierarchy (the dominant model) or is consistent with it (the interactive bureaucracy model)?

Advocates of the dominant bureaucracy model have argued that bureaucrats are not accountable because they (1) possess and employ bureaucratic discretion and (2) are not subject to hierarchical political control. Although we have provided clear evidence supporting the first of these two premises, our analysis in Table 5.2 provides little support for the second assumption. Instead, we find strong and broad evidence of hierarchical political control across two of the three branches of the federal government. We find statistical evidence of a response to our discrete measure of House influence in the expected positive direction, meaning that the more attention the House committee pays to water-related issues, and the higher the average LCV scores of committee members, the more inspections EPA NPDES officials conduct. Likewise, we also find a positive effect related to the tonal stimulus exerted by the House committee. The evidence in support of a tonal impact from House hearings is consistent with Wood and Waterman's basic thesis that political influence is not always conveyed in a discrete manner at one particular time period.

We also find that our measure of Senate influence is related to the number inspections conducted, but not in the manner we had a priori hypothesized. The negative coefficient for the Senate suggests that the greater the number of hearings held by the Senate committees, and the higher the LCV scores of committee members, the fewer the number of inspections conducted. We believe the explanation for this negative coefficient derives from the fact that the Republican party controlled the Senate during much of the time period under investigation (1981–86). It appears that the Democratic-controlled House was perceived by EPA personnel as being more committed to water pollution control efforts than was the Republican-dominated

Senate. Given these expectations, bureaucrats then responded in a predictable fashion.

They did not, however, respond to the appointment of Anne Burford as EPA administrator. Because, however, the NPDES program took considerable time to implement (see Landy et al. 1994), Burford and her cohort of conservative appointees (to other posts at the EPA) did not have to exert a great deal of energy to reduce the level of NPDES enforcements. Rather, all they had to do was to ensure that enforcement activity did not increase, a task they apparently managed with considerable success. On the other hand, when the Congress forced Burford to resign, President Reagan appointed the more environmentally minded William Ruckelshaus as the new EPA administrator. He commenced his term of office with the now famous, at least within the halls of the EPA, "Gorilla in the Closet" speech, in which he urged EPA personnel to enforce the law aggressively. Anecdotal evidence suggests EPA employees were more than willing to respond. As several EPA officials stationed in Washington told us, the halls of the EPA were replete with personnel wearing "I Survived the Ice Queen" T-shirts, a less than conciliatory farewell message for the departing Anne Burford. As our results demonstrate, the arrival of Ruckelshaus was associated with an increase in inspection activity. As expected, we find no evidence that the Thomas appointment impacted the level of inspection activity. Rather, it did represent a continuation of Ruckelshaus's more decidedly pro-enforcement agenda.

With regard to our other measure of presidential influence, there was no relationship between the number or tone of presidential statements and the number of inspections conducted. On the other hand, we found a positive association between the budget and the number of inspections. As with previous research (Wood and Waterman 1991, 1993, 1994; Waterman and Wood 1993) we found not only that the budget is positively associated with enforcement actions, but that it is also the most important hierarchical determinant in the model. Finally, with regard to the judicial branch, we found evidence of a tonal stimulus from penalties assessed by the federal courts. The greater the amount of the penalty assessed by the courts, the larger the number of inspections conducted by NPDES personnel.

With regard to our other independent variables, we did not find that the media exerted influence over EPA activity, nor did we find that the unemployment rate was related to the number of inspections conducted. Likewise, there was no seasonal impact on inspections. In summary, the model presented in Table 5.2 empirically demonstrates that Congress (through the hearings process and by forcing Reagan to appoint the pro-environmental William Ruckelshaus) exerted considerable influence over how NPDES personnel enforced the law. Congress and the president also exerted influence through the budgetary mechanism. Finally, consistent with the findings of Moe (1985) and Wood and Waterman (1993), we found that the activities of the courts are related to bureaucratic behavior. We did not find evidence of a separate presidential impact on the number of inspections conducted, however. Still, we did find considerable evidence of hierarchical control of the bureaucracy.

This finding is strong evidence that bureaucratic discretion and hierarchical political control coexist with regard to the NPDES program. To put it somewhat differently, it is evidence that bureaucratic discretion exists, but that bureaucrats are still held at least partially accountable to hierarchical political actors. This is evidence consistent with the interactive bureaucracy model.

With regard to the issue of primacy the evidence is more mixed. Region 1, with three nonprimacy states, conducted more inspections on average, region 6, with four nonprimacy states, conducted less inspections on average, and the coefficient representing region 10 was not statistically significant.

In Table 5.3 we turn our attention to a higher-level enforcement action; the number of referrals for judicial action to the Justice Department issued by each regional office during each quarter in the series. To control for the size of each region, and for past bureaucratic activity, we incorporated the dependent variable from Table 5.2; the number of inspections divided by the number of permittees for each region. Because inspections occur as a first step in the enforcement process and judicial action occurs much later, we lagged the independent variable to test for several possible lagged effects. We ran models lagging the variable from zero to four times. The model that performed the best incorporated a lagged effect of one quarter. The coefficient is significant, but negative, suggesting that the greater the number of inspections conducted, the fewer the number of cases referred to the Justice Department. This finding suggests that regions that are more active with regard to lower-level enforcement activities also are less active with regard to higher-level actions. This finding is consistent with the results we presented earlier in this chapter (see Table 5.1) and in Chapter 3.

Our findings with regard to the various hierarchical actors is more straight forward, however. With regard to political hierarchy, it is not surprising that we find strong evidence of court influence on the behavior of EPA personnel. In fact, the courts, as represented here by the amount of the penalty assessed against violators within each region, exhibited the strongest impact on the number of referrals issued of any variable in the analysis. As expected, the effect is positive, meaning that an increase in the penalty assessed promotes additional referrals to the Justice Department.

Table 5.3

Pooled Regression of Referrals in Ten EPA Regions, 1979–1988

	Referrals (logged)	
Constant	1.09** (0.21)	t = 5.15
Inspections/permits: Lagged once	−0.0325** (0.017)	t = 1.96
Ruckelshaus appointment	0.17** (0.07)	t = 2.31
Presidential statements	0.02** (0.01)	t = 3.81
Presidential statements: Moving average	−0.04** (0.01)	t = 3.71
Court penalties assessed, regional level (logged)	0.09** (0.01)	t = 19.16
Unemployment rate	−0.09** (0.02)	t = 4.43
Region 1	−0.25* (0.07)	t = 3.51
Region 7	−0.31** (0.08)	t = 3.98
Region 8	−0.21 (0.10)	t = 2.16
Region 9	−0.34 (0.07)	t = 5.06

GLS adjusted R^2 = .64.
N = 370.
Statistics represent the regression coefficient over its standard error.
**Indicates significance at the 0.05 level.

We also find a positive impact between our discrete measure of presidential statements and referrals. This positive impact suggests that EPA personnel resisted negative rhetoric from the White House, a conclusion also reached by Wood and Waterman (1993, 1994). We also find, however, that the response to the tonal stimulus of presidential statements over time was negative and of about twice the magnitude of the response to the discrete cue. This means that negative presidential rhetoric over time had a negative impact on the number of NPDES referrals. Obviously, as negative comments were issued over time, EPA personnel responded to the accumulation of these negative signals. The combined effect of the discrete and tonal stimulus responses is that short-term resistance to presidential rhetoric mitigated, to some extent, the long-term accumulated tonal impact of presidential influence on this particular measure. Still, accumulated signals were more powerful determinants of the behavior of EPA personnel.

With regard to presidential appointments over time, we again find that only the Ruckelshaus appointment was related to the dependent variable, and again in the expected positive direction. Once again, neither the Burford nor the Thomas appointments exhibited a statistically significant impact on EPA enforcement behavior. Again, this is evidence of congressional influence over EPA enforcement behavior. There is, however, no statistical association between the other measures of congressional influence and referrals. Furthermore, the budget was not statistically related to referral activities. This can be explained by the powerful association between the budget and the dependent variable in Table 5.2. By including the dependent variable from that prior analysis into the model we examine in Table 5.3, we are concomitantly controlling for much of the influence the budget exerts on the issuance of referrals. In fact, if we remove the inspection variable from Table 5.3 and replace it with the budget for each regional office, the budget variable does contribute in the expected positive direction.

Of the nonhierarchical measures, we find that the unemployment rate is related to judicial referrals. As expected, the higher the unemployment rate, the fewer the referrals that are issued by the regional offices to the Justice Department. We again find, however, that there is no relationship between media interest in water issues and NPDES enforcement activity.

In summary, the major hierarchical impact on regional referral activity was the penalty assessed by the courts in each region. Given the judicial implications of our dependent variable, we would expect the courts to be more closely associated with referral activities than the Congress or the president. We also found considerable evidence of hierarchical political control by the president and more limited evidence of congressional influence over the enforcement behavior of their bureaucratic agents.

We also found evidence of bureaucratic discretion, but only in four of the ten EPA regions. In each of the four regions (regions 1, 7, 8, and 9) referral activity was lower on average than we would have expected. This finding, that two of the three Western states acted in a less vigorous manner in enforcing the law, is consistent with the expectations of the former head of the EPA Water Office and other EPA personnel we interviewed. It suggests that as we move to higher-level enforcement activity, the Western states are indeed less aggressive in enforcing the law.

Finally, with regard to primacy, only one of the three regions with the most nonprimacy states exhibited a statistically significant coefficient. Region 1 exhibited less enforcement activity on average.

Discussion

As we hypothesized earlier in this chapter, there are three possible relationships between hierarchy and discretion. First, as many scholars already have argued, discretion could promote a bureaucracy that is unaccountable to elected superordinates. Under the conditions of the dominant bureaucracy model, we would have expected to have identified evidence of bureaucratic discretion, but no concomitant evidence of responsiveness on the part of bureaucratic agents to elected officials. Our findings therefore clearly contradict the assumptions of the dominant model, which has been advocated by such scholars as Lowi (1979). Our analysis demonstrates that bureaucrats are indeed accountable to political principals.

A second possibility, the obsequious bureaucracy model, is that political hierarchy could mitigate attempts at bureaucratic discretion. Our results with regard to inspections provide little support for this conclusion. Although there is clear evidence of congressional control of the bureaucracy, we also found evidence of variations in enforcement activities in seven of the EPA's ten regional offices. When we turned our attention to referrals we identified variations in only four of ten regions. This decrease from seven to four was not, however, likely due to increased hierarchical control, but rather to the stricter standards involved in referring cases to the Justice Department. As we move up the hierarchy of enforcement actions, it becomes more difficult for EPA personnel to employ their discretionary authority.

Finally, a third possibility is that both top-down and bottom-up effects can coexist simultaneously. Indeed, in both our analysis of inspections and referrals our conclusions point to this third alternative, the interactive bureaucracy model, as the most viable explanation of how bureaucratic discretion operates in the federal bureaucracy.

What does our analysis and this theory of coexistence suggest? It suggests that prior analyses that have asserted that bureaucratic discretion is a threat to democracy may be overstated. This assertion was based on the idea that discretion undermines democracy, inasmuch as bureaucrats are not responsive to elected officials. We have demonstrated that this assumption is not supported by the empirical evidence in the case of surface-water pollution control. Thus, although we may have other legitimate reasons for being concerned about the existence of bureaucratic discretion (e.g., environmentalist concerns of poor performance in some regional offices), our analysis suggests that we should not be concerned that discretion undermines democracy. Of course, we must note that we have examined but one division within one federal regulatory agency. Variations in the relationship between bureaucratic discretion and hierarchical control may exist across agencies, across policy areas, and across different levels of government. Thus, we recommend replication of our analysis in other bureaucratic settings, involving different policy areas, and different levels of government. Only in this way can we begin to derive a clearer sense of how bureaucratic discretion is related to political hierarchy in the broad setting of American bureaucracy.

What Is Bureaucratic Discretion?

The above results leave us with one vitally important question to answer. What is bureaucratic discretion? We know that it is more than a dummy variable representing regional variations in enforcement. Therefore, what is it that bureaucrats actually respond to? We think this is a vitally important question because most scholars have dedicated a greater effort to attacking or defending the existence of bureaucratic discretion than they have toward explaining what the concept actually represents. Lowi and many of the scholars we cited earlier in this chapter obviously perceive discretion as a threat to democracy. But they do not tell us very much about what they think bureaucratic discretion actually entails. According to Lowi (1979: 92–93) and Bryner (1987: 1) discretion is equated with a broad delegation of authority by Congress to an administrative agency. The problem with this definition is that it really tells us very little about what bureaucrats actually do. In fact, discretion is defined in terms of what the principals do (e.g., they delegate broad authority or they don't). This definition doesn't tell us whether bureaucratic agents employ the broad discretion once they get it or whether the broad discretionary authority is needed, due to the intractability of the externality being regulated or the diverse regulatory environment under which it occurs. As such, then, we cannot really come to a clear understanding of what discretion actually entails.

A second definitional approach to discretion is provided by Calvert, McCubbins, and Weingast. They argue that discretion is related to an unwillingness on the part of bureaucrats to respond to cues from their hierarchical superordinates, the so-called principals of the principal-agent model. They wrote (1989: 605), "agency discretion occurs when the agency succeeds in choosing a policy in line with agency goals, when those goals differ from what the executive and legislature expected at the appointment stage." The problem with this definition is that we have presented evidence in this chapter that demonstrates that EPA NPDES personnel did respond to Congress, the president, and the courts, and yet still employed a considerable measure of bureaucratic discretion when they enforced the law. Additionally, as with prior evidence presented by Wood and Waterman (1991, 1993, 1994) we demonstrated that multiple principals often possess contradictory goals simultaneously. Consequently, the Congress may be urging the EPA to move in one policy direction, while the president may be exerting pressure on EPA personnel to take policy in an entirely different direction. According to the definition proposed by Calvert and associates, agency discretion would necessarily exist in any case in which multiple principals disagree, because agents would be forced to choose between competing principal goals. Thus, discretion would not simply represent a failure of bureaucrats to respond to principal cues for action. In short, then, as with the first definition, discretion is more a function of principal behavior, than a function of the agent's behavior. In a time of divided government, the latter definition would suggest that broad exertions of bureaucratic discretion will be the norm in American politics.

Our analysis also raised the possibility that a so-called individual principal may actually exhibit characteristics of multiple principals. For example, within Congress, which is generally considered to be one principal, the House may be urging the EPA to enforce the law more vigorously, while the Senate may be sending an entirely different signal to EPA personnel. The issue of multiple principals with divergent goals or single principals with divided goals can greatly complicate the utility of any definition that equates discretion with the goal preferences of principals and their agents. This is so because we are explicitly assuming that principals have one set of goals that bureaucrats can then decide to respond to or to ignore. As our results indicate, this was not the case with regard to the issue of surface-water regulation in the 1980s. Different goals were expressed by different principals and even, in the case of Congress, by the same principal. Thus, if we apply the above definition to the case of surface-water regulation in the 1980s, EPA bureaucrats, by definition, had to employ considerable bureaucratic discretion, because their actions could not be entirely in accord with the contradictory goals expressed by competing principals. This is so even if we focus on the appointment stage, as recommended by Calvert and associates (1989). When Anne Burford was appointed as the new administrator of the EPA, considerable differences of agreement were expressed regarding environmental goals by the executive and legislative branches of government. The same can be said with the later appointment of William

Ruckelshaus. Serious differences continued to exist between the president and Congress, as later represented by Ronald Reagan's veto on two separate occasions of a new Clean Water Act, and Congress's 1987 override of the second presidential veto. EPA personnel thus were forced to choose between competing principals, which obviously put them in the position of exerting some level of bureaucratic discretion. But is responding to diverse principal goals all that bureaucratic discretion actually entails?

If discretion is more than Congress's propensity to delegate broad authority to the bureaucracy or an unwillingness on the part of bureaucrats to respond to cues from hierarchical political actors, then what is it? Is it merely the propensity of bureaucrats to act as they please, subject only to their own whim? Do they merely respond to whatever factors they wish, without constraint and without direction? Or does bureaucratic discretion mean that bureaucrats have the ability to respond to dynamic factors related to the particular regulatory environment that their agency interacts with on a daily basis?

As we have hypothesized in this book, the nature of the regulatory environment is a critical factor in determining the manner in which bureaucrats enforce the law. With a more diverse regulatory environment, such as is characteristic of surface-water pollution, we would expect bureaucrats to possess and employ considerable bureaucratic discretion. This, according to our theory, does not mean that they can do whatever they wish, or that they can ignore with impunity the will of their political principals. It means instead that bureaucrats must react to the regulatory environment related to the externality they deal with on a daily basis. The more diverse the nature of that externality (e.g., the more difficult it is to identify the source of the externality involved, the more and diverse the settings in which violators and violations can exist, and so on), the more flexibility bureaucrats will require in enforcing the law. Likewise, the bureaucratic response will be dictated by other factors in the regulatory environment including differing organizational structures of the agencies involved and varying economic conditions. In short, then, we argue that in the case of surface-water pollution control, bureaucrats use their discretion to respond to this highly diverse regulatory environment.

In the remainder of this book we consider bureaucratic discretion not simply in political terms, but in relationship to a diverse set of factors of which politics is only one (e.g., political, economic, demographic, and organizational factors, as well as conditions related to the externality involved). We examine the factors bureaucrats actually respond to, which allows us to better describe what bureaucratic discretion actually entails. In so doing, we demonstrate that bureaucratic discretion, in the case of surface-water regulation, should be defined as a pragmatic response to a diverse regulatory environment.

6

Enforcement at the State Level

Primacy and State Organizational Structures

Before we can address the question of what bureaucratic discretion entails, we must first examine another question: What do bureaucrats respond to? In the last chapter we demonstrated that they respond to hierarchical cues from their political principals. The statistically significant coefficients for the dummy variables, representing bureaucratic discretion, also suggested that they respond to other factors in the regulatory environment. But which factors? We included only two nonhierarchical factors in the models analyzed in Chapter 5, one representing a measure of the state of the economy (the unemployment rate) and another reflecting media interest in water pollution issues. Of these two variables we identified evidence (in the case of referrals to the Justice Department) suggesting that bureaucrats respond to the state of the economy. We found no relationship, however, between media interest and the level of the NPDES enforcement response.

Although the economy and media interest represent two factors related to water pollution control's regulatory environment, they clearly do not represent the broad diversity of that regulatory environment. We therefore ask, what other factors do NPDES personnel respond to? In this and the next chapter, we introduce and examine a variety of factors related to the water pollution control regulatory environment. In this chapter we focus on one factor: organization. We examine three types of organizational structure: region, primacy, and the type of organizational structure that state government's employ when they enforce the NPDES program. We argue that organizational structure plays an important role in determining the level of the NPDES enforcement response.

Thus far in this book we have focused our attention primarily on federal-level NPDES personnel. Because much of the actual enforcement work is done by state personnel, working under the guidelines of the NPDES program, we shift our attention in this chapter and the next to a discussion of the role the states play in surface-water pollution control efforts. We use EPA enforcement data, representing the regulatory efforts of both state and federal personnel, to analyze the level of enforcement across the fifty states. By switching to an examination of the states we are able to examine, in much greater detail, a variety of factors related to the diversity of water pollution control's regulatory environment.

State Organization of the NPDES Program

As noted we have examined NPDES enforcement almost exclusively from the perspective of federal level bureaucrats. It is tempting to concentrate our attention solely on the activities of the Environmental Protection Agency, the lead agency in charge of federal environmental enforcement. After all, the EPA is clearly the highest-profile agency in the country dealing with water pollution issues. But, as we pointed out in Chapter 2, it is really only one of many such agencies, even at the federal level. When we move beyond the federal level there are some 59,000 water-supply utilities and thousands of state and local water, improvement, and other special districts involved in water-quality and water-supply activities (Smith 1992: 111). Each of the fifty states also plays a role in the enforcement of the Clean Water Act of 1972 and other subsequent legislation. The 1972 act specifically provided for an active state role in the enforcement process. Section 101(b) of the Act states, "It is the policy of the Congress to recognize, preserve, and protect the primary responsibilities and rights of states to prevent, reduce, and eliminate pollution, to plan the development and use . . . of land and water resources, and to consult with the [EPA] administrator in the exercise of his authority under this Act."

In fact, the states were granted a larger role in the implementation of the Federal Water Pollution Control Act (i.e., the Clean Water Act of 1972) than they were in carrying out the provisions of the 1970 Clean Air Act. As Walter Rosenbaum (1985: 162) wrote, "The responsibility for implementing the FWPCA and most other federal water regulations rests heavily with the states." In comparison to the much more limited state role prescribed by the Clean Air Act, Rosenbaum wrote, "the FWPCA permits each state to designate the primary use for waters within its jurisdiction; in effect, this means substantial authority to establish rigorous or lenient water pollution standards."

Amendments to the 1972 FWPCA have further increased the state's role in surface-water enforcement. As a result, as Evan Ringquist (1993: 4) wrote, "Over the past fifteen years, many states have been far more active in controlling pollution than has the federal government. By focusing our attention on federal efforts at environmental protection, we are missing some of the nation's most important and innovative efforts at pollution control." Likewise, Zachary Smith (1992: 111) wrote, "Although the federal role in water pollution control has expanded significantly, states and localities have primary responsibility for the implementation of water pollution policy." Davis and Lester (1989) also noted that the states play a vital role in funding environmental programs. Furthermore, with cutbacks in federal spending becoming a way of life for the states, many of them have taken on an even greater burden for their regulatory programs in recent years (Lester 1990).

Despite the common misconception that environmental enforcement occurs predominantly at the federal level, many states have played the primary role in water pollution control. As we noted in Chapter 2, the federal EPA, following guidelines established in the 1972 FWPCA, sets the general guidelines and policy for the NPDES program. States can then establish their own programs so long as they meet or exceed the standards provided for the NPDES program by the federal EPA. At present thirty-eight states have been awarded primacy for their NPDES programs. This means that they play the primary role in the permit-issuance, compliance-monitoring, and NPDES enforcement processes. In Table 6.1 we present a breakdown of the fifty states by region and by whether they have been awarded primacy. The twelve states that do not have primacy are geographically dispersed across the nation. As we have noted before, three are from region 1, one is from region 4, four are from region 6, one is from region 8, one is from region 9, and two are from region 10. They include large states (e.g., Texas and Florida), states with low (Idaho) and high (Massachusetts) political support for the environment (as measured by their House and Senate delegations' League of Conservation Voter Scores), states with little available water (New Mexico), and states with considerable water supplies (Florida and Maine). In short, the states without primacy do not appear to share obvious common qualities.

In an attempt to determine if there is a pattern to the primacy and non-primacy states, we ran a probit analysis (because of the dichotomous nature of the dependent variable) that examined several possible explanatory factors encompassing such relevant variables in each state as the level of political support for the environment (the state LCV scores), economic capacity (per capita mean personal income), the level of industrialization and agriculture, several measures of water quantity and water usage, and a measure of the perceptions of state officials regarding the most important of source of pollution; for a detailed explanation of each of these independent variables see Chapter 7. As can be seen in Table 6.2, of all of these vari-

Table 6.1

States and EPA's Ten Regional Offices:
Primacy and Nonprimacy States for the NPDES Program

Region 1:	Connecticut	Region 6:	Arkansas
	Maine*		Louisiana*
	Massachusetts*		New Mexico*
	New Hampshire*		Oklahoma*
	Rhode Island		Texas*
	Vermont	Region 7:	Iowa
Region 2:	New Jersey		Kansas
	New York		Missouri
	Puerto Rico		Nebraska
	Virgin Islands	Region 8:	Colorado
Region 3:	District of Columbia		Montana
	Delaware		North Dakota
	Maryland		South Dakota*
	Pennsylvania		Utah
	Virginia		Wyoming
	West Virginia	Region 9:	American Samoa
Region 4:	Alabama		Arizona*
	Florida*		California
	Georgia		Guam
	Kentucky		Hawaii
	Mississippi		Johnson Atoll
	North Carolina		Midway Islands
	South Carolina		No. Marianas
	Tennessee		Nevada
Region 5:	Illinois		Trust Territories
	Indiana	Region 10:	Alaska*
	Michigan		Idaho*
	Minnesota		Oregon
	Ohio		Washington
	Wisconsin		

Source: Data provided by EPA.
*Indicates a state does not have primacy over its NPDES program.

ables only one was correlated with a state's decision to seek primacy: the level of industrialization in a state. The relationship was positive, suggesting that the greater the level of industrialization in a state the more likely it will be to seek primacy over its NPDES program.

In addition to this analysis, we also asked a number of state environmental officials from nonprimacy states why their state does not have primacy over its NPDES program. We received some starkly different answers to this question. For example, officials in New Mexico told us that they have so little water within their boundaries that it simply does not make sense for the state to seek primacy for its NPDES program. Water quantity was not

Table 6.2

Probit Analysis: Determinants of Primacy

Constant	−0.31
	(0.50)
Level of industrialization	4.71*
	(2.16)
McKelvey pseudo R-square	.17
N	50

The statistics represent the regression coefficient over its standard error.
*Indicates significance at the 0.05 level.

an issue in other states, however. For example, officials in Idaho and Arizona suggested that the key reason their states did not have primacy was that development took precedence over the environment among state lawmakers. The most commonly provided answer to our inquiries, however, related to the states' limited fiscal resources. A number of state officials told us the major reason why the EPA retained primacy in their state was because they could not afford to run their own program. Even some states that have primacy have experienced problems in this regard. Over the past several years, West Virginia has found itself on the brink of surrendering its NPDES primacy back to the EPA. Likewise, in 1982 Iowa was forced to abandon its municipal water-monitoring program, which enforced provisions of the Safe Drinking Water Act. This factor should be of great concern to citizens concerned with the environment, particularly because many states now find themselves navigating in increasingly perilous fiscal waters.

In addition to a broad grant of primacy for the NPDES program, primacy can also be awarded to a state for general permitting authority (e.g., for entire water basins), for industrial pretreatment authority, and for authority to regulate federal facilities (see Ringquist 1993: 70). As Ringquist (1993: 72) noted, as of October 1992 thirty-three states had primacy for general permitting authority, twenty-seven states had primacy for industrial pretreatment authority, and thirty-four states had primacy to regulate federal facilities. As EPA officials informed us, however, no state has primacy to regulate reservations for Native Americans within their jurisdiction. The EPA deals with all reservations, even if they are located in primacy states. This exception aside, most states have chosen to accept the responsibility for primacy over their NPDES programs. This is one indication of their inclination to play an active role in the enforcement of the Clean Water Act.

Table 6.3

State Organizational Structures

Health Agency	MiniEPA	Superagency	Other
Colorado	Alabama	Connecticut	California
Hawaii	Alaska	Delaware	Texas
Idaho	Arizona	Georgia	Virginia
Kansas	Arkansas	Iowa	West Virginia
Montana	Florida	Kentucky	
North Dakota	Illinois	Massachusetts	
South Carolina	Indiana	Michigan	
Tennessee	Louisiana	Missouri	
Utah	Maine	Nevada	
	Maryland	New Jersey	
	Minnesota	North Carolina	
	Mississippi	Pennsylvania	
	Nebraska	Rhode Island	
	New Hampshire	South Dakota	
	New York	Vermont	
	Ohio	Wisconsin	
	Oregon		
	Washington		
	Wyoming		
	Oklahoma*		
	New Mexico*		

Source: Ringquist (1993: 39).
*Oklahoma and New Mexico have shifted to environmental departments in recent years. Both previously employed a health-agency organizational structure. Because the permit issuances and enforcement actions examined in this chapter occurred while these states still operated under health agency organizations, New Mexico and Oklahoma will be treated as states with health agencies for the purposes of the forthcoming analysis (see Tables 6.7, 6.11, and 6.13; see also Tables 8.5 and 9.1).

Another indication is the type of organizational structure a state employs to house their environmental programs. In Table 6.3 we present data on the three main types of organizational structures employed by the states. Some states pattern their agencies after the federal EPA or what Ringquist (1993: 39) has called a "MiniEPA." These are patterned after the organizational structure of the federal EPA. Twenty-one states now use this organizational format. They consist of a wide range of states from different geographical regions. It also represents states with different levels of political support for the environment (as measured by the House and Senate delegation scores). Again, as with the nonprimacy states, no pattern is readily apparent with regard to the type of state most likely to adopt a miniEPA format.

Sixteen states employ what Ringquist has called a "superagency" organizational structure, which combines environmental programs with energy, natural resources, and wildlife programs. According to Ringquist (1993: 38), "While 'superagencies' can enhance comprehensive environmental management, it is equally likely that environmental protection may be deemphasized in favor of an agency's natural resource development responsibilities." Of the sixteen superagency states, as with the miniEPA states, no pattern is easily discernible. The sixteen superagency states are from different regions of the country and exhibit widely different levels of political support for the environment.

On the other hand, the nine states that employ health agencies do exhibit a pattern. These states are overwhelmingly from the West, with only a few exceptions. With the notable exception of Hawaii, they also tend to exhibit less political support for the environment (e.g., they rank lower on the House and Senate environmental support scores) than states using other organizational structures. A possible reason why these states chose to place their environmental programs in health agencies emerged in our interviews with state officials. They suggested that health agencies are less likely to actively promote environmental measures than either of the other two organizational structures. An official from Oklahoma, for example, which in July 1993 established the Department of Environmental Quality (thus separating itself from its state Department of Health), noted that the change signified a significant commitment to the goal of environmental protection. Officials in New Mexico, which likewise recently shifted to a miniEPA format, also told us that the shift represented a renewed commitment to environmental protection.

To test why states have adopted a health agency to administer water pollutant programs, we again ran a probit analysis with the same independent variables described above. As can be seen by the five probit models presented in Table 6.4, the only factors related to a state's decision to employ a health agency were our various measures of water usage in the states. For example, the more gallons of water a state uses, per capita, the more likely it will be to employ a health agency. The decision to employ a health agency is also positively associated with the percentage of water used by a state for irrigation purposes, and negatively associated with the percentage of water usage for thermoelectric purposes. What do these various results indicate? The positive association with water usage for irrigation purposes suggests that when agriculture plays a more important role in a state's economy, then it will be more likely to employ a health agency to administer its water program. On the other hand, states where water usage is greater for thermoelectric purposes are less likely to use health agencies.

Table 6.4

Probit Analysis: Determinants of State Organizational Structure

Health Agencies:
  Model 1
    Constant   −1.09**
                                (0.26)
    Water usage   0.001*
    Per capita   (0.001)   t = 1.89
    McKelvey pseudo
      R-square   .15
    N   50

  Model 2
    Constant   −1.32**
                                (0.31)
    Water usage   0.02**
    Irrigation purposes   (0.01)   t = 2.74
    McKelvey pseudo
      R-square   .23
    N   50

  Model 3
    Constant   −0.20
                                (0.32)
    Water usage   −0.014*
    Thermoelectric   (0.006)   t = 2.23
    McKelvey pseudo
      R-square   .17
    N   50

Superagencies:
  Model 4
    Constant   −0.13
                                (0.23)
    Water usage   −0.014**
    Irrigation purposes   (0.006)   t = 2.29
    McKelvey pseudo
      R-square   .21
    N   50

  Model 5
    Constant   −1.08**
                                (0.37)
    Water usage   0.012**
    Thermoelectric   (0.006)   t = 2.02
    McKelvey pseudo
      R-square   .14
    N   50

The statistics represent the regression coefficient over its standard error.
  *Indicates significance at the 0.10 level.
**Indicates significance at the 0.05 level.

Statistically speaking, we found an inverse relationship between our analysis of health agencies and our analysis of states employing the so-called superagency organizational format. Thus, states that use a greater amount of water (percentagewise) for thermoelectric purposes are more likely to employ a superagency than a health agency. States that use a greater percentage of their water for irrigation are less likely to use a superagency. Interestingly, our analysis found no statistically significant correlations between water usage, or any of our independent variables, and the states that have adopted a miniEPA format.

Although most states employ either a miniEPA, a superagency, or a health agency format, four states fall into the nebulous "other" category, meaning they use other organizational arrangements for their environmental programs. Of these four, California has by far the most confusing organizational arrangement of all. California has a Division of Water Quality, but it is not responsible for enforcement of the NPDES program. Instead, nine regional boards, with members appointed by the governor, each with their own staff, do most of the actual enforcement work. State officials told us that this organizational arrangement greatly undercuts a uniform or aggressive pursuit of strict environmental enforcement by the state of California.

The States and the Federal EPA

Whatever type of organizational structure a state selects, all primacy states still interact on a continuing basis with the EPA. In fact, the NPDES EMS manual notes, "A strong Federal/State relationship is essential to the effective operation of a program as comprehensive and complex as the NPDES program" (EPA 1986: 5). According to the EPA's "Guidance for Oversight of the NPDES Program" (EPA 1986, Emergency Management System: 5–6),

> The Oversight Guidance requires that Regions and States negotiate individual agreements that clearly define performance expectations for the NPDES program, as well as the respective roles and responsibilities of the Region and the State in administering the NPDES program. The Guidance is based on the assumption that where a State has an approved NPDES program, it has the primary responsibility to initiate appropriate enforcement action to ensure compliance by permittees.

The phrase to "negotiate individual agreements" is a key to the relationship between the EPA and the states. As Helen Ingram (1977) argued, the federal government does not have a hierarchical relationship over the states. Rather, the relationship between the states and the federal government is best characterized as one of bargaining and persuasion. This cooperative relationship does not mean that the EPA does not have any means to enforce compliance, however. In those states with "primary responsibility to initiate appropriate enforcement action," the federal EPA does act in an oversight capacity. As the EMS manual states (EPA 1986, Guidance for Oversight Agreement Document: 6), "USEPA has oversight responsibility for . . . [the NPDES] program, including the responsibility to ensure that enforcement actions are taken on a timely and appropriate basis, and may initiate direct Federal enforcement action." Under the NPDES Compliance Inspection Plan, for example, there are procedures for an "ongoing evaluation of the State inspection programs, including periodic random audits of inspection reports and case files" (EPA 1986, Chapter VA: 3). If, through an audit or other oversight mechanism, it is determined that a state has not satisfactorily performed its responsibilities under the NPDES program, then Section S309 of the Clean Water Act specifies that the "EPA must take enforcement action." According to the EMS manual (EPA 1986: 6), "The Guidance (for Oversight Agreement) requires the development of protocols for notification and consultation to foster effective communications and the timely resolution of issues between Regions and States, and contains criteria for direct Federal Enforcement action."

One of the most common means of "direct Federal enforcement action" is for a regional office to issue a notice of violation (NOV) if it has been determined that a state is not appropriately performing its enforcement responsibilities in a particular case. The NOV is sent "to an approved State with a copy to the permittee informing them of the permittee's violation of a State-issued NPDES permit or a State-issued S404 permit." As described in the EPA's EMS manual (EPA 1986, Chapter 2: 3), "The NOV specifically describes the violation and describes the action required by the State to avoid further action by USEPA." Consequently, through an examination of the number of NOVs issued we can examine one measure of the federal EPA's commitment to oversight of the states. Figure 6.1 presents the number of notices of violation issued per month from February 1986 through June 1994. As can be seen, the EPA was hardly aggressive in its oversight of the states prior to the advent of the Bush administration in January of 1989. One possible reason for the low number of NOVs issued during this time might be the inordinate period of time it took for the EPA to get regulations approved for surface-water pollution control. As Rosenbaum (1985: 158) wrote, "Not until 1978, several years later than the law [the Clean Water Act of 1972] had mandated, did the EPA issue the important general regulations prescribing the acceptable pretreatment standards for water pollution discharged by industry into municipal treatment systems.

By the end of that year, implementation of the standards had been smothered by litigation; more than 200 cases had been initiated in state and federal courts challenging the new standards."

Besides these suits which involved pretreatment standards, other political factors likely slowed the path toward aggressive EPA oversight of the states. For example, as Waterman (1989) argued, the Reagan administration attempted a veritable revolution in environmental politics. That revolution was designed to slow the path toward regulation and to delegate considerable authority back to the states. The data presented in Figure 6.1 clearly show that only a limited number of NOVs were issued during the latter years of Reagan's presidency. In January 1989, however, George Bush became president. His administrator of the EPA, William Reilly, was a former president of the Conservation Foundation. In addition, the Bush administration supported passage of the Clean Air Act (CAA) of 1990 and was characterized by greater support, or at least less overt opposition to environmental standards (i.e., covert attempts were undertaken by Dan Quayle's Council on Competitiveness to undercut environmental regulations). As can be seen in Figure 6.1, once George Bush assumed the presidency the number of notices of violations issued by the EPA increased dramatically. Although the number of NOVs has fluctuated over time, it is clear that the average is much higher than in the period prior to George Bush's ascension to the presidency. Clearly, as measured by the number of NOVs issued, then, the EPA has played a much more active oversight role in recent years.

Beyond its oversight role, the EPA also interacts with the states in other ways. The most important of these involves providing funding for various state programs. According to the EPA's EMS manual (EPA 1986, Chapter VA, NPDES Inspection Strategy), "State inspection programs have been funded through the Clean Water Act S106 grants to the states." The EPA also provides oversight of grants for sewage-treatment facilities. Some 75 billion dollars of federal funds have been distributed to the states and localities to build and ameliorate sewage-treatment facilities since 1972 (World Resources Institute 1994: 71). The EPA has also provided additional funding through the Superfund program. In recent years, however, these allocations have been reduced or eliminated altogether and present political trends suggest that in an age of tight federal budgets, matching funds and grants to the states for pretreatment and other water-related programs will not likely be forthcoming.

A final note on the state/EPA relationship is that even in states with primacy, the EPA performs the important task of what former EPA administrator William Ruckleshaus described as "the Gorilla in the Closet." This

Figure 6.1. **Notices of Violation**

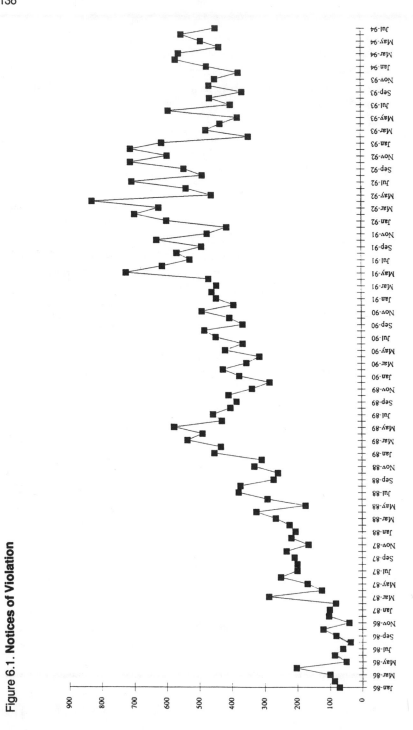

means that if states run into problems with particularly recalcitrant permittees, they know they can always turn to the EPA for assistance. Our analysis of primacy in Chapter 3 also suggested that the states often pass higher-level cases to federal EPA personnel.

In our interviews with state environmental officials many directly cited Ruckelshaus's comment in describing their relationship with the EPA. Many officials noted that the EPA gives them considerable latitude to enforce the law, so long as they are living up to the letter of the law. They also noted that the EPA is there when they need it. Hence, to many of the state environmental officials we interviewed the oversight role of the EPA was evaluated in highly positive terms.

The Permit Review Process

As the previous discussion has demonstrated, the Clean Water Act of 1972 provides for an active state role in the implementation of the NPDES program. The next question we ask is, how active have the states actually been in the enforcement process? Evan Ringquist (1993: 73) wrote that the states have played an active role: "States undertake far more monitoring and enforcement actions than does the EPA. In 1988, the states regulated twice as many 'major' NPDES permittees as did the EPA (5,000 versus 2,500) and over three times as many 'minor' NPDES sources (40,000 versus 12,000). In addition, state backlogs in issuing NPDES permits were only one-half as long as federal permit backlogs."

We likewise demonstrate that in permitting, compliance-monitoring, and enforcement activities the states have played an active and critically important role in the NPDES program. This is the positive side of the enforcement story. On the negative side, our comparison of the individual states demonstrates that not all of them are equally committed to active enforcement of the NPDES program (for more on state variations in environmental enforcement see Bowman 1984, 1985a, 1985b; Regens and Reams 1988; U.S. General Accounting Office 1982a). In addition, we demonstrate that state employees are more aggressive in issuing permits and conducting inspections than they are with regard to higher-level enforcement activities.

We turn our attention first to the NPDES permit program. One measure of a commitment to environmental enforcement is reflected in the number of permits issued under the NPDES program. In Table 6.5 we present a summary of the number of major NPDES permits issued in each of the states by both state officials and regional EPA employees. We break these figures down into municipal and nonmunicipal categories. In Table 6.6 we

Table 6.5

Number of Major NPDES Permits Issued per State

State	Municipals PL 92-500 and non–PL 92-500	Non-Municipals Private owned	State owned	Federal owned	Other unknown	Total
Alabama	117	99	0	7	0	223
Alaska	20	166	0	0	0	187
Arizona	19	11	3	6	0	40
Arkansas	65	33	0	2	0	100
California	155	77	0	9	0	246
Colorado	67	36	0	8	0	112
Connecticut	63	53	0	1	1	118
Delaware	14	17	0	0	0	32
Florida	147	128	0	3	0	293
Georgia	119	53	0	5	0	177
Hawaii	10	13	0	4	0	27
Idaho	27	33	2	2	0	64
Illinois	182	82	0	3	0	267
Indiana	108	65	0	4	0	179
Iowa	79	28	0	1	0	112
Kansas	41	9	0	3	0	57
Kentucky	63	52	0	4	0	122
Louisiana	95	150	0	2	0	247
Maine	66	31	0	1	0	98
Maryland	44	44	0	9	0	98
Massachusetts	96	68	0	0	0	165
Michigan	92	89	1	0	0	184

(continued)

Table 6.5 *(continued)*

State					
Minnesota	54	27	0	0	81
Mississippi	51	32	0	1	85
Missouri	78	48	0	2	129
Montana	26	19	0	0	45
Nebraska	42	18	0	0	67
Nevada	7	3	0	0	10
New Jersey	109	96	2	3	211
New Hampshire	42	25	0	2	69
New Mexico	25	10	0	1	36
New York	231	129	3	3	367
North Carolina	132	90	0	4	228
North Dakota	16	7	0	2	25
Ohio	176	109	0	3	289
Oklahoma	58	32	0	4	95
Oregon	46	24	0	0	70
Pennsylvania	253	148	0	2	404
Rhode Island	19	10	0	0	29
South Carolina	95	87	0	1	183
South Dakota	23	5	0	2	30
Tennessee	91	38	0	15	144
Texas	370	213	0	5	588
Utah	27	11	0	1	39
Vermont	27	7	0	0	34
Virginia	61	53	0	8	123
Washington	45	43	0	4	93
West Virginia	39	66	0	0	105
Wisconsin	85	51	0	0	136
Wyoming	16	13	0	0	29

Source: Data provided by EPA.
The total also includes two categories not listed in this table: public non–POTW and public–private owned facilities.

Table 6.6

Number of Minor NPDES Permits Issued per State

State	Municipals	Non-Municipals				Total
	PL 92-500 and non–PL 92-500	Private owned	State owned	Federal owned	Other unknown	
Alabama	167	1,216	29	25	30	1,684
Alaska	24	529	3	84	3	648
Arizona	29	41	1	22	1	107
Arkansas	277	350	46	54	0	768
California	97	800	24	22	2	1,067
Colorado	192	258	18	9	0	511
Connecticut	24	527	9	11	53	652
Delaware	3	43	0	0	2	61
Florida	77	339	11	27	1	507
Georgia	338	549	1	16	2	910
Hawaii	4	39	1	7	0	54
Idaho	78	105	12	7	0	213
Illinois	538	1,225	91	18	18	2,286
Indiana	301	666	86	4	0	1,594
Iowa	650	714	48	0	73	1,608
Kansas	410	513	20	7	8	1,122
Kentucky	173	1,577	80	59	0	2,452
Louisiana	314	782	24	22	0	1,154
Maine	62	160	12	25	0	279
Maryland	141	562	18	24	34	918
Massachusetts	38	294	10	13	1	394
Michigan	320	1,047	37	13	9	1,522
Minnesota	497	397	18	16	6	1,015

(continued)

Table 6.6 *(continued)*

Mississippi	275	803	45	33	58	1,414
Missouri	531	1,111	54	38	308	2,273
Montana	61	87	3	11	0	174
Nebraska	326	567	3	2	14	989
Nevada	9	62	4	3	2	84
New Jersey	75	840	32	15	38	1,109
New Hampshire	37	67	8	3	1	122
New Mexico	23	99	2	11	0	139
New York	354	1,158	73	13	4	1,722
North Carolina	197	889	45	6	1	1,560
North Dakota	265	80	4	13	0	390
Ohio	621	3,036	75	22	54	4,234
Oklahoma	248	273	5	5	0	574
Oregon	165	696	56	13	15	1,008
Pennsylvania	584	3,409	98	42	31	4,558
Rhode Island	19	71	4	4	17	105
South Carolina	165	758	74	17	2	1,076
South Dakota	240	53	15	18	0	332
Tennessee	475	857	4	38	10	1,448
Texas	802	1,606	37	55	0	2,523
Utah	26	59	1	1	0	89
Vermont	60	32	0	2	0	106
Virginia	602	1,080	5	44	6	2,351
Washington	178	312	15	27	8	564
West Virginia	203	3,166	51	23	5	3,606
Wisconsin	41	466	1	1	6	958
Wyoming	15	718	16	19	8	838

Source: Data provided by EPA.

The total also includes categories not listed: public non–POTW and public–private owned. This accounts for the apparent discrepancy in the totals provided.

then present a similar breakdown of the number of minor permits issued in each state. As can be seen, in every state, whether it is a primacy state or not, more minor than major permits have been issued. When we examine particular categories of permit issuances, however, this picture changes somewhat. For example, when it comes to permits for municipalities, California has issued more major than minor permits. This is evidence of California's greater concern with municipal discharges, a concern we first demonstrated at the federal level in Chapter 3. Other states that exhibit a similar pattern toward municipalities include Connecticut, Florida, Hawaii, Maine, Massachusetts, and New Hampshire. By narrow margins, Nevada, Utah, and Wyoming have also issued more major than minor permits to municipalities.

When we examine the absolute numbers of major and minor permits delineated in Tables 6.5 and 6.6 we can also see that there are considerable variations in the numbers issued across the states. To bring some order to this process, in Table 6.7 we rank order the number of major and minor permits combined by state. As can be seen, Pennsylvania, with 4,962 permits, ranks first, whereas Hawaii, with 81 permits, ranks last. It is unclear from a visual examination of Table 6.5 whether there is a regional component to the issuance of NPDES permits. An examination of the ten states that have issued the most permits suggests there may not be a regional component. Among them are eastern states (New York and Pennsylvania), border states (West Virginia and Kentucky), Rustbelt and midwestern states (Illinois, Ohio, and Missouri), two southern states (Virginia and Alabama), and a southwestern state (Texas). To provide a clearer picture, however, we broke down the number of permit issuances by region in Table 6.8. We also broke them down into four categories; major, minor, total, and the average number of total permits issued per state in each region. As is apparent from the table, there are wide discrepancies across the regions in terms of permit issuances. The most permits have been issued in regions 3, 4, and 5 (more than twelve thousand each), whereas the least permit issuances have occurred in regions 1 and 9 (fewer than two thousand each). When we control for the number of states in each region, region 3 has issued the most permits at 2,541. The most active regions in terms of permit issuances are, in order, regions 3, 5, 2, 7, and 4. Regions 2 and 3 include East Coast states, regions 5 and 7 include Rustbelt and midwestern states, and region 4 includes southern states. The regions that have issued the least permits come from the West (regions 8, 9, and 10), the South and Southwest (region 6), and New England (region 1), which ranks last. Because, as we noted in Table 6.1, regions 1, 6, and 10 have the most nonprimacy states, the data in Table 6.8 appear to provide strong evidence that primacy is related

Table 6.7

States Ranked by Number of Major and Minor NPDES Permits Issued

Rank	State	Number of Permits
1	Pennsylvania	4,962
2	Ohio	4,523
3	West Virginia	3,711
4	Texas	3,111
5	Kentucky	2,574
6	Illinois	2,553
7	Virginia	2,474
8	Missouri	2,402
9	New York	2,089
10	Alabama	1,907
11	North Carolina	1,788
12	Indiana	1,773
13	Iowa	1,720
14	Michigan	1,706
15	Tennessee	1,592
16	Mississippi	1,499
17	Louisiana	1,401
18	New Jersey	1,320
19	California	1,313
20	South Carolina	1,259
21	Kansas	1,179
22	Minnesota	1,096
23	Wisconsin	1,094
24	Georgia	1,087
25	Oregon	1,078
26	Nebraska	1,056
27	Maryland	1,016
28	Arkansas	868
29	Wyoming	867
30	Alaska	835
31	Florida	800
32	Connecticut	770
33	Oklahoma	669
34	Washington	657
35	Colorado	623
36	Massachusetts	559
37	North Dakota	415
38	Maine	377
39	South Dakota	362
40	Idaho	277
41	Montana	219
42	New Hampshire	191
43	New Mexico	175
44	Arizona	147
45	Vermont	140
46	Rhode Island	134
47	Utah	128
48	Nevada	94
49	Delaware	93
50	Hawaii	81

Table 6.8

Permits Issued per Region

Region	Major	Minor	Total	Mean per state
1	444	1,536	1,980	330.0
2	578	2,831	3,409	1,704.5
3	762	11,494	12,256	2,451.2
4	1,455	11,051	12,506	1,563.3
5	1,136	11,609	12,745	2,124.2
6	1,066	5,158	6,224	1,244.8
7	365	5,992	6,357	1,589.3
8	280	2,334	2,614	435.7
9	323	1,312	1,635	408.8
10	414	2,433	2,847	711.8

to NPDES permit issuances. Table 6.8 indicates that there is a regional component to the issuance of NPDES permits. Still, because we have not examined other factors related to the diversity of the regulatory environment, we cannot provide a more rigorous test of this thesis until the next chapter.

In Table 6.9 we examine the impact of organizational structure on the number of permit issuances. The results demonstrate that other forms of organizational structure, beyond region, have an impact on the number of permits issued. Part A of the table compares the number of major and minor permits issued by primacy and nonprimacy states. As the above quote by Ringquist noted, primacy states clearly perform the major portion of the permit-issuance process. As of the end of 1993, 72.3 percent of all major permits had been issued by primacy states, whereas only 27.7 permits had been issued in nonprimacy states. Likewise, 87.5 percent of all minor permits had been issued by primacy states, whereas only 12.5 percent had been issued by nonprimacy states. Because there are thirty-eight primacy states and only twelve states without primacy, we might expect these types of variations in the aggregate numbers. When we control for the number of primacy and nonprimacy states in part B of Table 6.9, however, we found that nonprimacy states actually have been more active in terms of the issuance of major permits by a relatively narrow margin of 54.8 to 45.2 percent. With regard to minor permits, however, the primacy states have by far been more active in issuing permits, by a margin of 68.9 to 31.1 percent. Because major permits are subject to more frequent inspections, inspections of a more stringent type, as well as more stringent enforcement standards (see Chapter 2), this finding is important. It suggests that regional EPA officials take a more active role in issuing permits that require a more stringent regulatory oversight. Part of the reason for this discrepancy between major

Table 6.9

Impact of Primacy and State Organizational Structure on the Issuance of NPDES Permits

Part A: Total major and minor permits, with percentages

	Major		Minor	
Primacy	4,980	(72.3%)	48,880	(87.5%)
Nonprimacy	1,912	(27.7%)	6,992	(12.5%)

Part B: Major and minor permits, average by state

	Major		Minor	
Primacy	131.0	(45.7%)	1,286.3	(68.9%)
Nonprimacy	159.3	(54.8%)	582.7	(31.1%)

Part C: Major and minor permits, by organizational structure of the state agency

	Major by state/average		Minor by state/average	
Health	827	75.2	5,790	526.4
MiniEPA	2,882	151.7	21,851	1,150.1
Superagency	2,121	132.56	18,684	1,167.8
Other	1,062	265.5	9,547	2,386.8

and minor permits may be that regional EPA personnel have greater discretion in assigning points that count toward whether a permittee will be classified as a major or minor permittee (see Chapter 2).

In part C of Table 6.9 we examine the issuance of permits according to which organizational format a state employs. In this analysis, as well as in the other analysis presented in this chapter and Chapter 7, we have classified Oklahoma and New Mexico as having health agencies. Our reason for doing so was that although they have switched to miniEPAs in recent years, most of the permits and other enforcement actions we examine were conducted while they employed health agencies.

Our first conclusion is that states that employ a miniEPA organizational structure are the most active in issuing major permits, followed next by the superagencies, and then by the health agencies, which lag far behind. This is true both with regard to the total number of major permits issued and the average number issued per state. Actually, the four states that use "other" forms of organizations rank at the top, but because two of these states are Texas and California (large population states), we have decided to concentrate on only the other three organizational formats. MiniEPAs issued the most minor permits, followed again by superagency states and then, far behind, states with health agencies. When we examine the average number of minor permits issued per state, however, superagency states have a slight advantage on miniEPA states, with health agency states again lagging far behind. Overall, these figures suggest that miniEPAs and superagencies play a far more active role in the permitting process than do health agencies, a conclusion that is consistent with our a priori expectation that state health agencies would be the least aggressive organizational actors in the enforcement process.

The results from Tables 6.8 and 6.9 suggest that organizational structure matters. Although a more rigorous test of this thesis will be carried out later in the book (see Chapters 7 and 8), our preliminary results indicate that organizing the EPA into regions, delegating primacy to the states, and placing state programs in different organizational structures has important implications for NPDES enforcement.

Compliance Monitoring

We next examined EPA data on compliance-monitoring activity by the states and the federal EPA from four of the EPA's ten regional offices (region 1 from the Northeast, region 6 from the South and Southwest, and regions 9 and 10 from the West). We examined data that provide a unique analysis of only a brief period of time, from June 1988 through April 1989. Still, these data are interesting because they allow us to break the number of inspections down by the lead agency—that is, a state agency, the EPA, a joint inspection with the EPA in the lead, or a joint inspection with the state taking the lead. Although the number of joint inspections is negotiated between the EPA and the states, the distribution of state and federal inspections should provide us with a means of determining how aggressive the state role has been in NPDES enforcement.

As can be seen in Table 6.10, 75.3 percent of all inspections in these four EPA regions were conducted by the states. An additional one percent were joint inspections in which the states took the lead. Thus, more than three-quarters of all basic monitoring activity during this period was conducted by the states. Furthermore, most of the EPA's monitoring activity occurred in states that do not have primacy over their NPDES programs.

Next we broke monitoring behavior down by the type of inspection conducted. Most inspections are compliance-monitoring (nonsampling) inspections, which as we noted in Chapter 2, mostly involve a site visit combined with a review of relevant monitoring reports, the discharge monitoring report (DMR) filed by the permittee. The NPDES manual, however, also requires the states and the EPA's ten regional offices to conduct more

Table 6.10

Inspections by Lead Agency, Inspection Type, and Type of Permittee

Lead agency	Inspections	
	Total	Percentage
EPA	655	18.6
State	2,644	75.3
Joint inspection (EPA lead)	179	5.1
Joint inspection (state lead)	35	1.0

Lead agency	Type of inspection			
	Sampling		Nonsampling	
	Number	Percentage	Number	Percentage
EPA	58	6.6	282	18.5
State	789	89.4	1,156	75.7
Joint inspection (EPA lead)	28	3.2	70	4.6
Joint inspection (state lead)	8	1.0	19	1.9

Type of permitee	EPA		State		Joint EPA		Joint state	
	Number	Percentage	Number	Percentage	Number	Percentage	Number	Percentage
Industry	191	17.6	855	78.7	31	2.9	10	0.9
Municipality	367	23.0	1,147	72.0	62	3.9	16	1.0
Utility	18	12.6	116	81.8	8	5.6	1	0.7
Government facility	25	18.9	103	78.0	2	1.5	2	1.5

rigorous inspection types, such as compliance-sampling inspections. Given our a priori expectation that the federal government would have greater available resources for enforcement purposes, we anticipated that although the states were more active in the total number of inspections conducted, the EPA would be more aggressive with regard to inspection type. But as can be seen in the second part of Table 6.10, the states actually have been more aggressive with regard to inspection type as well! The number of compliance inspections matches the percentages in the first part of Table 6.10 almost identically. The states conducted 75.3 percent of the total number of inspections, but 75.7 percent of compliance evaluation (nonsampling) inspections were conducted by the EPA. And although 18.6 percent of all inspections were conducted by the EPA, 18.5 percent of compliance evaluations were conducted at the same level. With regard to compliance-sampling inspections, however, only 6.6 percent were conducted by the EPA. 89.4 percent of all compliance-sampling inspections were conducted by the states! Thus, not only have the states been more active in terms of the total number of inspections conducted, but they also have been more vigorous with regard to the types of inspections conducted.

The states likewise are aggressive in their compliance-monitoring activities regardless of the type of permittee involved. As can be seen in the third part of Table 6.10, the states conducted 70 percent or more of the total inspection activity with regard to each type of permittee (i.e., industry, municipalities, utility companies, and government facilities). Thus, it is clear from Table 6.10 that when it comes to compliance-monitoring activities, we should be paying much closer attention to the states.

Enforcement

A similar picture emerged when we examined the aggregate data on NPDES enforcement. Although the EPA played a more aggressive role in conducting higher-level enforcements than it did with regard to compliance-monitoring activities, the results presented in Table 6.11 suggest that the states have continued to play an active role at this stage of the enforcement process, as well. When we present a breakdown of the total number of enforcement actions conducted by the EPA and the states from 1989 to 1992, the percentages indicate that enforcement activity is roughly shared between the federal and the state level. The EPA conducted 8,589 enforcement actions during this four-year period, or 51.5 percent of the total number of such actions, whereas the states conducted 8,098, or 48.5 percent. Although the states have not been as active in conducting actual enforcement actions as they have been in the area of compliance monitoring, the

Table 6.11

Enforcement Actions by EPA and States, 1989–1992

EPA	8,589	51.5
States	8,098	48.5

Source: Data provided by EPA.

results suggest they have still played a vitally important role in the implementation of the Clean Water Acts.

Although the aggregate data indicate that the states indeed are active in NPDES enforcement, the data for the individual states paint a less optimistic picture. In Table 6.12 we present data on enforcement activity from each of the fifty states for the same time period. As can be seen, there are considerable variations in the number of enforcement actions across the states. For example, the states in which the most enforcement actions were conducted were Texas, Louisiana, New Hampshire, and North Carolina. Two of these are Southern states, one a Southwestern state, and one a New England state. With the exception of North Carolina, they also are nonprimacy states, meaning that the EPA retains primary jurisdiction over NPDES enforcement in these states. The states with the least number of enforcement actions are North Dakota, Delaware, Hawaii, and Montana. Two are western states, one is an eastern seaboard state, and one is located on the Pacific Ocean.

As we did with the number of permit issuances, we also examined the number of enforcement actions to determine if any regional variations can be determined. When we did this in Chapter 3, with federal enforcement data only from 1978 to 1986, we found evidence of considerable variations across EPA regions. We present similar variations in part A of Table 6.13. We again find that regions 6 and 2 are most active in enforcing the law (although the order has changed—region 6 here has conducted the most actions, followed next by region 2). We also find that regions 1, 3, 7, 8, 9, and 8 are relatively inactive in terms of overall enforcements. When we calculated a weighted average of enforcement actions per region (weighted by the number of states per region) region 6 was still the most active, followed by regions 2, 4, 5, and 10. The least active regions were regions 3, 1, 7, 9, and 8. As can be seen, one of the states that was least active, region 1, has multiple nonprimacy states, while region 6, with the most nonprimacy states, ranked highest. Thus, with regard to primacy, the analysis of the ten EPA regions is not consistent.

Table 6.12

Total Enforcement Actions Conducted by Federal and State Officials in the Fifty States, 1989–1992

State	Total	Percentage
Alabama	260	1.6
Alaska	140	.8
Arizona	51	.3
Arkansas	710	4.3
California	118	.7
Colorado	69	.4
Connecticut	74	.4
Delaware	4	.0
Florida	385	2.3
Georgia	150	.9
Hawaii	5	.0
Idaho	28	.2
Illinois	214	1.3
Indiana	303	1.8
Iowa	128	.8
Kansas	21	.1
Kentucky	786	4.7
Louisiana	1,918	11.5
Maine	122	.7
Maryland	80	.5
Massachusetts	154	.9
Michigan	290	1.7
Minnesota	239	1.4
Mississippi	630	3.8
Missouri	109	.7
Montana	11	.1
Nebraska	36	.2
Nevada	18	.1
New Hampshire	33	.2
New Jersey	1,580	9.5
New Mexico	229	1.4
New York	572	3.4
North Carolina	1,225	7.3
North Dakota	1	.0
Ohio	545	3.3
Oklahoma	576	3.5
Oregon	93	.6
Pennsylvania	234	1.4
Rhode Island	83	.5
South Carolina	120	.7
South Dakota	47	.3
Tennessee	98	.6
Texas	3,040	18.2
Utah	26	.2
Vermont	20	.1
Virginia	59	.4
Washington	179	1.1
West Virginia	34	.2
Wisconsin	21	.1
Wyoming	24	.1

Table 6.13

Impact of Region, Primacy, and State Organizational Structure on EPA Enforcement Actions

Part A: Enforcements by region

Region	Total	Average per state
1	486	81.00
2	2,152	1,076.00
3	411	82.20
4	3,654	456.75
5	1,612	268.66
6	6,473	1,294.60
7	294	73.50
8	178	29.67
9	192	48.00
10	440	110.00

Part B: Enforcements—Primacy vs. nonprimacy states

	Total		Average by state	
Primacy	9,169	(57.7%)	241	(30%)
Nonprimacy	6,723	(42.3%)	560	(70%)

Part C: Enforcements by organizational structure of the state agency

Organization	Total	Average per state
Health	1,184	107.6
MiniEPA	6,534	343.9
Superagency	4,923	307.7
Other	3,251	812.8

To provide a more rigorous test, in part B of Table 6.13 we broke down the number of enforcement actions into primacy and nonprimacy states. The figures presented in Table 6.11 demonstrated that the states perform almost one-half (48.5 percent) of all NPDES enforcement activity. The data in Table 6.13 indicate that the nonprimacy states are almost as active as the primacy states. A full 42.3 percent of all enforcement activity is conducted in just the twelve nonprimacy states, whereas only 57.7 percent of activity is conducted in the thirty-eight primacy states. But when we control for the total number of primacy and nonprimacy states, a markedly different picture emerges. On average, each of the twelve nonprimacy states conducted 560 enforcement actions or 70 percent of all enforcement activity. This means that 70 percent of all enforcement activity occurred in just the twelve nonprimacy states! What does this mean? It means that although the aggregate figure presented in Table 6.11 suggested an active state role in enforcement, the states clearly have not been as active as regional EPA personnel have been once we control for the total number of primacy and nonprimacy states. These figures are strong evidence that the states are less committed to aggressive enforcement than is the federal EPA. In short, the results presented in part B of Table 6.13 are deeply disturbing.

To determine which states are least likely to enforce the law aggressively, in part C of Table 6.13 we again broke down enforcement actions by the type of organizational structure employed by each state. As with our analysis of permits in Table 6.9, our results again show that states that use health agencies to implement their water programs are less aggressive in enforcing the law. With only 1,184 total actions and a weighted average of 107.6 per state, states employing health agencies lag far behind states with other organizational structures. Again, the miniEPA and superagency states provide more stringent outputs. When we look at the weighted averages, miniEPA states are more aggressive (6,534 total actions and 343.9 actions per state) than superagencies (34,923 actions and 307.7 actions per state). Again, we exclude states with "other" organizational formats from this analysis because there are only four of them (and two are Texas and California).

These results again demonstrate that organizational structure matters. They also suggest that the regional officials of the EPA have been more aggressive in their enforcement of the NPDES program than have state officials. This is a matter of considerable concern, particularly because the direction of environmental enforcement in recent years appears to be toward delegation of authority from the federal level and a resulting more prominent state role in enforcement.

Regulatory Program Strength

Our measures of enforcement in this chapter have thus far included data from both the federal EPA and the states. This has allowed us to compare the federal and state role in enforcement. But we also want to examine the individual commitment of individual states to enforcement of the NPDES program. Consequently, in this section we examine data on the regulatory strength of the water-quality programs in the fifty states compiled by FREE (1988) and updated by Evan Ringquist (1993). We present the rankings for each state in Table 6.14. As Ringquist (1993: 157) wrote,

> The evaluation matrix used to create the measure of state water program
> strength borrows heavily from the 1988 FREE rankings and the state policy

Table 6.14

Ringquist's State Water Program Strength Score

State	Score	State	Score
Alabama	5	Montana	8
Alaska	2	Nebraska	9
Arizona	5	Nevada	6
Arkansas	5	New Hampshire	6
California	8	New Jersey	11
Colorado	6	New Mexico	5
Connecticut	10	New York	10
Delaware	8	North Carolina	11
Florida	8	North Dakota	6
Georgia	10	Ohio	8
Hawaii	8	Oklahoma	6
Idaho	6	Oregon	11
Illinois	11	Pennsylvania	9
Indiana	7	Rhode Island	8
Iowa	9	South Carolina	7
Kansas	8	South Dakota	6
Kentucky	8	Tennessee	5
Louisiana	3	Texas	2
Maine	7	Utah	8
Maryland	11	Vermont	10
Massachusetts	6	Virginia	11
Michigan	11	Washington	7
Minnesota	12	West Virginia	5
Mississippi	7	Wisconsin	13
Missouri	8	Wyoming	9

Source: Ringquist (1993: 158).

innovation index found in the Green Index. . . . The FREE submatrices provide information regarding the level of state responsibility for the federal NPDES and municipal wastewater treatment grant program, the percentage of NPDES permittees in significant noncompliance with their permits, the number of EPA enforcement activities undertaken to back up the failure of state efforts under the CWA, and the scope and strength of the state's non-point source pollution control program. To the FREE rank score based on this data, I add one point for each of the following strengths or innovations in a state's water pollution control program; an approved industrial pretreatment program, a toxic water pollution control program, authority to regulate federal facilities under the CWA, a wetlands protection program, and a ground-water protection program.

In part A of Table 6.15 we broke down the state program strength scores by region. This provided some extremely interesting results. What was

Table 6.15

Impact of Region, Primacy, and State Organizational Structure on Ringquist's State Program Strength Measure

Part A: State program strength by region

Region	Total	Rank
1	7.8	5
2	10.5	1
3	8.8	3
4	7.6	6
5	10.3	2
6	4.2	10
7	8.5	4
8	7.2	7
9	6.8	8
10	6.5	9

Part B: Stage program strength by primacy vs. nonprimacy state

	Average per state
Primacy	8.5
Nonprimacy	5.2

Part C: State program strength by organizational structure of state agency

Organization	Average per state
Health	6.6
MiniEPA	7.6
Superagency	9.0
Other	6.5

immediately apparent to us was that region 6, which had ranked as the most active region in terms of enforcement activity, ranks last in regard to its weighted average (per state) regulatory program strength score. This reflects the fact that most of the enforcement activity conducted in region 6 has been conducted by federal EPA personnel, particularly in the states of Texas and Louisiana. As we have noted repeatedly, four of the six states in region 6 do not have primacy.

Other results in part A of Table 6.15 are also interesting. The region with the highest program strength scores is region 2. This is interesting inasmuch as two former administrators of the EPA Water Office informed us that New Jersey had one of the worst compliance records in the country. Among other top regions on this ranking are regions 5, 3, 7, and 1. The regions that rank lowest are regions 4, 8, 9, 10, and 6. The regions that score lowest on this ranking are from the West, the Southwest, and the

South, whereas those that score highest are from the Rustbelt, the Midwest, and the East.

In part B of Table 6.15 we broke down the regulatory program strength scores by whether a state has primacy or not. Clearly, we expected to find a relationship of some sort here, insofar as primacy is one of the criteria used in the construction of the index. Because, however, the index includes a variety of other criteria, we thought it worthwhile to present the results regardless of our expectations. Not surprisingly, we found that the weighted average of nonprimacy states ranks far lower than that for primacy states, by a margin of 5.2 to 8.5.

In part C of Table 6.15 we also broke down the program rankings by the type of organization each state uses to enforce water pollution programs. Again, states with health agencies rank lowest of the three types with an average score of 6.7, although the four so-called other states rank lowest at 6.6. It is clear that the more aggressive activity in these four states, as represented by our results on permit issuances and enforcement actions, is largely the result of EPA personnel rather than state officials. As for the other two types of state organizations, superagencies rank highest at 9 with states with miniEPAs ranking second at 7.6.

Conclusions

The results from Table 6.15 again show that there is considerable variation in state-level enforcement, as well as variation in the commitment of the fifty states to the implementation of the NPDES program. We find these variations disturbing, but not surprising. Given the diverse nature of the regulatory environment, we had expected to find considerable variation across regions and states. As we argued in Chapter 3, the diverse regulatory environment and the resulting pragmatic enforcement style (and accompanying bureaucratic discretion) actively encourage such variations. In short, because federal and state environmental officials interact with a diverse regulatory environment (consisting of multiple sources of pollution, different water problems across states and regions, different levels of political support, different levels of water usage, different types of water usage, and so forth) we expect each of these three factors (pragmatic enforcement, bureaucratic discretion, and regional and state variations in enforcement) to occur.

A legitimate criticism of the approach adopted in this chapter is that we have not controlled for a variety of other factors, beyond organizational structure, which also may explain variations in permit issuances and enforcement behavior. We also have not controlled for one type of organizational structure on another. As we noted at the beginning of this chapter, however, our sole purpose here has been to introduce and examine variations in organizational structure across regions and the fifty states. In the next chapter we provide a more detailed examination of the factors that promote a diverse regulatory environment in the area of surface-water pollution control. In that chapter, we provide a more statistically rigorous test of the effects of organization on NPDES enforcement behavior. We also present the rest of the puzzle with regard to the question of what factors NPDES personnel respond to and what is meant by the term "bureaucratic discretion."

7

Explaining Variations in NPDES Enforcement

What do bureaucrats respond to? What is bureaucratic discretion? We raised these two key questions at the end of Chapter 5. Then in Chapter 6 we provided a discussion of the role of organizational structure in NPDES enforcement. In this chapter we fill in the remaining pieces of the puzzle by examining in detail the nature of surface-water pollution control's regulatory environment. We first discuss a number of diverse factors that bureaucrats may respond to. Then we provide an empirical test of the regulatory diversity thesis.

Before we turn to our analysis of these diverse factors, we first wish to thank Evan Ringquist for his cooperation in providing some of the data we analyzed during the course of this chapter. We are taking the somewhat unusual step of thanking him directly in the text because we have noted a declining proclivity in recent years on the part of scholars and lay people to read footnotes, and we did not want his contribution to be overlooked.

Political Influence

Despite the active participation of the states in the permit, compliance monitoring, and enforcement process, our analysis from Chapter 6 demonstrated that there are considerable variations in state-level enforcement of surface-water pollution control laws. One reason cited for these variations has been the role that political influence plays at the state level. For example, Walter Rosenbaum (1985: 164) wrote, "In many states local water polluters have economic and political weight quite disproportionate to their national stature. Often a handful of industries constitute practically the whole of a state's economic base. Intense and effective political pressure often can be exerted by such interests to impede implementation of the law."

In a later edition of his work, Rosenbaum (1991: 198) continued that local regulatory agencies have a greater tendency than the federal EPA to "accommodate regulatory interests . . . to enforcement of designated water uses and the associated emission controls." Rosenbaum then concluded, "Regulated interests often are likely to press vigorously for a major state role in the administration and enforcement of water quality standards, believing that this works to their advantage more than implementation through the EPA's regional and national offices."

Our interviews with state environmental personnel provided considerable support for Rosenbaum's claim that the states represent a highly political arena. For example, a top-level enforcement official from New Mexico stated that political pressure occurs on a case-by-case basis. He then delineated how, during the tenure of a past Republican governor, considerable pressure was exerted on agency personnel to ease enforcement practices. In one case he even asserted that "a sweetheart deal" was worked out between the governor's office and the number three violator on the state's enforcement priority list. Likewise, an official from Alaska complained that after his office assessed penalties against a particularly egregious violator, a past "governor . . . simply gave the money back."

The governor was not the only state official identified as having influence over state water-enforcement policy. Business interests were also prominently identified in our conversations with state personnel. An official in Arizona, for example, stated that business interests have undue influence. He then added, this is a "very conservative state." Development is "the most important issue." A number of officials from various states also identified environmental groups as having considerable political influence. A top water official from Alaska, for example, said that environmental groups were "loud and obvious" and thus tended to attract a lot of attention from agency personnel.

It should be noted that studies of the federal EPA have also demonstrated that politics plays an important role in the enforcement process (Wood 1988; Waterman 1989; Harris and Milkis 1989; Wood and Waterman 1991; Waterman and Wood 1993). Wood and Waterman (1993; 1994) examined, along with three other EPA divisions, the enforcement of the EPA NPDES program and found that such actors as the president, Congress, the federal courts, and even the media exerted influence over NPDES enforcement outputs. Our own analysis in Chapter 5 likewise demonstrated that a variety of hierarchical political actors (e.g., the president, Congress, the courts) have exerted influence over the NPDES program. It should also be noted that once we turn our attention from the national government to the states, support for environmental regulation appears to vary even more considerably from state to state. Some states appear to be firmly committed to aggressive environmental regulation, but others tend to be less forthright in their support.

One means of measuring this variation in state-level support for the environment is provided by the League of Conservation Voter (LCV) environmental support scores for each states's House and Senate delegations. These LCV scores are important because they not only reflect support for environmental issues in Congress, but also represent a measure of political support for the environment in each state. As we would expect, Table 7.1 demonstrates that there are wide variations in support for the environment across the states. For example, when we examined support scores for the year 1992, we found House scores ranged from a high of 100 percent in Vermont to a low of 0 percent in Alaska and Wyoming. In the Senate, Massachusetts scored the highest at 96 percent, whereas Idaho, Mississippi, Utah, and again Wyoming scored the lowest with a score of 0 percent.

From a regional perspective, with the exception of New Hampshire, the New England states exhibited the most pro-environmental House and Senate delegations in the country. Likewise, eastern seaboard states like New York, New Jersey, Delaware, and Maryland had very environmentally minded congressional delegations. The picture changed, however, when we turned our attention to other regions of the country. In the Rustbelt and midwestern regions environmental support scores were consistently lower than they were in the eastern states. They were higher, though, than the LCV scores for the southern, southwestern, Rocky Mountain, and western states. Additionally, there was considerable variation within regions. For example, Illinois, Michigan, Minnesota, and Wisconsin had more environmentally minded legislators than some other Rustbelt or midwestern states. In these regions, Iowa, Kansas, and Missouri ranked at the low end of the scale. As we turned our attention to the South, environmental-support scores were lower than in the Midwest, with Florida and Georgia, both coastal states, showing the highest level of support. In the Southwest, both Texas and New Mexico ranked low in both legislative bodies. In the West there was greater variation than in most other regions, with Alaska, Arizona, Montana, and Wyoming ranking near the bottom of the scale and California and Oregon ranking considerably higher.

In short, there are considerable variations across regions, with the New England and East Coast states ranking highest, and the southern, southwestern, and western states ranking among the lowest in the nation on the 1992 LCV rankings. There are also some striking variations within regions, with coastal states such as California, Georgia, and Florida ranking higher than other states in their regions. Interestingly, when one looks at the states with

Table 7.1

League of Conservation Voter Scores for the 1992 U.S. House and U.S. Senate Delegations from the Fifty States (in percent)

State	House	Senate
Alabama	23	13
Alaska	0	8
Arizona	11	13
Arkansas	20	46
California	47	54
Colorado	34	29
Connecticut	69	92
Delaware	56	55
Florida	44	46
Georgia	32	75
Hawaii	94	67
Idaho	44	0
Illinois	47	80
Indiana	46	25
Iowa	18	29
Kansas	33	17
Kentucky	21	17
Louisiana	13	25
Maine	81	75
Maryland	59	80
Massachusetts	80	96
Michigan	44	75
Minnesota	70	75
Mississippi	19	0
Missouri	38	8
Montana	22	29
Nebraska	29	46
Nevada	38	67
New Hampshire	50	25
New Jersey	58	88
New Mexico	27	29
New York	62	63
North Carolina	30	34
North Dakota	56	9
Ohio	35	88
Oklahoma	30	21
Oregon	58	34
Pennsylvania	32	59
Rhode Island	91	75
South Carolina	40	21
South Dakota	69	33
Tennessee	32	54
Texas	25	25
Utah	42	0
Vermont	100	88
Virginia	24	38
Washington	43	55
West Virginia	48	59
Wisconsin	46	71
Wyoming	0	0

Source: World Resources Institute (1994: 230–79).

the most environmentally minded delegations in both the South and the West they tend to be states that border the ocean. Of course it should be noted that the data we present here are from the 1992 House and Senate delegations. These figures will surely change following the monumental political shifts engendered by the 1994 midterm elections. As the House and Senate delegations change, we would of course expect the state rankings to change, especially because as Dunlap (1989) and Bruce, Clark, and Kessel (1991) have concluded, Democrats tend to have higher environmental LCV scores than Republicans. In summary, when we look at the political landscape we find considerable variation in political support for the environment across states and regions. Some states clearly are more politically committed to environmental protection than are others. In addition, it is clear from our interviews that political influence is overtly exerted in many states. With regard to the LCV scores, we will hypothesize that enforcement (e.g., permit issuances and enforcement activity) should be more aggressive (e.g., more permits should be issued and more enforcement actions conducted) in states with more pro-environmental House and Senate delegations.

LCV scores represent but one measure of political influence. In addition, in the empirical analysis we present later in this chapter, we will consider three other measures. We examine two measures of voter participation: the percentage of citizens registered to vote in each state in 1988 and 1992 and the percentage of actual voters in the 1988 and 1992 presidential elections. Our hypothesis is that enforcement will be more aggressive in states where public participation is higher.

It also is possible that state governmental factors exert an independent impact on enforcement outputs, in addition to the congressional and voter participatory measures we have considered above. Therefore, our last measure of political influence is a measure of legislative professionalism, reflecting the professionalism of the fifty state legislatures. We would expect greater levels of enforcement to occur in states with more professional legislatures (see Ringquist 1993).

Interest-Group Influence

As many of the interviews cited above suggest, different types of interest groups (e.g., environmental, business) may also exert influence on the level of the NPDES response. A highly diverse array of scholars have argued that interest groups play an important role in regulatory politics. Some have argued that interest-group influence is a benign manifestation of our nation's pluralist governmental process (Truman 1951), whereas others have argued that interest groups have venally captured the regulatory agencies that initially were designed to oversee them (Huntington 1952; Kolko 1963, 1965; Kohlmeier 1969; Lowi 1979). Although they disagree about the motives of interest groups, or the effects of interest-group liberalism on our political system, all agree that interest groups play a vital role in the regulatory process. In this chapter we examine several types of interest groups.

From a theoretical perspective, of the various types of interest groups the most relevant would appear to be environmental groups, inasmuch as their very purpose for coming into existence was to help preserve the environment. They therefore have a clear, vested interest in environmental regulation. Although many environmental groups operate nationally, there are variations in environmental-group support across the fifty states. We examined Ringquist's (1993: 162) measure of environmental-group strength in the states, which consists of 1987 membership (per one thousand persons in each state) in the Sierra Club, Friends of the Earth, and the National Wildlife Foundation. On this measure a diverse set of states ranked high. Vermont, New Hampshire, California, Alaska, Oregon, Connecticut, Minnesota, Montana, Maine, Washington, Wyoming, Massachusetts, and Maryland exhibited the highest number of environmental-group members. These represent mainly New England and western states. At the other extreme were Mississippi, Alabama, Kentucky, Louisiana, Tennessee, Arkansas, South Carolina, Texas, Georgia, West Virginia, Oklahoma, and Utah. As can be seen, most of these states are Southern states. In short, there appears to be a strong regional component to environmental-group membership.

There are a large number of environmental groups active in the states, but it is important to note that they do not all share the same policy goals and objectives. As Evan Ringquist (1995c: 152) wrote,

> Though environmental groups still make up the largest block of players in the environmental quality advocacy coalition (the seven largest groups had 7.7 million members in 1990), they can no longer be seen as a unified force. The environmental movement has matured and diversified to include large, multi-issue groups (Sierra Club); smaller, more narrowly focused "purist" groups (Friends of the Earth); nonpartisan research and policy development centers (Resources for the Future); law and science groups (Environmental Defense Fund); "radical" deep ecology groups (Earth First!); and increasingly active independent state and local groups (Clean Water Action). While these groups may share certain core values, they display a dazzling variety of policy positions and political tactics.

This diversity of "policy positions and political tactics" is evidence of fractionalization, which may suggest that, despite their impressive numbers, environmental groups in America are not united politically. That would suggest that environmental-group influence may be on the wane. Along with variations in political positions, membership in environmental groups also has fluctuated over time. Environmental-group membership soared during the late 1960s and early 1970s (Jones 1975), but declined substantially late in the decade. As Mitchell, Merting, and Dunlap (1992) note the conservative politics of the Reagan era then contributed to a dramatic increase in the membership of environmental groups. Waterman (1989: 134–35) likewise provided evidence of a surge in membership and contributions to environmental groups during the early 1980s. On the other hand, in recent years environmental-group membership appears to be on the decline again. With Republican challenges to the Endangered Species Law and Clean Water Act during the 1995–96 congressional session, as well as severe proposed cuts in funding for the EPA, there may yet be another resurgence in environmental-group membership. Still, the variety of different environmental groups and their fluctuating membership suggest that environmental-group influence may be on the decline. This is a hypothesis we examine later in this chapter.

Environmental groups represent an organized measure of interest in the environment. On the other hand, the so-called outdoorsman also is interested and interacts in environmental matters, but is not organized as an environmental interest group. Although outdoorsmen clearly do not share the same goals as traditional environmentalists, they do have a vested interest in the environment. Environmental degradation depletes the amount of water and land that would otherwise be available for fishing and hunting activities. Because outdoorsmen regularly interact with the environment, they also are more likely to be aware of ongoing environmental degradation, or conversely the results of ongoing steps to improve the quality of the environment. As a result, outdoorsmen are likely to be both aware of ongoing environmental degradation and supportive of protecting the environs in which they hunt and fish.

Unlike the other interest groups we will examine, outdoorsmen, although they are often organized into various sports-related groups, represent a latent measure of interest-group support for the environment; that is, the purpose of their organizations is not to exhibit support for the environment. Therefore, outdoorsmen differ from our other interest-group measures. They may be an important factor in environmental matters, because they have a vested interest in preserving the environment. We will therefore examine their potential influence on surface-water pollution control enforcement outputs. For a direct measure of the "outdoorsman" we would have preferred a representation related directly to water, such as the number of fishing licenses issued in each state. Because we were unable to secure this particular measure, however, we have used instead the number of hunting licenses issued per one thousand people in each state as our surrogate measure for "outdoorsmen."

When we examined this measure we found the largest number of hunting licenses were issued in Western states such as Idaho (586.4), North Dakota (575.3), Montana (569.8), South Dakota (538.2), Wyoming (470.9), and Oregon (351.7), with a large number of licenses also issued in Midwestern states such as Wisconsin (302.2), Iowa (263.4), Nebraska (225.1), Michigan (212.8), and Missouri (203.8). Although there is a clear regional component to the states where the most hunting license have been issued, there is less of an observable pattern to the states where the fewest licenses have been issued. These include Hawaii (11.7), Rhode Island (20.0), California (23.1), Florida (29.0), Massachusetts (34.6), Connecticut (34.6), New Jersey (38.1), Maryland (42.4), Illinois (56.3), South Carolina (60.8), North Carolina (65.0), New York (73.7), and Nevada (83.6). Many of these are New England and East Coast states, but they also include southern, midwestern, and western states. Furthermore, not all New England states are represented by low levels of hunting license issuances. Vermont issued 205.4 licenses per thousand people, Maine 163.2, and New Hampshire 114.3. Of the East Coast states, Pennsylvania issued (187.7), whereas such border states as West Virginia (339.4), Tennessee (188.4), Georgia (146.5), Kentucky (139.9), Arkansas (139.0), and Virginia (137.2) also have issued a substantial number of hunting licenses. Therefore, although western and midwestern states are more likely to issue hunting licenses, clear variations are not as readily observable among the states that issue fewer licenses. We therefore cannot dismiss hunting licenses as merely a surrogate for region.

Along with environmentalists and outdoorsmen, who have an incentive to preserve wilderness areas, other interest groups often find themselves in economic conflict with the environmental movement. For example, polluting industries and mining groups are directly affected by water-quality regulations. Because they seek NPDES discharge permits, and therefore the right to discharge into local waters, they are more likely to favor a relaxed regulatory role. This is particularly true inasmuch as both can contribute heavily to water pollution. Despite the high level of trust that EPA NPDES enforcement personnel exhibit regarding industry, industry was described by the Council on Environmental Quality (1993: 227) as the sixth most important polluter of rivers (see also Chapter 3). Likewise, mining companies contribute considerably to water pollution problems. For example, as Michael Hayes (1992: 98–99) wrote, auger mining (boring horizontally into exposed coal seams) is often employed to extract as much coal as possible from the seam after contour mining techniques cease to be efficient. Auger mining inevitably generates an acid water discharge that also runs down the mountainside, resulting in highly toxic pools and/or the pollution of nearby streams. Additional water pollution results from the dumping of sediments into streams and the oxidation that results from exposure of sulfur-bearing rock to water and sunlight. The resulting sulfates and sulfides increase the acidity of streams, with devastating consequences for both plants and fish.

As with environmental groups and outdoorsmen, polluting-industry and mining-company strength varies considerably across the states. With reference to Ringquist's (1993: 162) measure of polluting-industry strength, which is the "value added by manufacturing as a percentage of gross state product in 1986 produced by those industries most responsible for water pollution," there are clear variations. Polluting-industry strength is strongest in such diverse states as Indiana, Wisconsin, Ohio, South Carolina, Tennessee, Arkansas, New Jersey, Illinois, Pennsylvania, Maine, and Vermont. Clearly, there is no clear-cut regional pattern to these industrial states. States that rank lowest on this measure include Alaska, Wyoming, Nevada, North Dakota, Montana, and Hawaii—western states.

Mining industry strength is represented by "the value of mining output in 1986 as a percentage of gross state product" (Ringquist 1993: 162). Mining activity is highest in states such as Alaska, Wyoming, Louisiana, West Virginia, New Mexico, Oklahoma, Texas, and North Dakota, and considerably lower in most other states. No clear regional pattern is therefore apparent in the data.

Finally, agricultural groups also can exert considerable influence on policy outputs. Because, as the Council on Environmental Quality (1993: 227) reports, pollution in U.S. rivers is overwhelmingly caused by runoff from agricultural sources, one would expect to find that states with a greater percentage of output from farms would be more strictly regulated. Because, however, most agricultural runoff is classified as a nonpoint source, and the NPDES program is primarily interested in point-source pollution, we could also expect that NPDES personnel would play a less active role in enforcement in states where agricultural interests are more predominant. As Ringquist (1993: 162–63) wrote, "Few water quality regulations have focused on agriculture because of the decentralized nature of nonpoint pollution problems." We have measured agricultural group strength in two ways: "as the average percentage of gross state product attributed to all crops and livestock in 1985 and 1986" and as the net farm income as gross state product for 1986 (Ringquist 1993: 163). The states ranking highest on these

measures are North Dakota, South Dakota, Wyoming, Nebraska and Iowa—
all midwestern and western states.

In summation, we have suggested that a wide variety of interest groups
potentially can influence the politics of environmental protection. We examine these groups (environmental groups, outdoorsmen, polluting industry, mining interests, and agricultural interests) later in this chapter. The
latter three of these groups clearly bring an economic component to their
interest in environmental matters. Economic factors can also influence environmental enforcement in other ways. For this reason we turn next to a
discussion of several possible economic influences on NPDES enforcement.

Economic Influence

In the last two sections we discussed variations in political influence across
the fifty states. As many scholars have noted, economic factors provide an
alternate explanation for variations in state-level policy outputs. For example, Dye's (1966) research found a strong correlation between state wealth
and education policy in the American states. In a recent study of environmental policy, Lowry (1992: 69–72) found an association between personal
income per capita in a state and the ranking of its stationary water program.
He also found a statistically significant relationship between personal income and both a state's water expenditures for stationary water source
pollution control and "state reception of waste treatment grants." On the
other hand, Ringquist's (1993: 167) integrated model of state policy influence found no such correlation between per capita income and the strength
of state water pollution control programs; although he does acknowledge
(ibid.: 170) that it has a strong indirect effect on the strength of a state's
water pollution control program.

Other literature also suggests that state wealth may be related to enforcement outputs. For example, early research on environmental politics concluded
that conservation issues were largely the concern of the upper-middle class (see
Harry, Gale, and Hendee 1969; Devall 1970). Most recent public-opinion studies have found no association between income or social status and attitudes
about the environment (Buttel and Flinn 1978; Van Liere and Dunlap 1980;
Mohai and Twight 1987). Still, one study by Elliott, Regens, and Seldon (1995:
50) found a significant association between income and environmental
attitudes. They concluded, as "real income [per capita] increases, the public's
willingness to support increased spending on environmental protection also
increases." Consequently, although there is considerable disagreement in the
findings related to economic influence, there are clear reasons for considering
state wealth as a possible determinant of enforcement outputs.

. Most scholars have been content to use the measure of a state's per capita income, but in fact it represents just one possible measure of economic influence. In his economic model of state policy influence, Ringquist (1993: 159) also identified a positive correlation between the level of industrialization in a state and the strength of its state water pollution control program. It is therefore possible that there could be a similar positive association between the level of industrialization in a state and the number of NPDES permits issued or enforcement actions undertaken.

Likewise, the unemployment rate also can be associated with enforcement outputs. As we demonstrated in Chapter 5, the unemployment rate was negatively associated with the number of referrals to the Justice Department. In Chapter 4, Rouse and Wright found that approximately three-quarters of all NPDES personnel say they consider the condition of the state of the economy when they enforce the law. Other scholars also have found evidence that the unemployment rate is associated with environmental attitudes. For example, Elliott, Regens, and Seldon (1995: 50) noted that during "periods of economic retrenchment other concerns, such as joblessness or inflation, are at the forefront of the political agenda." Likewise, Buttel (1975) conceded that during difficult economic times the public turns its attention away from environmental matters and toward economic concerns. Given our earlier findings, and the results of these studies on environmental attitudes, we again postulate that the unemployment rate is associated with enforcement outputs, in a negative direction.

Unemployment is but one measure of a tradeoff between the economy and the environment. Another possibility raised by the "environmental justice" literature is that the level of poverty in a state is associated with enforcement activity. As Bullard (1990) has argued, communities housing poor people and minorities are more likely to suffer the ravages of exposure to various contaminants and thus a higher level of environmental risk (see also Cable and Cable 1995; Szasa 1994; Paehlke and Rosenau 1993; Bryant and Mohai 1992; Colquette and Robertson 1991; Godsil 1991). Therefore, if NPDES enforcement personnel respond to the level of the environmental threat in a particular state, we should expect to find a positive association between the percentage of the population living below the official poverty line and the level of enforcement activity.

Obviously, if as Regens (1991) argued, there is a tradeoff between spending for environmental matters and spending for other purposes we also need to consider the level of state expenditures for environmental programs. As we would expect, there is considerable variation in state-level spending. As Ringquist (1995c: 152) wrote, "States fund environmental regulation programs, to varying degrees. In the early 1980s, states provided from 19 percent (Rhode Island) to 76 percent (California) of the cost of running pollution control programs, and state contributions have increased since that time."

We would expect that a positive association would exist between state expenditures and enforcement activity; that is, the more money a state spends on its environmental programs the more enforcement outputs it will generate. Although this is a logical assumption, Appleton (1985) found no such association between the resources devoted to implementing consumer protection laws in the states and actual enforcement of those laws. Likewise, Ringquist (1993: 159) found no association between per capita state expenditures and the strength of a state's water pollution control program. Despite these past findings, we believe it is necessary to control for state expenditures in order to derive a reliable measure of the impact of other economic variables on the level of enforcement outputs. Any model that did not incorporate state expenditures would, at least from a theoretical perspective, be underspecified.

In conclusion, there are a number of possible economic influences on enforcement activity. Therefore, along with our measures of political and interest-group activity, we consider a variety of economic factors. Past research (Ringquist 1993; Lowry 1992) examined the impact of political and economic factors on water quality enforcement. As we have noted throughout this book, one of our main concerns is that the diversity of the surface-water pollution control regulatory environment can have a direct impact on the behavior of state and federal NPDES personnel. Although political and economic factors are indeed vital to our understanding of this diverse regulatory environment, we also need to consider a variety of factors directly related to water issues such as measures of water quantity, water usage, and the sources of water pollution problems. We turn to a discussion of these issues in the next section of the chapter.

Water Usage and Quantity

In an earlier work we (Hunter and Waterman 1992: 407) wrote, EPA enforcement "officials have told us that the variability in the types of water problems is a critically important factor which accounts for their use of greater flexibility in the enforcement of the CWA." Can the same be said for NPDES enforcement by both state and federal personnel? In Chapter 1 we examined the diverse nature of water pollution problems in the fifty states. In this section we examine differences in water quantity and water usage among them.

As studies by Ingram (1990), Ostrom (1990), and Munro (1993) have demonstrated, the politics of water quantity is an important issue in many western states. In our own interviews with state environmental officials, most western state officials identified issues related to water quantity as being high on their agenda. On the other hand, this was a much less prevalent theme of the environmental officials we talked to from eastern states, who were more likely to identify water quality as their major concern. When they did discuss water quantity, they generally did so in terms of preserving wetlands areas. In other words, preserving natural habitats appeared to be a greater concern than freeing water for economic development purposes.

One possible reason for these variations in perceptions across regions is that water quantity varies considerably from region to region and state to state. As Zachary Smith (1992: 107) wrote, "In the United States, many areas, most notably in the West, either or will soon be suffering from water shortages." Thus, while water quality is certainly an important issue, many state officials are equally interested in water quantity. As George Tchobanoglous and Edward Schroeder (1985: 3) wrote, "The major issues associated with the use of water by humans are quantity and quality. Within limits, water quantity is more important than water quality in determining the extent and type of development possible in a given geographical location."

In Table 7.2 we present data on water quantity for each of the fifty states. As can be seen from a perusal of column one of the table, there is indeed considerable variation in the amount of water available. Such big land-area states as Alaska, with 86,051 square miles of water, Michigan, with 40,001, Florida, with 11,761, and Wisconsin, with 11,190, rank at the very top in terms of water quantity. On the other end of the scale are smaller states such as West Virginia, with 145, New Mexico, with 234, Arizona, with 364, and Vermont, with 366 square miles of water. By looking at Table 7.2, we can also compare the water quantity in various states. For example, California has roughly as many square miles of water as Minnesota, whereas tiny Rhode Island has more than three times as much water as New Mexico, a much larger southwestern state. Likewise, such geographically disparate states as Pennsylvania, Oklahoma, South Dakota, and New Jersey have similar water-quantity levels. In short, when we look at the water-quantity figures, we find that there is considerable variability across states and regions, and even within regions of the country. We would expect these variations to have an impact on how NPDES personnel enforce the law. We hypothesize that the greater the amount of water in a state, the greater the level of the enforcement response (i.e., more permits issued, more enforcement actions undertaken) will be.

Although water quantity is important, so is the way each state uses its

Table 7.2

Water Area and Water Usage in the Fifty States

State	Water* area	Per capita water usage per day**	Public supply***	Thermo- electric	I&M****	Irrigation
Alabama	1,673	2,103	7.6	80.5	9.9	0.8
Alaska	86,051	712	21.2	7.4	32.8	0.0
Arizona	364	1,715	10.0	0.9	2.1	85.8
Arkansas	1,107	2,492	5.4	18.4	3.0	65.5
California	7,734	1,636	11.0	24.5	2.3	61.6
Colorado	371	4,027	5.5	0.8	1.6	91.2
Connecticut	698	1,149	10.6	84.9	3.9	0.1
Delaware	535	2,426	5.3	67.9	24.8	1.6
Florida	11,761	1,280	11.4	66.8	4.0	17.1
Georgia	1,522	823	17.2	61.0	12.0	8.3
Hawaii	4,508	1,894	10.0	45.1	0.9	42.1
Idaho	823	21,463	1.3	0.0	1.5	92.4
Illinois	2,325	1,256	13.2	80.7	4.4	0.5
Indiana	550	1,431	8.9	55.8	34.3	0.6
Iowa	401	991	15.0	65.3	9.4	2.4
Kansas	459	2,273	6.3	7.3	1.7	83.4
Kentucky	679	1,131	10.7	81.2	6.3	0.2
Louisiana	8,277	2,446	6.5	57.3	20.2	14.2
Maine	4,523	1,231	8.4	70.4	16.4	0.1
Maryland	2,633	1,381	12.4	80.9	5.5	0.5
Massachusetts	2,717	1,611	8.3	87.5	1.6	0.2
Michigan	40,001	1,217	12.0	73.6	12.1	1.8
Minnesota	7,326	639	21.3	51.9	16.1	7.4
Mississippi	1,520	968	13.1	26.7	9.4	35.3
Missouri	811	1,185	11.4	80.7	1.9	5.0
Montana	1,490	10,705	2.0	0.8	0.7	96.0
Nebraska	481	6,277	2.7	22.1	1.7	72.7
Nevada	761	2,913	8.0	0.6	0.9	89.6
New Hampshire	382	809	12.4	60.7	26.7	0.1
New Jersey	1,303	894	16.1	65.5	16.4	1.9
New Mexico	234	2,119	8.0	1.8	2.5	86.0
New York	7,251	842	20.1	71.5	7.1	0.3
North Carolina	5,103	1,300	8.7	82.9	6.2	1.5
North Dakota	1,710	1,827	7.2	76.9	1.1	13.3
Ohio	3,875	1,161	12.3	82.7	4.3	0.1
Oklahoma	1,224	400	43.1	10.6	8.9	35.0
Oregon	2,383	2,238	7.6	0.2	4.6	87.3
Pennsylvania	1,239	1,196	12.5	71.3	15.4	0.1
Rhode Island	500	407	29.8	63.8	4.9	0.7
South Carolina	1,896	1,916	6.2	76.0	16.6	0.5
South Dakota	1,224	960	14.2	0.6	6.8	68.1
Tennessee	926	1,706	8.2	71.7	19.1	0.1
Texas	6,687	1,458	12.2	43.5	10.9	32.1
Utah	2,736	2,441	10.5	0.6	4.9	83.1

(continued)

Table 7.2 *(continued)*

State	Water* area	Per capita water usage per day**	Public supply***	Thermo-electric	I&M****	Irrigation
Vermont	366	222	51.6	0.8	43.7	0.8
Virginia	3,171	1,153	9.5	79.4	9.3	0.7
Washington	4,721	1,401	15.0	6.1	8.0	70.3
West Virginia	145	3,021	3.2	77.4	18.9	0.1
Wisconsin	11,190	1,360	9.8	80.7	6.8	1.2
Wyoming	714	13,522	1.8	3.8	3.0	91.0

Source: World Resource Institute, *The 1994 Information Please Environmental Almanac*, 230–79.

    *Water area is presented in square miles.

    **Per capita water usage per day is reported in gallons.

    ***Public supply, thermoelectric, I&M, and irrigation figures are presented in terms of percentage of water withdrawn for this purpose in each state.

    ****Represents withdrawal of water for industrial and mining purposes.

water resources. In columns 2 through 6 of Table 7.2 we present data on actual water usage in the fifty states. Again the picture that emerges is one of considerable diversity, not only in terms of the total per capita water used each day, but also in terms of the purposes for which that water is used. We present four categories of water usage: water used for the public supply, thermoelectric purposes, industry and mining activities, and irrigation purposes. As can be seen, most states use a relatively small percentage of their water for their public supply. Vermont at 51.6 percent and Oklahoma at 43.1 percent are two obvious exceptions. Twenty-three states use less than 10 percent of their water for public purposes. Another twenty-one states use between 10 and 20 percent for public purposes. Only six states use more than 20 percent of the water they withdraw for this purpose. Thus, there is less diversity regarding the percentage of water withdrawn for public purposes than one might have expected.

The same cannot be said for water withdrawn for thermoelectric purposes. It ranges from a low of 0 percent in Idaho to a high of 87.5 percent in Massachusetts. Sixteen states use less than 10 percent of their withdrawn water for thermoelectric purposes, whereas twenty-eight states use 50 percent or more of their water for the same purpose. Furthermore, there does not seem to be an easily identifiable regional explanation for these variations. The differences between the states are striking. States from the East (Connecticut), the South (Virginia), the Deep South (Alabama), the Midwest (Illinois, Missouri, and Wisconsin), and several so-called border states

(West Virginia, Maryland, and Kentucky) all use approximately the same percentage of water for thermoelectric purposes.

With regard to industry and mining, there is less variability. Thirty-four states use less than 10 percent of their withdrawn water for industrial or mining purposes. This is surprising given the general emphasis in the environmental literature on the prominent role that industry and mining interests play as contributors to water pollution problems. In fact, industry and mining concerns withdraw relatively little water in comparison to thermoelectric plants. In addition, in most states, more water is withdrawn for the public water supply than for industrial and mining purposes.

Although there is little variability with regard to industry and mining, there is considerable variability with regard to water withdrawn for irrigation purposes. Twenty-eight states withdraw less than 10 percent of their water for irrigation. On the other hand, sixteen states withdraw more than 50 percent of their water for this purpose. A simple visual examination of the data in Table 7.2 reveals that in many states there is an inverse relationship between the amount of water withdrawn for thermoelectric purposes and water withdrawn for irrigation. Unlike thermoelectric water withdrawal, however, there appears to be a definite regional component to irrigation water usage. The states that withdraw the largest percentage of their water for irrigation purposes are western states. The states that have withdrawn the highest percentages for this purpose are Montana (96 percent), Idaho (92.4 percent), Colorado (91.2 percent), and Wyoming (91 percent).

Although there are substantial variations with regard to water quantity and water usage, there does not appear to be as much variation with regard to whether states withdraw ground or surface waters. In Table 7.3 we present data on water withdrawn from surface and ground sources for each of the fifty states. As can be seen, much more water is withdrawn from surface-water sources (the ones regulated by the NPDES program) than from groundwater sources. Although there is considerable variation related to the amount of water withdrawn, most states use a greater amount of surface water than groundwater. Only six states (Arkansas, Kansas, Mississippi, Nebraska, New Mexico, and Oklahoma) withdraw more water from the ground than from surface sources. In addition, groundwater usage tends to be highest in western states. Thus, our analysis agrees with Zachary Smith's (1992: 106) conclusion that "roughly 75 percent of freshwater comes from surface sources." This is not to suggest, however, that groundwater is not important. As Regens and Reams (1988: 54) noted, "It supplies approximately 40 percent of all irrigation water used by agriculture as well as approximately one quarter of all industrial sector water withdrawals. In addition, groundwater is the primary source of drinking water for more than

Table 7.3

Water Withdrawal: Comparing Ground and Surface Waters

State	Groundwater	Surface water
Alabama	403	7,680
Alaska	112	529
Arizona	2,740	3,830
Arkansas**	4,710	3,130
California	14,900	31,900
Colorado	2,800	9,190
Connecticut	165	4,680
Delaware	89	1,280
Florida	4,660	13,200
Georgia	996	4,360
Hawaii	590	2,150
Idaho	7,590	12,100
Illinois	945	17,100
Indiana	621	8,810
Iowa	495	2,370
Kansas**	4,360	1,720
Kentucky	247	4,070
Louisiana	1,340	8,010
Maine	85	1,060
Maryland	239	6,180
Massachusetts	338	5,180
Michigan	707	10,900
Minnesota	797	2,480
Mississippi**	2,670	963
Missouri	728	6,200
Montana	218	9,100
Nebraska**	4,800	4,150
Nevada	1,070	2,280
New Hampshire	64	1,250
New Jersey	566	12,200
New Mexico**	1,760	1,720
New York	840	18,100
North Carolina	435	8,510
North Dakota	141	2,540
Ohio	904	10,800
Oklahoma**	905	760
Oregon	767	7,660
Pennsylvania	1,020	8,810
Rhode Island	25	501
South Carolina	282	5,720
South Dakota	251	341
Tennessee	503	8,690
Texas	7,880	17,300
Utah	971	3,510
Vermont	45	587
Virginia	443	6,420
Washington	1,450	6,490

(continued)

Table 7.3 *(continued)*

State	Groundwater	Surface water
West Virginia	728	3,860
Wisconsin	681	5,830
Wyoming	403	7,200

Source: U.S. Government, *The American Almanac 1993–1994: Statistical Abstract of the United States,* 223.

  *Presented in millions of gallons of water withdrawn each day.

**States that withdraw more water from ground than surface sources.

50 percent of the total population, and 95 percent of the residents in less populated, rural areas depend entirely on it for domestic uses."

Extrapolating from Regens and Reams, because groundwater is more closely associated with nonpoint pollution sources, and because western states use more of their withdrawn waters for irrigation purposes, concerns over nonpoint pollution sources should be highest in western states. We can therefore hypothesize that because western states use more of their withdrawn water for irrigation, there should be a negative correlation between irrigation withdrawals and the NPDES enforcement response. We would expect a positive relationship between the amount of water used for industrial or mining interests and the NPDES response, inasmuch as NPDES personnel should be more aggressive in enforcing the law in those states where the threat of pollution from mining and industrial interests is highest. Additionally, we would expect a positive association between withdrawals for thermoelectric and public supply purposes and the response of NPDES personnel. Likewise, because Sapat (1995) already has found an association between groundwater withdrawal and various state-level responses to groundwater pollution, we would expect a positive response between the amount of water withdrawn by a state from surface waters and the level of the NPDES response.

Perceptions of the Sources of Water Pollution

Although water-quantity and water-usage issues clearly could be relevant to the level of the NPDES response, another relevant factor could be perceptions of the sources of water pollution problems in each state. One such source of variation is the distinction between point and nonpoint sources of pollution. Point sources are those sources with an identifiable discharge point. On the other hand, nonpoint sources are sources that have no clearly identifiable discharge point. Nonpoint discharges derive from such diverse sources as agricultural and urban runoff from streets, which end up in nearby and even distant waterways. Controlling runoff is much more difficult than is the control of pollution from an identifiable discharge site, inasmuch as it is much more difficult for EPA personnel to identity the polluter involved in a particular case (Ingram and Mann 1994; Lowry 1992; Chesters and Schierow 1985). As a result, the General Accounting Office (1977, 1980a) urged Congress to pay more attention to nonpoint sources of pollution, which it did in passing the 1987 Water Quality Act. Even so, because there is no point source for agency personnel to monitor, violations from nonpoint sources are far more difficult for enforcement personnel to ameliorate than emissions from point sources.

The Clean Water Act of 1972 largely deals with point sources of pollution. Because most state and federal personnel we interviewed informed us that nonpoint sources are by far the more difficult sources of pollution to deal with, the Clean Water Act of 1972 clearly did not adequately deal with one of the most difficult and important factors promoting water pollution. Concern over which source, point or nonpoint, is more important varies considerably across states and regions. According to Ringquist (1993: 72–73), Illinois, Indiana, Massachusetts, North Carolina, Wisconsin, and Wyoming, plus the states contiguous to the Chesapeake Bay, have the most "extensive and innovative nonpoint source programs" in the country. Ringquist also lauded Washington State for its Centennial Clean Water Program, which he described as "a nice mix of innovations in controlling both point and nonpoint source water pollutants" (ibid.: 73). Lowry (1992: 112–19) also stated that Iowa has one of the strongest nonpoint-source pollution programs in the nation. Not all states are equally committed to nonpoint pollution control, however. In an analysis of state water-management administrators in Wisconsin and Ohio, William Gormley (1987: 290) found that "Wisconsin administrators" were "more concerned about nonpoint problems than federal administrators, while Ohio administrators" were "less concerned." Gormley explained these differences by noting that "Wisconsin has made more significant progress in combating water pollution from point sources than any other state in the Midwest." As a result, "Wisconsin regulators are anxious to approach the 'new frontier' of nonpoint pollution."

In Table 7.4 we present data on the opinions of state and interstate water pollution control administrators on which source, point or nonpoint, represents a "more significant problem" in their state. As can be seen from the survey compiled by the Association of State and Interstate Water Pollution Control Administrators (ASIWPCA 1984), and as we anticipated a priori, western states are much more likely to view nonpoint water pollution as

Table 7.4

State Views on the Importance of Point and Nonpoint Sources of Pollution

States saying nonpoint sources are less important than point sources

Texas	Indiana
New Mexico	Maine
Alabama	Vermont
Georgia	New Hampshire
South Carolina	Rhode Island
Connecticut	

States saying point and nonpoint sources are of equal importance

Oklahoma	Michigan
Louisiana	Illinois
Mississippi	Missouri
Tennessee	Iowa
North Carolina	Kansas
Virginia	Nebraska
Maryland	Colorado
Pennsylvania	New York
New Jersey	

States saying nonpoint sources are more important than point sources

California	Wyoming
Oregon	Montana
Washington	South Dakota
Idaho	North Dakota
Nevada	Wisconsin
Arizona	Minnesota
Utah	Arkansas
Kentucky	Ohio
West Virginia	Delaware
Massachusetts	Florida
Alaska	Hawaii

Source: Association of State and Interstate Water Pollution Control Administrators, Nonpoint Source Committee, Water Quality Management Task Force, *Analysis of the States' Responses to ASIWPCA Nonpoint Source Pollution Survey*, February 1984.

their main problem. Administrators from all of the western states express similar perceptions on this question. Likewise, most southern and midwestern state administrators believe that point and nonpoint sources are of equal concern. Of the states that identify point sources as being more important most are from New England (five of the six New England states) or the Southwest (Texas and New Mexico). Propinquity to the ocean does not appear to be clearly related to concerns over the source of pollution. Although administrators from three Pacific Ocean states (California, Oregon, and Washington) identified nonpoint sources as being the most important, only administrators from three of the Atlantic Ocean states (Delaware, Florida, and Massachusetts) voiced the same opinion. Still, region appears to be a powerful determinant of administrator's perceptions of the relative importance of point and nonpoint sources. Because point sources of pollution are usually described as being more relevant to surface-water concerns, we hypothesize that states that show a greater concern with point sources of pollution will be more aggressive in enforcing the NPDES program.

State Demographics

As we have just noted, there are considerable variations across the states with regard to water quantity, water usage, and the perceived source of water pollution problems. Each of these factors are directly related to what we have called the diversity of the regulatory environment across the fifty states. Another factor related to this diversity is the population of each of the fifty states. At first glance it would appear that state demographic variables such as population would have little immediate relevance to water pollution control outputs. When we focus on global environmentalism, however, one of the central concerns is overpopulation and the demand that population places on the world's ecosystem (see Brown 1995: Chapter 1). Still, most studies of environmental enforcement have focused on political and economic criteria, (see Wood and Waterman 1994; Ringquist 1993), rather than population and other demographic variables. One notable exception is Lowry's (1992: 105) study, which found that "Section 208 allocations [under the Clean Water Act for federal funding of waste-treatment management programs] were almost entirely dependent on [the] population of each state." Still, funding for this program was based on the criterion of "urban-industrial concentrations." Thus, the rationale why population would be related to Section 208 funding is clear. On the other hand, why should we expect a state's population to be related to the level of the NPDES response?

Because the central theme of this book is that the nature of the regulatory environment has a direct impact on the manner in which bureaucratic personnel enforce the law, we argue that such factors as population (how many people live in a state), population density (how many people, per square mile, live in a state), and the percentage of a state's population living in metropolitan areas (where people live in a state) may be important determinants influencing regulatory outputs; and perhaps outcomes, as well (see Chapter 8). Population could be a relevant variable in an analysis of water pollution control for at least two basic reasons. First, the more people that live in a state, the greater the strain it likely places on that state's ecosystem.

In the specific case of water pollution, more people could translate into greater levels of pollution. According to this explanation, population would be a demand factor directly related to the nature of the water pollution problem. A second possible explanation for the relevancy of population is related to bureaucratic perceptions of risk. According to this alternative explanation, larger state populations would translate into a greater perceived need for more vigorous pollution control by enforcement personnel. With more people living in more diverse settings potentially at risk, environmental personnel would feel a greater need to pursue water pollution control enforcement more aggressively.

Thus, for different reasons, population may very well be related to enforcement outputs. Likewise, population density may be related, as well. The greater the density of people living within a state the greater the level of pollution and therefore the higher the level of enforcements. Or again high density areas may be perceived as areas of higher risk by agency personnel. How the population is stratified could also be related to enforcement outputs. Much research, for example, has shown that minorities disproportionately fall victim to the effects of pollution (see Wernette and Nieves 1992; Pollock and Vittas 1995). This research suggests that environmental enforcement would be weaker in states with larger minority populations. Likewise, other researchers have argued that whites are more concerned about the environment than African Americans (see Taylor 1989). Extrapolating from this "concern gap" thesis, one could hypothesize that there would be greater levels of enforcement in states with larger white populations, because white people would be more attentive to environmental problems. In recent years, however, a number of studies have debunked this "concern gap" thesis. Dunlap and Jones (1987), for example, found no differences between African Americans and whites regarding their concern over water pollution problems. Likewise, Mohai (1990) and Jones and Carter (1994) found relatively equal levels of concern between whites and African Americans on a variety of environmental issues, though Jones and Carter (1994: 575) also added "that it is more likely that certain environmental concerns will have more salience for African Americans than whites" (see also Caron 1989). Summarizing, support for the "concern gap" thesis would be found if states with larger white populations exhibited greater levels of enforcement or if states with larger African American populations exhibited lower levels of enforcement. Most past public opinion research has focused on the differences between African Americans and whites, but one could also extrapolate that enforcement would be less aggressive in states with a larger percentage of Hispanics in residence. For these reasons we will examine the possible impact of the percentage of white, African American, and Hispanic denizens of each state on NPDES enforcement.

Population is not the only demographic variable that could be related to the enforcement vigor of agency personnel. Several studies of public opinion have found that age is a strong determinant of attitudes on the environment (see Buttel 1979; Honnold 1984; Mohai and Twight 1987; Dunlap 1989; Ladd 1982; Mitchell 1984; Jones and Dunlap 1992; Kanagy, Humphrey, and Firebaugh 1994). Evan Ringquist (1993: 27) even noted that "age appears to be the only real defining characteristic regarding concern for the environment: younger generations are more concerned about the environment than are older people." It is therefore possible that the younger a state's population is, the greater the level of NPDES enforcement response will be in that state. We examine two measures of age in the analysis to follow. The first is the median age of each state's population. Because there is relatively little variance in this measure across states, we also will examine the percentage of each state's population that is sixty-five years old or older.

Several other studies have pointed to religion as an important determinant of public attitudes on environmental matters (Guth et al. 1995; Kanagy, Humphrey, and Firebaugh 1994; Shaiko 1987). According to these studies, certain denominations are more or less committed to the environment than others. We therefore examine three measures of religion: the percentage of church members in each state, the percentage of Catholics, and the percentage of Baptists.

An Empirical Test

In Chapter 6 we discussed various organizational variations across the fifty states. Then in the first part of this chapter we demonstrated that there are considerable variations across the fifty states in terms of political support for the environment, interest group influence, economic capacity, water quantity, water usage, perceptions of the source of water pollution problems, and various state demographics. In this section we empirically address a fundamental question: Does the diversity across the fifty states, which we identified in the first section of this chapter, have an actual impact on the enforcement response of NPDES personnel? In other words, does the diversity of the regulatory environment really matter? If so, which factors are the most influential determinants of enforcement behavior? To test these questions we apply the various enforcement measures we introduced in Chapter 6 as dependent variables in our analysis. These include the total number of major and minor permits issued by federal and state officials in the fifty states (logged) and the total number of enforcement actions conducted by federal and state NPDES personnel in the fifty states from 1989 to 1992 (logged). We have combined enforcement actions conducted by state and federal level personnel because we are interested in the overall NPDES response to various factors in the regulatory environment. This means that we will not be able to determine if federal and state personnel respond in differing ways to different factors in the regulatory environment. Although we believe that is an interesting question that deserves attention, we will leave it for a future analysis.

The independent variables for our analysis are summarized below in six categories: organizational, political, interest-group, economic, water, and demographic variables.

Organizational Variables

Because we argued in Chapter 6 that organizational structure can have an impact on the level of the NPDES enforcement response, we incorporate various measures representing organization in our model. These include a simple dummy variable to measure whether a state has primacy over its NPDES program or not. If a state has primacy it is coded as a one, if not then it is coded as a zero. We also examine whether the type of organization used by each of the states (i.e., miniEPA, health agency, superagency) has an impact on the level of its enforcement response. Again, these three variables are represented by dummies coded one if a state employs a particular organizational structure and zero if it does not. Finally, we provide a more thorough test of the influence of region on the level of the NPDES enforcement response, by examining dummy variables representing each of the ten regional offices.

Political Variables

We are interested in whether political support has any impact on environmental enforcement. To test this possibility we use the LCV environmental support scores for the House and Senate delegations for each of the states for the year 1992. We employ these measures, rather than the more direct state-level measure used by Ringquist (see 1993: 160), because our measure of permits and enforcement actions conducted reflects activity at both the state and federal level. Furthermore, the Senate scores should represent statewide support for environmental initiatives, whereas the House scores should be a better representation of district-level support for the environment. Although the LCV scores represent environmental support from federal actors elected from each state, and represent a surrogate measure of congressional influence, the legislative professionalism score provides a measure of state-level elite behavior. To measure the political interest of individual citizens within each state we employ the percentage of the population that was registered to vote in 1988 and 1992, as well as the percentage of the population that actually voted in 1988 and 1992 in each individual state.

Interest-Group Variables

We include measures for various interest-group influences on NPDES enforcement. These include Ringquist's (1993: 161–63) measures of polluting-industry strength, environmental-group strength, mining strength, and agricultural strength. In addition, we include a measure representing a latent interest in environmental matters: outdoorsmen, represented as the number of hunting licenses (logged) purchased per one thousand residents of each state.

Economic Variables

We use several measures of economic influence across the fifty states. As with most past studies of environmental enforcement, we use the per capita income of each state to represent its basic economic capacity. We also use per capita expenditures in each state as a measure of state commitment to environmental programs. Additionally, we employ a measure of the level of industrialization in each state (see Ringquist 1993: 158). Because of our earlier findings from Chapter 5, we also include a measure of the unemployment rate in each state. Finally, because the "environmental justice" literature argues that there is a correlation between poverty and the level of the environmental response in each state, we also include a measure representing the percentage of the population of each state living below the official poverty line.

Water Variables

As a measure of water quantity, we use two measures. The first is the log of the total water area in each state. The second is the percentage of the total number of square miles of water in each state divided by the total land area of each state. This second measure gives us a percentage of the water to land area for each state. For water usage we have developed a measure of the percentage of water withdrawn from surface waters (surface waters divided by the total amount of water withdrawn). We also use several measures including the per capita water usage per day, water withdrawn for public supply, thermoelectric, industry and mining, and irrigation usage in the model. Each of these is represented in percentage terms. Because there is a high correlation between several of these variables, for example, irrigation and thermoelectric usage, we use only one of these variables in the model at a time. We also include three measures related to perceptions of the source of pollution in each state. These are dummy variables representing states whether respondents to the ASIWPCA survey believed that either nonpoint sources of pollution were most important, point and nonpoint sources were identified as being of equal concern, or point sources of pollution were more important.

Demographic Variables

Our main demographic measure is the population of a state. We measure this in three separate ways. First, we use the raw number of people living in each state, which is logged because of the skew of the distribution. Second, we use census data on the population of each state per square mile to measure population density; again, this measure is logged. Third, we use the percentage of the population living in metropolitan statistical areas. Because many scholars have asserted that whites are more interested in environmental issues than African Americans or Hispanics, we also include measures for the percentage of the white, African American, and Hispanic population living in each state. Many scholars also have argued that age is associated with attitudes on environmental issues. We therefore include the average age of the population in each state as representation of the possible impact of age on NPDES enforcements and the percentage of the population of each state over sixty-five as a second measure representing age. Finally, because much recent research has found a correlation between religious beliefs and attitudes on the environment, we include three measures for religion. The first is the percentage of the population of each state which identified itself in the 1990 census as churchgoers. The second is the percentage of the population that identified themselves as Catholic. The third is the percentage of the population that identified themselves as Baptists.

We will not restate our hypotheses related to each of our independent variables. Instead we refer the reader back to the body of this chapter, and for the organizational measures to Chapter 6. There we present our expectations regarding the relationship between each independent variable and the level of the NPDES enforcement response.

Because of the inordinately large number of independent variables in our analysis, and obvious concerns about multicollinearity between them (e.g., many of our water-usage variables are clearly associated with other), we initially ran individual models for each postulated type of influence. As Ringquist (1993) did, we ran models for political, interest-group, and economic influence, plus models for our water and demographic variables. Because variables within categories also are related to each other, we likewise ran correlations between each of the independent variables in and across the various models to check for possible multicollinearity. Finally, we combined the results from each of these models to form an integrated model. Due to concerns about space, we will present only the results of the integrated models in this chapter. Except for the models in which we control for region, we will examine only those variables that are statistically related to our dependent variables at the 0.5 (two-tailed) or 0.10 (one-tailed) level of significance.

We begin first with an analysis of the number of major permits issued in the fifty states. The results of our analysis are presented in Table 7.5. The results presented in model 1, which does not control for region, support our hypothesis that the diversity of the regulatory environment is an important determinant of the behavior of NPDES enforcement personnel. We find clear evidence that four of our six categories of variables have a direct impact on major permit issuances: demographic, water, interest-group, and economic variables. The first measure in model 1 of Table 7.5 represents the population of each state. We hypothesized that the more people there are living in a state, the more aggressive the enforcement response from state and EPA NPDES personnel will be. Not only do our results support this hypothesis, but if we delete population from the regression model, the adjusted R-square is also reduced by over one-half. Clearly, then, not only does a state's population have a positive impact on the number of permits issued, it is the dominant factor in the model.

Population measures how many people live in a state. Our second demographic variable, the percentage of the metropolitan population, tells us where they live. Interestingly, although we found a positive association between the overall population of a state and the number of major permits issued, we find a negative relationship between the percentage of a state's population living in a standard metropolitan statistical area and the dependent variable. This suggests that NPDES personnel are not primarily motivated by concerns related to population risk. If they were, we would expect to find a positive association between the percentage of the metropolitan population and permit issuances, because more people live in metropolitan areas in most states than in rural areas. Given our hypothesis that population is related to demand for pollution, we would have expected to find a positive association between metropolitan population and permit issuances, as well. What, then, accounts for the negative coefficient? The negative coefficient is likely related to the tendency in many urban areas for industry to discharge directly into municipal wastewater-treatment systems (see Chapter 3). As a result, although there is a greater concentration of the population in urban areas, and therefore greater demand is placed on the ecosystem,

Table 7.5

Determinants of the Number of Major NPDES Permits Issued by State and Federal Officials in the Fifty States

	Model 1: Major permits logged	Model 2: Major permits (logged)
Constant	−8.00** (1.15)	−8.48** (0.96)
Demographic variables Population (logged)	0.73** (0.08)	0.75** (0.07)
Percentage of population living in metro areas	−0.01** (0.004)	−0.01** (0.003)
Water variables Water area in each state (logged)	0.13** (0.05)	0.14** (0.04)
Nonpoint sources of pollution more important (dummy)[a]	−0.27** (0.11)	−0.10 (0.10)
Interest group variables Mining industry strength	0.03** (0.007)	0.03** (0.01)
Polluting industry strength	0.05** (0.01)	0.05** (0.01)
Economic variables Per capita mean income	0.0001** (0.0000)	0.0001** (0.0000)
Organizational variables Region 9 (dummy)	—	−0.63** (0.17)
Region 10 (dummy)	—	−0.46** (0.15)
Adjusted R-square	.85	.90
N	50	50

The statistics represent the regression coefficient over its standard error.
  *Indicates significance at the 0.10 level.
**Indicates significance at the 0.05 level.
[a]The dummy for states that consider point sources of pollution to be more important is positive and statistically significant at the 0.05 level for major permits, but not for minor permits.

much of this demand is shifted onto a relatively few municipal treatment permittees. The end result is that fewer major permits are issued in metropolitan areas than we might have expected a priori. Another possible explanation is provided by Rosenbaum (1985: 148), who wrote, "A congressional staff study in the early 1980s found more than 4 out of 10 community water systems were either failing to meet water quality standards or neglecting to test the water at all. . . . Among the worst offenders are many of the 100,000 small facilities serving limited populations." It is possible, then, that the EPA has responded to such evidence and is providing stricter enforcement in areas with smaller populations.

The next two measures in our model are water variables. The first of these is simply a measure of the total water area available in each state and thus is related to water quantity. Simply put, the results indicate that more major NPDES permits will be issued in states with greater water quantity. This is further evidence that demand is related to the nature of the NPDES response. As with our two demographic variables, our finding regarding water quantity also demonstrates that the nature of the regulatory environment greatly drives the enforcement responses of NPDES personnel. The second water variable makes this point even more clearly. It is a dummy representing the perceived source of pollution, as represented in the AS-IWPCA poll of state administrators. We find that fewer major permits are issued in states where administrators perceive nonpoint sources of pollution as being more important. Likewise, although the results are not presented in Table 7.5 because of multicollinearity between the point and nonpoint measures, we also found that in states where administrators considered point sources to be more important, a greater number of NPDES major permits were issued. These results make perfect sense, because the NPDES program primarily deals with point-source pollution problems. Thus, we have evidence that the perceived source of pollution is directly related to the NPDES enforcement response.

Although the first four variables represent the diversity of the regulatory environment, the next two deal with the nature of the polluters in each state. We find that the greater the level of mining and polluting-industry strength in a state, the greater the number of major permits that will be issued. Although these variables measure the strength of these interest groups, they also are a surrogate for the prevalence of mining and industry in the various states. Thus, from the perspective of the diversity of the regulatory environment thesis, we can interpret these findings to mean that permit issuances are directly related to the types of industries present in the states, in this case mining and polluting industries. In summary, the findings in Table 7.5 provide strong evidence that the diversity of the water pollution regulatory environment has a major impact on the level and direction of the bureau-cratic response.

The final measure in the major permit model is economic, suggesting that as the mean per capita income of a state increases, the number of major permits issued also increases. This finding is consistent with Lowry's (1992) findings and suggests that states with a greater economic capacity (e.g., greater wealth) are capable of responding more aggressively at the enforcement stage.

Not only are the results of our model supportive of our contention that scholars should pay closer attention to the nature of the regulatory environ-ment in explaining enforcement outputs, but the overall fit of the model is also quite impressive, with an adjusted R-square of .85. Clearly, the one factor that accounts for most of this variance is the population of the states. Without considering this demand factor it is not possible to adequately explain the enforcement response of NPDES personnel.

The results in model 1 of Table 7.5 may explain much of the regional variation we identified in the pooled regression models from Chapter 5. To test this possibility, in model 2 of Table 7.5 we controlled for a possible independent effect exerted by the regional offices. Our expectation was that because we incorporated various factors related to the diversity of the regu-latory environment into the model, we would find limited evidence of re-gional variations in the level of the NPDES enforcement response.

The results presented in model 2 provide strong support for our a priori expectations. We found evidence of variations in only two of the ten regional offices. The negative and statistically significant coefficients for these regions come largely at the expense of the dummy variable repre-senting the importance of nonpoint pollution sources in the states. Al-though the nonpoint variable was significantly related to major permit issuances in model 1 of Table 7.5, it is no longer correlated with it in model 2. As we noted earlier in this chapter, most states that consider nonpoint sources of pollution to be of greater importance are from the West (see Table 7.4). Regions 9 and 10 represent nine western states that likewise perceive nonpoint sources as being of greater importance. Be-cause the regression coefficients for both regions are negative, as was the coefficient for the nonpoint dummy in model 1, we can extrapolate that much of the variation exhibited by these two regional offices is really related to the nature of their perceptions of pollution problems. In short, the evidence from model 2 demonstrates that there is little evidence of regional variations.

In Table 7.6 we replicate the analysis and examine minor permit issu-ances as the dependent variable. As was the case with major permit issu-

Table 7.6

Determinants of the Number of Minor NPDES Permits Issued by State and Federal Officials in the Fifty States

	Model 1: Minor permits (logged)	Model 2: Minor permits (logged)
Constant	−10.70** (1.40)	−10.51** (1.34)
Demographic variables Population (logged)	1.07** (0.10)	1.07** (0.09)
Percentage of population living in metro areas	−0.02** 0.006)	−0.02** (0.005)
Water variables Nonpoint sources of pollution more important (dummy)[a]	−0.39** (0.15)	−0.46** (0.14)
Water usage for thermoelectric purposes[b]	0.01** (0.003)	0.01** (0.003)
Interest group variables Mining industry strength	0.06** (0.01)	0.06** (0.01)
Agricultural strength	0.12** (0.05)	0.13** (0.05)
Outdoorsmen: hunting licenses (logged)	0.23** (0.11)	0.17 (0.11)
Organizational variables Primacy for NPDES program (dummy)	0.78** (0.17)	0.82** (0.16)

(continued)

ances, the population of a state is again overwhelmingly the most influential factor in the model. As with major permits, there is a positive association between a state's population and the number of minor permit issuances. Likewise, we also find a negative relationship between the percentage of a state's population living in standard metropolitan statistical areas and minor

Table 7.6 *(continued)*

	Model 1: minor permits (logged)	Model 2: minor permits (logged)
State environmental organization (dummy)	Health	Health
	−0.30* (0.11)	−0.27 (0.17)
Region 10 (dummy)	—	0.59** (0.28)
Adjusted R-square	.84	.85
N	50	50

The statistics represent the regression coefficient over its standard error.
  *Indicates significance at the 0.10 level.
**Indicates significance at the 0.05 level.
[a]The dummy for states that consider both point and nonpoint sources of pollution to be of equal importance is positive and significant for minor permits, but not for major permits.
[b]Water usage for irrigation is also statistically related to minor permit issuances. Because of a high degree of multicollinearity between thermoelectric water usage and irrigation water usage, the two variables cannot be included in the model simultaneously. When the model is run with irrigation usage, the coefficients for all other variables are practically the same as they are in the minor permit model presented. The coefficient for irrigation usage, however, is negative.

permit issuances. Our reasoning for the impact of these coefficients on minor permit issuances is the same as that explicated above for major permits.

Although the demographic variables exert a similar impact, the water variables exert a somewhat differential impact on minor permit issuances. Water quantity was related to the number of major permits issued, but not to minor permit issuances. Instead, water usage is related to permit issuances. More minor permits are issued in states where a greater level of water is withdrawn for thermoelectric purposes. Although we do not present the results, due to multicollinearity between thermoelectric and irrigation usage, fewer permits are issued in states where a greater level of water is withdrawn for irrigation purposes (as we noted above, mostly the western states). As with the major permit model, states where administrators consider nonpoint pollution to be of greater importance issue fewer minor permits. Consequently, the perceived source of pollution is related to both major and minor permit issuances. There is a difference between the two models, however. In the major permit model, the dummy representing states where administrators consider point sources to be more important was also related to permit issuances. It is not related to minor permit issuance, however. On the other hand, more minor permits are issued in states where administrators perceive both point and nonpoint sources of pollution as being of equal importance; this was not statistically related to major permit issuances. Thus, although we find considerable similarities with regard to the water variables between the two models presented in Tables 7.5 and 7.6 (comparing models 1 in both tables), there are some interesting differences as well. Despite these differences, both models demonstrate that the nature of water issues in the states are related to permit issuances.

As with the results of the major permit model, we also find that minor permit issuances are related to several interest-group measures. Again, as in the major permit model, we find a positive association between permit issuances and mining strength, indicating that where mining interests are more prevalent, more minor permits will be issued. We also find a positive association between one of our measures of agricultural strength, net farm income as a percentage of gross state product for the year 1986, and minor permit issuances. This finding is understandable when we consider the combined results from models 1 of Tables 7.5 and 7.6. They suggest that NPDES personnel are more likely to issue more major permits in states where industry is prevalent and more minor permits in states where agriculture is prevalent.

Somewhat surprisingly, we also found that there is a positive association between our measure of outdoorsmen, the number of hunting licenses issued in each state (logged), and the number of minor permits issued. As we postulated earlier in this chapter, this measure represents a latent measure of interest-group support for the environment. Because "outdoorsmen" regularly interact with the environment, and because they are therefore likely to be aware of ongoing environmental degradation of wilderness areas, we do not find the positive association between permit issuances and hunting licenses to be particularly surprising, despite the tendency to consider hunters and other outdoorsmen to be anti-environmental. The fact that they depend on and regularly interact with the environment gives them a vested interest in it.

Last, we find no evidence of an economic influence on the issuance of minor permits. We do, however, find a relationship between two organizational factors and the dependent variable. As our preliminary analysis in Chapter 6 suggested, primacy states are more likely to issue minor permits than nonprimacy states. Our more rigorous analysis presented in Table 7.6 confirms this expectation. Likewise, our findings from Chapter 6 suggested that health agencies are less likely to issue minor permits. Again, the results from model 1 of Table 7.6 confirm this finding, but only at the 0.10 (one-tailed) level of significance. As we hypothesized, the results from the minor permits model demonstrate that organizational structure exerts an important impact on permit issuances. Although this is an important finding, we also note that we found no evidence that primacy or state structure impacts major permit issuances.

As we did in Table 7.5, in model 2 of Table 7.6 we control for regional variations in NPDES enforcement. The results again demonstrate that once we include measures of the diversity of the regulatory environment in our model, there is little evidence of regional variations. We find a statistically significant coefficient for only one regional office (region 10). Once a dummy for region 10 is incorporated in the model, statistical support for the independent effect of state-agency structure and outdoorsmen is eliminated, which indicates some overlap between these measures. The important point, however, is that only one regional office shows any evidence of variations in the level of its enforcement response.

In Table 7.7 we turn our attention to the total number of enforcement actions (logged) conducted in each state by state and federal NPDES personnel. As can be seen in model 1 of Table 7.7, both primacy and state organization have a statistically significant impact on the dependent variable. As we found in Chapter 6, states with primacy, on the whole, conduct fewer enforcement actions than do states without primacy (where federal EPA personnel enforce the law). Likewise, we demonstrate that there is the expected negative relationship between states with health agencies and the number of enforcements conducted. Although we do not present the results here, if we substitute miniEPAs for health agencies there is a positive association (at the .10 level) between states employing miniEPAs and the number of enforcement actions conducted in the states. This is therefore further clear evidence that organizational structure has a direct impact on NPDES enforcement behavior.

We found no evidence that the quantity or usage of water is associated with enforcement outputs. On the other hand, perceptions of the source of the water problem are once again related to the level of the NPDES response. In states where administrators identified nonpoint sources as being more important, once again we found evidence of lower enforcement activity. Neither of the other two dummy variables representing perceptions of the source of water problems, however, were related to our measure of higher-level enforcement activity.

We also found that one of our economic variables was related to the number of enforcement outputs. The higher the percentage of people living below the poverty level in a state, the higher the level of the NPDES

Table 7.7

Determinants of the Number of Enforcement Actions Conducted by State and Federal Officials in the Fifty States

	Model 1	Model 2
Constant	−7.62**	−7.76**
	(2.33)	(1.90)
Demographic variables		
Population (logged)	0.79**	0.81**
	(0.15)	(0.13)
Water variables		
Nonpoint sources of pollution more important (dummy)	−0.69**	−0.35
	(0.28)	(0.26)
Economic variables		
Percentage of population below poverty line	0.13**	0.09**
	(0.03)	(0.03)
Organizational variables		
Primacy for NPDES program (dummy)	−0.80**	−0.35
	(0.33)	(0.30)
State environmental organization (dummy)[a]	Health	Health
	−1.14**	−1.29**
	(0.35)	(0.30)
Region 3 (dummy)	—	−1.16**
		(0.39)
Region 6 (dummy)	—	1.22**
		(0.50)
Region 9 (dummy)	—	−1.28**
		(0.45)
Adjusted R-square	.66	.76
N	50	50

The statistics represent the regression coefficient over its standard error.
**Indicates significance at the 0.05 level.
[a]When we substitute miniEPAs into the model for health agencies the results are nearly the same, but the coefficient for the miniEPA dummy is positive.

enforcement response. We also note that the coefficient for per capita mean income was negatively related to the total number of enforcements, though more weakly than the measure of the percentage of people living below the poverty level. Because minorities in our society are disproportionately poor, we substituted the percentage of the African American population for the percentage of people living below the poverty level. The results of that model were almost identical to the results presented in model 1 of Table 7.7, with a positive coefficient representing the percentage of the African American population, but a slightly smaller adjusted R-square. Finally, we found the same relationship when we substituted the percentage of Baptists in each state into the model. This may not be related merely to religious belief, however, but rather to economic and demographic factors. When we examined the relationship between African Americans and the percentage of the population living below the poverty level in each state, as independent variables, and Baptists as our dependent variable, the adjusted R-square was .67 and both independent variables were statistically related at the .05 level. Thus, we are convinced the association between enforcements and the independent variable is related to an economic criteria.

Our finding may appear counterintuitive at first, especially given the findings of Wernette and Nieves (1992), who found that minorities are disproportionately exposed to air pollution outcomes, and Pollock and Vittas (1995), who found that racial and ethnic subpopulations reside closest to toxic sources, a pattern particularly relevant for African Americans. In the next chapter, in fact, we demonstrate that African Americans are disproportionately exposed to water pollution outcomes. Given these findings we might have expected to find a negative relationship between African Americans in our enforcement model. When we considered the thesis of this book, however, that NPDES personnel respond to the diversity of the water pollution regulatory environment, the result from Table 7.7 makes sense. If the levels of pollution are higher in areas with a larger percentage of poor people and minorities, then we would expect to find NPDES personnel responding more aggressively in these states, simply because more pollution is present. In other words, because there is more pollution in areas where poor and African American people live, NPDES enforce the law more aggressively. This is because businesses and other types of permittees pollute to a greater extent in these areas (see Pollock and Vittas 1995). As we noted, this is a point we will return to in the next chapter.

Finally, we also found that one of our demographic variables was related to the level of the enforcement response. As with the models presented in Tables 7.5 and 7.6, the population of a state is once again the most important determinant of the level of the NPDES enforcement response. This is further support for our hypothesis that the diversity of the regulatory environment is an important determinant of enforcement outputs.

Finally, there is one important difference between the permit and enforcement models. Although four of the five interest group measures were related to either major or minor permit issuances, none were related to the level of the NPDES enforcement response. Again, given the prevalent role that interest groups play in many theories of the regulatory process (e.g., pluralism, iron triangles, capture theory, issue networks, advocacy coalitions), this finding is of interest. The combined results of Tables 7.5 and 7.6 demonstrate that interest groups do play an influential role in the overall enforcement process, but not necessarily in every stage of that process.

We also note that of our five interest-group measures, the only one that was not related to permit issuances or the number of enforcements conducted was our measure of the strength of environmental organizations. This conforms to the discussion we presented on the declining influence of environmental groups. It is, however, at least somewhat surprising considering that we did find that our measure of outdoorsmen, and three industry-based groups, are related to permit issuances. Our lack of statistical support for the influence of environmental groups may have much to do with the period under investigation, however. The enforcement actions analyzed in Tables 7.7 were largely conducted during the Bush presidency, although the permit issuances, given the requirement that permits are issued for five years, span the Bush and Clinton years. It is clear that even while environmentalists received a more positive reception from the Clinton administration than from either of his Republican predecessors, over the past two decades they have found less influence with executive-branch officials than they did during the halcyon days of the 1970s. Finally, we note that in Tables 7.5, 7.6, and 7.7 we found no evidence that any of our political variables were related to either permit issuances or enforcements conducted.

In model 2 of Table 7.7 we again examine the influence of region on NPDES behavior. As can be seen, dummy variables representing three regions (3, 6, and 9) were statistically significant. Of these, however, the dummy for region 6 largely captures the dynamic of the primacy dummy, inasmuch as a full third of all nonprimacy states are in this one region. Likewise, as was the case in Table 7.5, the dummy for region 9 is related to the dummy variable representing nonpoint sources of pollution. Of the dummies for the three regional offices, then, only region 3 is not correlated with any of the other variables in the model. Thus, it alone exhibits clear evidence of an independent effect. Thus, again, once we incorporate various measures representing the diversity of the regulatory environment into the equation, there is limited evidence of regional variations in enforcement behavior. Although some regional variations can be identified, it is clear that much of the variation in regional enforcement we identified in Chapter 5 is really related to factors contained in the regulatory environment of surface-water pollution control.

Implications for Bureaucratic Theory

Clearly, the findings presented in this chapter also tell us a great deal about the nature of political control of the bureaucracy. Over the past two decades, adherents of the principal-agent model have argued that principals actively seek to control the behavior of their bureaucratic agents. In so doing, these studies have focused almost exclusively on the motives and incentives of political principals (e.g., the president and the Congress). They have, however, largely ignored the influence of unelected political actors, such as interest groups. Likewise, they have dedicated relatively little attention to an examination of the motives of the bureaucratic agent (though see Wood 1988; Wood and Waterman 1994: chapter 5). Beyond such basic assumptions as bureaucrats are utility maximizers who shirk attempts at political control and have inherent information advantages over their political superordinates, we know relatively little about why or how bureaucrats actually behave. This book was written, in part, in an attempt to rectify this scholarly oversight and to tell us more about the role of the agent in the principal-agent model.

What then does our analysis tell us about political control of the bureaucracy? First, our findings show that there is a relationship between the nature of the regulatory environment and the behavior of bureaucratic agents. Principal-agent theory, as it is now postulated, has largely overlooked this relationship because its primary concern has been with an analysis of political hierarchy. Thus, although some studies have examined the effect of organizational structure on attempts at political control (e.g., Wood and Waterman 1991, 1993, 1994), most studies have tended to treat agents, in different settings, as if they are all driven by the same motivations and demands (see Waterman and Meier 1995). Our analysis suggests otherwise. In a diverse regulatory environment, such as is typified by surface-water pollution control, we hypothesized that agents would adopt a pragmatic enforcement style and would employ greater levels of bureaucratic discretion. Our empirical findings support this hypothesis. Clearly, then, our analysis demonstrates that future principal-agent studies must not only focus on measures of hierarchical control (e.g., top-down factors), but also must control for factors related to the task performed by the relevant bureaucratic agent and factors related to the regulatory environment (e.g. bottom-up factors). To ignore these factors is to present an underspecified model of political control.

What Is Bureaucratic Discretion?

We are now ready to answer two critically important questions. First, what is it that NPDES personnel respond to? As we have just noted, and as we presented in Chapter 5, studies of bureaucracy that have employed the basic assumptions of the principal-agent model have largely examined this question from a top-down perspective. Agents respond to political cues from their hierarchical superordinates. The evidence on this point is overwhelming, and we do not wish to challenge it. Rather, we wish to add to it a second important point. By focusing on top-down responses almost exclusively, principal-agent theorists have largely forgotten that agents also respond to a variety of nonhierarchical factors. As we have demonstrated in this chapter, they respond to a variety of factors related to the nature of their particular regulatory environment. It is these factors, so long ignored in principal-agent studies, that tell us much about what bureaucrats actually respond to and perhaps even why, in some cases, they do not respond to their political superiors. The combined evidence from this book demonstrates that bureaucrats respond to the president, the Congress, and the courts, but they also respond to demand factors (represented here by the population of each state), to economic factors, to issues related to the type of externality involved, to interest-group pressure, and so on. They also are constrained by the types of organizational structures imposed upon them. Thus, our analysis demonstrates that an exclusive focus on top-down impacts misses much of what bureaucrats actually respond to, for bureaucrats also respond to the diverse nature of their regulatory environment.

What, then, does this tell us about bureaucratic discretion? Specifically, what is bureaucratic discretion? In Chapter 5 we presented a definition that suggested that bureaucratic discretion is related to whether Congress delegates broad authority to the bureaucracy. We argued that this definition tells us what the principals do, but not what agents do. We also presented a second definition suggesting that agents respond to the goals of their political superordinates. We argued that this was not an appropriate definition for several reasons. Particularly, any time that multiple principals disagree over policy goals, agents would by definition have increased discretion, inasmuch as their goals would have to diverge from one principal or another. Likewise, in the case of a single principal expostulating contradictory goals, discretion would likewise be increased. Thus, to a large extent, the question of whether discretion exists or not would depend on the behavior of the principals in the model, rather than the agent.

Both definitions were based on a top-down view of the bureaucracy. Our bottom-up analysis of the EPA NPDES program, however, suggests another definition of bureaucratic discretion. We have demonstrated that bureaucrats respond to factors related to their regulatory environment. In fact, an analysis of the results from Tables 7.5, 7.6, and 7.7 demonstrates that bureaucratic behavior is a response to multiple and diverse factors conducive to the surface-water pollution control regulatory environment. Many of these factors are beyond the direct control of either principals or their agents. For example, unless we wish to alter the population of each state, move people from urban to rural areas, alter the economic make-up of each state, or alter the demographic and/or interest-group configurations existing within each state, political principals will not be able to control all of the relevant factors that bureaucrats respond to. Furthermore, as the regulatory environment becomes more diverse, bureaucrats will necessarily have even more factors they will need to respond to. Thus, the more diverse the regulatory environment, the broader the discretion agency personnel will require to enforce the law. The less diverse the regulatory environment, the less discretion agents will require in enforcing the law. Once we turn our focus to a bottom-up view of the bureaucratic world, then, the existence of bureaucratic discretion can be seen as directly associated with the bureaucrat's need to respond to the level of diversity in their regulatory environment. Bureaucratic discretion is therefore not simply the propensity of agents to respond to, or not to respond to, the goals of their political principals, but also the bureaucrat's need to respond to the level of diversity in their regulatory environment.

This approach to bureaucratic discretion has important implications for scholarly research. It tells us that scholars who have for too long treated bureaucratic discretion as a mere straw man may need to dedicate more time to defining what the concept entails with regard to the regulatory environment involved in a particular analysis. It also means that scholars will have to address the question of what the bureaucratic world would be without some measure of discretion. In the past, by conceptualizing discretion in mostly pernicious terms, scholars have argued that we should do away with it. But given the findings in this book, we ask, is that a realistic alternative? Our answer is a resounding no. We cannot eliminate bureaucratic discretion, nor should we. To do so would be to tie the hands of bureaucratic agents unduly, making it impossible for them to respond to important factors within their regulatory environment. Although we certainly do not make an argument for unbridled and unsupervised bureaucratic discretion, we believe that scholars should begin to rethink the concept and examine it from a bottom-up, as well as a top-down perspective. In so doing, we believe that the benefits, as well as the costs of bureaucratic discretion, will be better understood.

Conclusions

What do our findings suggest? First, they demonstrate that the diversity of the regulatory environment across the fifty states does matter in myriad ways. In the three models presented in this chapter we found that five of our six categories of variables were related to the level of the NPDES enforcement response. Of these, by far, the greatest impact was exerted by demographic variables, particularly the number of people living in a state. Simply stated, the more people there are in a state, the greater the level of the NPDES enforcement response. We also found that the greater the number of people living in metropolitan areas, the fewer major and minor permits that will be issued. We believe this is related to the tendency in many metropolitan areas for industry to place a greater burden on municipal wastewater-treatment facilities, as well as particularly egregious violators in small population areas. In addition to how many people live in a state and where they live, we also provided evidence that the stratification of the population on racial lines is an important determinant of water pollution outputs. We found a positive association between the percentage of the African American population living in a state and the number of enforcement actions conducted. Although we believe this association is mostly due to the economic condition of African Americans in our society (e.g., our finding in Table 7.7 that the percentage of people living below the poverty level and per capita income are also related to enforcement activity), this finding suggests that scholars should be paying more attention to various population measures when they model state and federal enforcement activity.

Second, we found an association between variables representing water quantity, water usage, perceptions of water pollution problems, and permit issuances. We also found that perceptions of the source of the water problem was related to the level of NPDES enforcement responses. This is further evidence that scholars should be paying closer attention to the diversity of the regulatory environment. NPDES enforcement personnel are clearly guided in their daily actions by that environment.

Third, we found that organizational structure matters, particularly with regard to the number of enforcement actions conducted by NPDES personnel and minor permit issuances. Both primacy and the organizational structure employed by a state (health or miniEPA agency) were related to enforcement outputs, and primacy and states with health agencies were related to minor permit issuances. Finally, we found that evidence of regional variations in enforcement behavior diminished substantially once we incorporated measures for the diversity of the regulatory environment.

Fourth, we found that economic factors are related to the level of the enforcement response. A state's per capita mean income was positively related to the number of major permits issued, but negatively related to enforcement activity. Likewise, the percentage of poor people living in a state was related to the level of the NPDES enforcement response. Neither the level of industrialization in a state nor its unemployment rate, however, were related to the level of the NPDES response.

Fifth, we found that a number of interest-group variables were related to the issuance of major and minor permits. Our findings with regard to mining, polluting industry, and agricultural strength suggest that this relationship is related not just to their political strength, but also to their presence in a state; that is, where a greater number of mining companies and industrial firms are located, we find evidence of a more active NPDES response in the realm of permit issuances. In addition to these organized interests, we also found an association between minor NPDES permit issuances and our measure of "outdoorsmen." This finding suggests that scholars may need to pay closer attention to a latent measure of environmental interest in the fifty states. We also found that environmental groups did not exhibit influence over the number of permit issuances or enforcement actions conducted.

Finally, although all of these findings suggest that the diversity of the regulatory environment is important, one nonfinding is also interesting. In each of our models we found no evidence that politics matters, at least not directly. None of our political variables (LCV scores, registration rates, voting rates, legislative professionalism) were related to permit issuances or the level of enforcement responses. Our findings on interest groups suggest that principal-agent studies should pay more attention to these unelected political actors. Our findings about organization suggest that principal-agent studies also need to focus more directly on organizational variations in hierarchical models. Finally, our results indicate that principal-agent studies need to more realistically examine the motives of the bureaucratic agent from a bottom-up perspective. Scholars must also consider what bureaucratic discretion actually entails before they recommend that it should be eliminated.

Our analysis in this chapter has focused on the relationship between the diversity of the regulatory environment and the level of the NPDES response. Still unanswered is the question of whether this diversity also is related to policy outputs. We address that question in the next chapter.

8

Water Outcomes: The Neglected Arena

In the last chapter we demonstrated that the diverse nature of the regulatory environment is related to NPDES outputs. In this chapter we examine whether this diverse regulatory environment is related to policy outcomes as well. We will address this question in two ways. First, we use regression models to determine whether the variables we identified in the last chapter are related to three measures of water policy outcomes. Then, we will provide information from interviews and surveys conducted with officials from the EPA and state environmental departments to determine their attitudes on policy outcomes.

The Determinants of Policy Outcomes

In the last chapter we examined the determinants of policy outputs. Outputs are relatively easy to measure. They represent the actions that NPDES personnel conduct in the process of enforcing the Clean Water Act, such as issuing permits, conducting inspections, or issuing notices of violation or administrative orders—in short, the measures that we have presented and analyzed throughout this book. Although a focus on outputs is important, the real goal of enforcement is not to create outputs, but rather to influence outcomes. In the case of the NPDES program, the ultimate goal is to ameliorate outcomes—specifically, to improve the quality of the nation's surface waters. Our objective, therefore, will be to determine if the diversity of the regulatory environment we identified in the last chapter has an impact on actual water-quality levels, as well as on the responses of NPDES personnel.

Our first step in performing this analysis is to develop a reliable measure of water policy outcomes. Unfortunately, as Ringquist (1993: 93) wrote, this is not an easy task:

Deciding on the objects of measurement in air quality is relatively easy since almost all regulatory efforts over the past twenty-five years have been aimed at reducing emissions and concentrations of six criteria pollutants. There are no analogs to these criteria pollutants in water quality control, however. Water quality can be measured using biochemical oxygen demand, dissolved oxygen, suspended sediments, suspended or dissolved solids, nutrient loads, pesticide residues, inorganic toxins, heavy metal ions, or countless other constituents. Each of these water quality measures has its own effect on human and ecosystem health, so using any one, or even a small subset, to represent water quality can lead to misrepresentations of water quality. We can try to make an end run around this galaxy of specific water constituents by using more general measures of water quality, such as clarity, smell, conductivity, and whether or not waters support healthy native fish populations. The gains in information management associated with this strategy, however, are offset by losses in precision of measurement.

Despite the loss in the "precision of measurement," we examine three measures of policy outcomes analyzed by Ringquist. We do, however, address the loss of precision later in this chapter when we examine the attitudes of NPDES and state personnel regarding the nature of policy outcomes. The three dependent variables we analyze are Ringquist's (1993: 183) measures of the percentage change in average pollutant concentrations of phosphorus, dissolved oxygen, and dissolved solids between two time periods: 1973–75 and 1986–88.

The first of these, phosphorus, is a nutrient that "can stimulate algae blooms and growth of nuisance water plants, accelerate eutrophication (the aging of lakes and reservoirs), and cause problems with oxygen depletion as the plants die and decompose" (Conservation Foundation 1984: 114). Most increases in phosphorus and other nutrients have "occurred in the eastern United States (the New England, mid-Atlantic, South Atlantic–Gulf, and Ohio–Tennessee water-resource regions) and the Pacific Northwest." Additionally, between 1974 and 1981, areas in which phosphorus traces were increasing exceeded those areas where phosphorus trends were decreasing (ibid.: 110). It is therefore an important measure of possible degradation and/or improvement in water quality.

With regard to our second dependent variable, the Conservation Foundation (1984: 109) reported, "Dissolved oxygen, usually present in clean waters at levels of five parts per million or more, is necessary for fish and other aquatic life to survive. The decomposition of organic pollutants, such as those in municipal sewage, depletes the natural oxygen levels. Ten percent of U.S. inland lakes and rivers have levels of dissolved oxygen low enough to affect fish communities adversely." The Conservation Foundation reported improving dissolved oxygen levels as of the mid-1980s in

"New England, the Ohio–Tennessee and Missouri river basins in the Midwest, and in the South Atlantic–Gulf." On the other hand, decreasing levels were "observed in the Pacific Northwest and in California" (ibid.).

As for our third dependent variable, the Conservation Foundation (1984: 112–13) wrote,

> Total dissolved solids (TSDs) is a measure of all the inorganic salts and other substances dissolved in water. High levels of dissolved solids can make water unfit to drink, adversely affect fish and other freshwater aquatic life, accelerate corrosion in water systems and equipment that uses water, and depress crop yields. These problems are more likely in regions with low annual rainfall, such as the Southwest and High Plains, whereas lower concentrations occur in New England, the mid-Atlantic, the Southeast, Alaska, Hawaii, California, and the Pacific Northwest, regions with relatively high precipitation.

The Conservation Foundation (1984: 113) reported, "The Great Lakes, Rio Grande, and Upper Colorado River water-resources regions show the most improvement" in dissolved solid levels. On the other hand, degrading trends were prevalent "in the Missouri River, Arkansas–White–Red River, and Pacific Northwest regions."

As can be seen in these descriptions, the three dependent variables represent different types of threats to water quality. They also have exhibited a national impact on water quality. For these reasons we consider them appropriate preliminary measures of water-quality outcomes. As we will discuss later in this chapter, however, they are by far not the only means of operationalizing water-quality outcomes, nor should they be.

Along with these three dependent variables, our independent variables for the analysis will be our demographic, water, and organizational variables (i.e., primacy and state organizational structure) from the last chapter. We have chosen these three sets of variables because we specifically want to know if the diversity of the regulatory environment is related to policy outcomes; and these three sets of measures best represent the diversity of the regulatory environment. We present our results in Table 8.1.

Despite the strong association between population and policy outputs, as represented in Tables 7.5, 7.6, and 7.7, we find no evidence that population is related to either of our three measures of policy outcomes. This does not mean, however, that demographic variables are not related to outcomes. As can be seen in models 1 and 3 from Table 8.1, the percentage of the African American population living in a state is related to two policy outcome measures, changes in the percentage of phosphorus and dissolved solids—the latter at only the .10 level. What is interesting about these relationships is the direction of the impact. The positive coefficients in both models suggest

Table 8.1

Determinants of Water Pollution Outcomes in the States

Model 1: Phosphorous

Constant	−21.68**
	(9.55)
Demographic variables	
Percentage of the African American population in a state	1.67**
	(0.68)
Adjusted R-square	.11
N	42

Model 2: Dissolved oxygen

Constant	5.18**
	(2.45)
Organizational variables	
State enviromental organization—health	−7.56**
	(3.56)
Water variable	
Point and nonpoint pollution of equal importance (dummy)	5.96*
	(3.23)
Adjusted R-square	.16
N	35

Model 3: Dissolved solids constant

	−16.47**
	(8.03)
Demographic variables	
Percentage of the African American population in a state	0.64*
	(0.34)
Organizational variables	
Primacy for NPDES program (dummy)	16.44**
	(7.51)
State environmental organization—health	16.40**
	(7.31)
Adjusted R-square	.20
N	35

The statistics represent the regression coefficient over its standard error.
*Indicates significance at the 0.10 level.
**Indicates significance at the 0.05 level.

that the higher the percentage of African Americans living in a state, the poorer the water quality will be. This finding is therefore consistent with the writings of the proponents of the environmental-justice literature (e.g., Pollock and Vittas 1995; Wernette and Nieves 1992; Bunyan and Mohai 1992; Kelly and Robertson 1991; Godsil 1991) who have argued that minorities are disproportionately the victims of environmental degradation. As Gary Bryner (1995: 30) wrote with regard to air pollution outcomes, reducing or eliminating pollution is a basic requirement of justice and fairness. The people who suffer the adverse effects from air pollution are not the same as those who benefit from the economic activity that produces pollution as a by-product. The real costs of pollution-producing activities, in terms of adverse health effects, must not be borne by third parties who are not involved in the producing and purchasing of goods. It is unjust for the benefits of commercial activity to accrue to one group, while the burden of poor health and other problems caused by pollution be borne by a different group.

As our analysis demonstrates, the same could be said with regard to African Americans and water pollution outcomes. Clearly, then, the implications of our findings are disturbing. Not only do they raise issues about environmental justice, but they also suggest that although policy outcomes are related to the diversity of the regulatory environment, they are not related to it in the positive manner we would have hypothesized. For example, our findings regarding population in Chapter 7 suggested that the greater the population in a state, the greater the demand for water pollution control activities, and the greater the level of the NPDES response. That suggested an affirmative NPDES response to pollution problems. We also found that states with a higher percentage of poor people (and African Americans) also exhibited higher levels of enforcement. Still, our findings in Table 8.1 indicate that, when we turn our focus to policy outcomes, the results of the NPDES responses to pollution problems have not yet generated improved water-quality outcomes for African Americans. Clearly then, not all Americans are enjoying equally the benefits of water pollution control.

Beyond our demographic measures, the analysis presented in Table 8.1 also demonstrates that there is a link between organizational structure and water quality. Again, however, the direction of our findings provide room for concern. The results in models 2 and 3 demonstrate that a relationship exists between states that employ a health agency to enforce their environmental programs and the percentage of change over time in the levels of dissolved oxygen and dissolved solids. The negative coefficient in model 2, for dissolved oxygen, suggests that states that employ health agencies have poorer water quality than states that use other organizational structures (e.g., a miniEPA or superagency). Likewise, the positive coefficient in model 3, for dissolved solids, indicates the same conclusion. Additionally, the positive coefficient in model 3 for primacy indicates that states with primacy have poorer water quality than states in which the EPA enforces the NPDES program.

This is extremely powerful evidence that organizational structure matters but does not conform with our a priori expectations. In his analysis of these same three measures of water quality Ringquist (1993: 186) had identified a statistically significant association between his revised measure of state water-program strength (for a discussion of it see Chapter 6) and the level of dissolved solids and phosphorus. Therefore, we did anticipate a relationship between organizational structure and these two dependent variables. Our finding with regard to dissolved solids, then, was not unexpected, but not our finding with regard to dissolved oxygen, and our nonfinding with regard to phosphorus. Despite these divergences from our expectations, the results in Table 8.1 provide clear evidence that the nature of the enforcement response does have an impact on policy outcomes, but only indirectly. It also suggests that the recent movement on the part of several states away from health agencies and toward a miniEPA organizational format (e.g., New Mexico and Oklahoma; see Chapter 6) is a positive development, one that should be encouraged in other states.

With regard to our last category of independent variables, we found no evidence that water quantity or water usage were related to policy outcomes. We had expected a relationship between water quantity and water outcomes. As Rosenbaum (1985: 150) wrote, "The recognition that policies affecting water availability also affect water quality has come slowly and belatedly to the nation's governments. In the West and Midwest, for instance, federal subsidies intended to ensure farmers abundant water for irrigation have severely affected water quality in many regions."

Despite Rosenbaum's expectations, we found no correlation between water-quantity and water-policy outcomes. We did, however, find that one of our three measures of the perceived source of water pollution was related to changes in the levels of dissolved oxygen, but only at the .10 level. In states where administrators perceive point and nonpoint sources of pollution to be of equal importance there is evidence that water quality (as measured by dissolved oxygen) is actually improved. This is an important finding, because it represents the only independent variable in our analysis that is positively associated with water-quality outcomes.

In summation, we found that the diversity of the regulatory environment is related to policy outcomes, but not in the manner we had expected. Our findings raise serious concerns regarding the issue of environmental justice, as well as suggesting that we need to take a closer look at how organizational structure impacts water-quality outcomes. Clearly, structure does matter. The question is, can we design organizational structures that are better capable of promoting the goal of improved water quality? Our findings suggest that states with health agencies have the poorest water quality and that primacy is also related to decreases in water-quality outcomes. Still, our results must be treated as preliminary, and so we raise the question mainly as an incentive for other scholars to address it in greater detail.

Finally, in addition to our test of the diversity of the regulatory environment thesis, we also wanted to determine if our output measures, which we presented in Chapter 6 and then analyzed in Chapter 7, are related to water-quality outcomes. Ringquist (1993, 1995b) had found that there was a correlation between policy outputs and policy outcomes in relationship to reductions in atmospheric concentrations of sulfur dioxide and nitrogen dioxide, but he found no such similar evidence with regard to the three water-quality measures analyzed in Table 8.1. We likewise found no association between our measures of major permits, minor permits, or enforcement actions and the three measures of policy outcomes. In the next section we will try to provide an answer for why this is so.

Of Outputs and Outcomes

As we noted above, data on water-quality outcomes are far less revealing than in other areas of environmental protection. Partly for this reason, assessments of water quality in America have been mixed. For example, in its mid-1980s assessment of water quality the Conservation Foundation (1984: 105) concluded,

> Unlike the nation's relatively consistent and widespread improvements in air quality, success in cleaning up surface waters has been mixed. Many streams have improved, some of them dramatically: the "dying" Great Lakes, Erie and Ontario, are reviving, with fewer algae blooms and growing fish populations; Atlantic salmon have returned to New England's Connecticut and Penobscott rivers, and shell-fish bed and public-beach closings due to dangerous bacteria levels have become less frequent. But water quality in some streams and many lakes appears to be degrading, and in most there has been little change since the early 1970s.

In 1993 the Council on Environmental Quality (CEQ; 1993: 225) admitted, "Despite decades of research and regulation, the federal government still lacks a comprehensive assessment of the quality of the nation's waters." The CEQ then extrapolated from past studies and offered the following assessment of the nation's water quality: "Of several assessed water resources, about two-thirds met federal water quality standards and achieved state-designated uses such as fishing, swimming, and drinking. One-third of the assessed waters did not fully meet designated uses." Consequently, the CEQ report was more positive in its assessment of improvements in water quality than was the Conservation Foundation a decade before, though both found mixed evidence on the water-quality front. A more positive assessment was provided by Ringquist (1993: 8), who reported, "the data suggest that overall water quality levels have remained stable over the past twenty years (no mean achievement), and discharges and concentrations of some pollutants have decreased significantly." Still, his results also suggest mixed findings with regard to water quality nationwide.

What accounts for the limited and mixed evidence regarding the quality of our nation's waterways? Although data are copious regarding air pollution, reliable data on water quality are relatively scarce. Much of this scarcity is due to the nature of existing legislation. The Clean Air Act of 1970 specified a variety of air pollutants that were to be ameliorated over a specified period of time. EPA enforcement personnel, as well as scholars, could therefore turn to the legislation itself to determine congressional intent with regard to the outcomes to be affected. No such clear guidance was provided by the Clean Water Act of 1972 (e.g., the FWPCA of 1972). That legislation did not specifically identify measures of water quality to be ameliorated. Instead, as we discussed in Chapter 2, the legislation left the choice of identifying measures of water quality in the hands of state officials. The end result has been confusion over what counts as a water-quality outcome and how water-quality outcomes should be measured.

Due to past legislative mandates, then, the EPA has delegated the task of measuring water quality almost entirely to the states. As the Conservation Foundation (1984: 105) reported, "the federal Environmental Protection Agency (EPA) maintains no records and makes no estimates of the quantities of pollutants discharged by different types of sources to either ground or surface water." It then provided some additional reasons for this oversight:

> One possible reason is that the job has proven more difficult than originally thought, as evidenced by repeated failures to meet the deadlines established in the Clean Water Act. In particular, cleaning up discharges from municipal sewage-treatment plants has been much more expensive and proceeded much more slowly than originally scheduled; even when the plants are built, they may not be operated properly. Another reason is that some major sources of pollution, particularly storm-water runoff from agricultural land and city streets, have been largely ignored.

Clearly, water pollution problems have proven more intractable than originally anticipated, particularly with regard to nonpoint sources of pollution, which were all but ignored in the original 1972 legislation. Still, we believe the major reason why the EPA does not have a systematic database of water-quality measures is because of the dichotomy created by existing legislation, which places the task of enforcement in the hands of federal and state personnel and the task of measuring water quality in the hands of state officials. Furthermore, by emphasizing such nebulous terms as "swimmable waters" and "fishable waters," such existing legislation has provided little useful guidance to state environmental personnel in the task of developing reliable measures of water quality. Thus, unlike the case of air pollution, where federal legislation has encouraged clear measures of policy outcomes, in the case of water quality, existing legislation has had precisely the opposite effect.

Consequently, it should not be surprising that the states have employed a wide variety of often dubious methods to measure water quality. To better understand how they measure water quality we asked state environmental officials the following question: "In enforcing water-quality standards, what outcomes do you use to measure your success?" Officials from twenty-two states responded to that question. The answers we received were quite diverse. For example, officials from Arkansas, Illinois, Indiana, Iowa, Louisiana, Maine, Michigan, Nebraska, and New Hampshire answered that the number one outcome they used to measure water quality is "compliance" with NPDES regulations. In other words, environmental officials in these states directly equate outputs with outcomes. Officials from Louisiana were the most blunt of all. One official there stated that Louisiana relied on "beancounting" to measure water quality. Given our finding, along with Ringquist's, that there is no statistical correlation between outputs and outcomes in the area of water pollution control, this emphasis on beancounting is particularly disturbing.

Not all state officials, however, identified compliance as the primary means by which they measure water-quality outcomes. In Ohio officials said they use a "measure of aquatic life" to determine if water quality is improving. Officials from Maryland also identified the health of fish stocks and shellfish as their primary mechanism for evaluating water quality. An analysis of aquatic life is one of the primary means by which water quality can be determined. In fact, in our interviews with federal NPDES officials, this method was most often identified as an affordable and reliable means of measuring water quality (see the discussion below). This does not mean, however, that all states use a rigorous methodology in determining the quality of aquatic life. For example, officials from Rhode Island told us they rely on reports of bad news from citizens and other sources. If there are no reports of fish kills or complaints from recreational areas, Rhode Island state officials interpret this as evidence that water quality in their state is sound. Consequently, although state officials use a measure of aquatic life to determine the level of water quality in Rhode Island, it can hardly be characterized as a particularly rigorous measurement device. Likewise, officials from West Virginia stated that the primary method they use to measure water quality is to examine the diversity of fish stocks in their waters. In other words, they count the number of fish species that are alive in West Virginia waters. A decrease in number is interpreted as evidence of degradation of West Virginia waterways.

In other states, environmental officials directed their attention toward the quality of the water itself. As with states that examine aquatic life, there is considerable diversity in the approaches employed by officials from various states. For example, officials in Massachusetts told us they look for "visible improvement" in the waterways. By this they mean that they physically look at the water to see if there is any visible improvement in it. If it is not discolored or does not emit a noticeable odor, then state officials determine the water quality to be acceptable. Additionally, Massachusetts officials stated that they use the number of "miles of streams improved" as a measure of water quality. Given their emphasis on a visual inspection of Bay State water quality, however, it is doubtful that this measure is much more rigorous than their first criterion.

Officials from Alabama also identified the number of "miles of streams improved" as their primary criterion for evaluating water quality. Officials from Minnesota identified miles of streams and "ambient standards of water quality" as their primary criteria. Likewise, officials from Georgia said they monitor streams, whereas officials from Kentucky said they rely on the ambient monitoring data they provide to the EPA. Officials from New York also said they rely on actual measures of water quality.

Although an examination of aquatic life and water quality would appear to be more rigorous than the mere standard of swimmable and fishable waters delineated in existing federal water quality legislation, the results of our survey demonstrate that we should pay close attention to the actual methodology employed by state officials when they determine the quality of their waterways. A mere visual inspection of waterways, the simple counting of fish types, or a reliance on complaints from citizens alone is not nearly as reliable a method of measuring water quality as is conducting actual sampling inspections of state waterways. It is therefore apparent from our survey of state officials that there needs to be a greater emphasis on devising an appropriate methodology for measuring water quality. At present too many different methods are used, and too many of these are inappropriate. Given this point, we should not be surprised when we find that there is no correlation between outputs and outcomes in the area of surface water.

Additionally, other factors also mitigate against such a statistical association. For example, in 1991, the *Washington Post* commenced an investigation of the nation's water quality. As Ashworth (1995: 35) wrote,

It is probable that even the most cynical of the Post's reporters were shocked by what they turned up. Nineteen years after passage of the act, and six years after it was supposed to be in full effect, the Environmental Protection Agency, charged with enforcing the legislation, had not even written the rules covering four-fifths of the industries that it was supposed to regulate. Industries with no rules in place included hazardous waste treatment facilities, commercial solvent recyclers, industrial laundries, hospitals, and chemical-drum recyclers. Machinery manufacturers remained unregulated; so did used-oil recyclers and much of the transportation industry. All in all, of some 75,000 industrial facilities around the nation that the Clean Water Act was supposed to police, 60,000 did not even have standards in place for judging their performance. Nor did there seem to be much hope that the situation would improve soon.

As we noted in Chapter 2, state environmental officials in both Florida and West Virginia told us that one of their major problems is that many polluters still discharge into surface waters without an NPDES permit, this more than twenty years since the passage of the original 1972 legislation. As we also noted, officials in other states also told us that the discharge limit for NPDES permits is often set at too high a level. As a result, even when a permittee is in full compliance with the provisions of its permit, serious environmental degradation can still result. This is a particular problem for NPDES enforcement personnel in the states, because in many of them the people who negotiate and eventually write the provisions of the NPDES permits are not the same people who later enforce them. Many state enforcement personnel told us this creates serious problems for them at the enforcement level. Clearly, it is yet another reason why outputs and outcomes are not statistically associated with each other. It also demonstrates that despite all of the empirical evidence on NPDES enforcement that we have presented in the last several chapters, there are still significant gaps in the enforcement process.

There also are clear problems with reporting requirements for policy outputs. Although we have analyzed data on policy outputs throughout this book, and our results are largely based on this analysis (along with our many interviews with state and federal environmental officials), we must concede that we discovered many instances of disturbing irregularities regarding the compilation of output data by state officials. For example, as we described in Chapter 2, some states have treated permit modifications as a formal enforcement action, which can inflate the number of formal actions. Likewise, some states consider the issuance of a notice of violation as a formal action, despite the dictates of the EPA Enforcement Management System manual, which lists NOVs as informal actions. These irregularities can create serious accountability problems and make it difficult to compare output activity across the states, as well as difficulties in comparing outputs and outcomes.

Still, these irregularities are minor compared to what we learned from our interviews with state officials. Many of them noted that they are exceedingly sloppy in terms of record keeping. Officials in some states even suggested that this tendency toward sloppiness may be intentional. With record keeping and documentation comes accountability. Some officials therefore told us that records of many interactions with permittees are not kept, simply because they either do not want the EPA to know about it or because they do not want it made available for other purposes (e.g., legal proceedings).

There are, of course, other less sinister reasons for poor record keeping. State officials also have told us that poor record keeping on enforcement outputs is related to the decentralized nature of the enforcement tasks. Agency personnel in the field will generally report major actions, but often lower-level actions (e.g., meetings with permittees) are not faithfully reported. In some states officials have told us they would rather have their personnel out in the field rather than have them doing paperwork in the office. They therefore place a lesser emphasis on keeping a reliable record of all their enforcement activities than they do on actually enforcing the law. Other state officials told us that poor record keeping was also due to budgetary problems; if they had more personnel, they could more effectively and reliably do their jobs. Finally, many states are still moving toward computerization of their data sets. As Waterman and Wood (1993) noted, computerization has promoted a more reliable compilation and management of data sets in many federal and state regulatory agencies. Thus, with computerization, we can anticipate some improvements in the reporting of output data by the states.

Consequently, nonstandard and poor reporting of enforcement actions may have contributed to the lack of a statistical association between outputs and outcomes. Clearly, and disturbingly, then, measurement problems are not related purely to problems with water-quality outcomes. We need to think about how to improve output measurement as well. Still, of the two, operationalizing water quality would appear to take precedence. As we have noted, there is no uniform method of measuring water-quality across the fifty states, and although some quantifiable measures do exist, as we demonstrated in Table 8.1, a major problem with surface-water regulation in the United States is that nearly twenty-five years after the enactment of the Clean Water Act of 1972, we still do not have a reliable means of measuring the legislation's relative success or failure. Some measures are available, but overall the measurement of policy outcomes in water quality has been unsatisfactory. Until we devise clear, consistent, reliable, and valid measures of water quality, there is little hope that we will ever provide evidence that outputs are related to improved water quality. Consequently, if we were forced to make just one recommendation based on our analysis of the NPDES enforcement process, it would be that a better method of measuring water quality must be devised. Until that happens, NPDES enforcement will never achieve its full potential.

If we could make two recommendations, then, we would defer to the opinion of many of the state and federal personnel we spoke with over the past decade. Clearly, the most commonly expressed opinion derived from our interviews with state and federal water pollution control officials was that the EPA's front office, the state governments, environmentalists, the media, and most academics, as well, place too much of an emphasis on policy outputs and not enough on policy outcomes; notice we ourselves dedicated several chapters to outputs and only one to outcomes. As the head of the NPDES program in one of the EPA's regional offices told us, "You can generate a lot of enforcement actions that give you very little [in terms of water quality], but it gives you something to count." He noted the propensity of EPA officials to engage in what Gormley (1989) has called "beancounting." The EPA official continued that the emphasis on evaluating EPA performance should be on outcomes, not outputs. He further stated, "if we're doing our job and enforcement is providing some deterrence, you'd think there'd be a time when the number of enforcement actions would decline. But when that happens we get a call from Washington asking us what's going on." In response, there is a push to increase the number of enforcements. The end result is not cleaner water, but more regulatory activity for its own sake.

Given this opinion, it would appear that the federal EPA would be moving away from outputs toward a greater commitment to outcomes. Past federal legislation has made such a move difficult if not impossible to make, however. The overwhelming emphasis on regulatory outputs therefore may be the primary weakness of the 1972 Clean Water Act and of the NPDES enforcement process. Essentially, the way the federal laws are written, the emphasis is placed directly on outputs. Because the EPA in fact plays a limited role in measuring outcomes, it has almost by necessity emphasized outputs over outcomes. To do otherwise would have left the EPA with no real role in the NPDES process. Thus, past legislation has created an artificial dichotomy that makes it more difficult for NPDES enforcement personnel to match outputs and outcomes. We therefore should not be surprised by the findings that there is no correlation between permit issuances and outcomes or enforcement outputs and water-quality outcomes. Simply stated, current legislation encourages this dichotomy.

Measuring Water Quality

The question therefore becomes, how can we best measure water quality? As we have demonstrated, there is at present no one clearly defined answer to this question. In the remainder of this chapter we therefore discuss several possible alternative methods of operationalizing water quality. Unfortunately, each has its advantages and disadvantages. Despite this, a method (or multiple methods) has to be selected. We believe this step to be imperative. Additionally, given current concerns over the cost of regulation, a theme we turn to in the final chapter of this volume, we need to consider not only the reliability and validity of any potential measurement scheme but also its relative cost. This, of course, only complicates matters even more, making it even more difficult to decide on a reliable measure of water-quality outcomes.

Clearly, one obvious means of measuring water quality would be to employ the methods we analyzed in Table 8.1—for example, phosphorus, dissolved oxygen, and dissolved solids. We could add to these a variety of other similar measures including suspended solids, "such as soil sediment and other solid particles" (Conservation Foundation 1984: 112) and heavy metals and organic toxic substances. We could examine a variety of trace elements, including arsenic, barium, boron, cadmium, chromium, copper, iron, lead, manganese, mercury, selenium, silver, and zinc. We could also examine such pollutants as ammonia, calcium, chloride, fecal coliform bacteria, fecal streptococcus, magnesium, nitrate-nitrite, phytoplankton, potassium, silica, sodium, sulfate, and organic carbon. We could test for the presence of such pesticides as Alpha-hexachlorocyclohexane, gamma-hexachlorocyclohexane or lindane, endosulfan, or pentachlorophenol. We could also test for the presence of such benzene-like hydrocarbons and derivatives as bis–2-ethylhexyl-phthalate, fluoranthene, and pyrene. Likewise, we could examine such properties as alkalinity, conductivity, pH levels, turbidity, and even temperature. In short, there is no shortage of possible pollutants, compounds, metals and/or other properties that we could analyze. Such measures would appear to provide us with a vast list of different ways to operationalize water quality. But despite the array of alternative measures we have presented, which is far from a comprehensive list (note the absence of DDT, and so on) there are serious problems with this approach. First and foremost, although the list of possible pollutants is indeed impressive, it cannot escape the problem posed by time. Succinctly stated, there can be a considerable lag between the time when efforts are first undertaken to clean up a waterway and the period in which positive results are first exhibited. This lag time is far longer than for air pollution control. This is particularly true with regard to groundwater. Slow-moving water in underground aquifers is particularly resistant to ameliorative efforts because the water in the aquifer moves so slowly that it cannot easily cleanse itself once polluted. Likewise, many stagnant surface-water systems can take years and even decades to begin showing evidence of improvement. Thus, unlike air pollution, which can sometimes be ameliorated by a stiff wind, pollution in surface water can be a nearly intractable problem. What this means in practical terms is that ameliorative action taken twenty years ago may not yet have been reflected in improved water quality in terms of any of the measures we analyzed earlier in Table 8.1. As Ringquist (1993) correctly noted, this lagged time effect is yet another reason why statistical models may not yet show a significant relationship between outputs and outcomes.

Unfortunately, time is an important and confounding variable in any analysis of water outcome data, and one that we cannot easily control for. In the analysis presented in Table 8.1, the data were presented for two separate three-year time periods and were represented by the change in outcomes between those two periods. Despite this attempt to deal with the lagged effect of ameliorative efforts on water pollution control, the poor fit of the models (reflected by the diminutive adjusted R-squares), despite the impressive number of explanatory dependent variables we considered, is one indication of the confounding influence time exhibits on water pollution outcomes. In short, time matters and there is no quick fix for it.

A second problem is related to the nature of the water systems themselves and the manner in which we pollute them. As we noted earlier in this chapter, officials in several states identified the number of "miles of streams improved" as a measure of water quality. We noted several egregious problems with the manner in which this measure was operationalized. But let us suppose that each state actually aggressively and competently conducted sampling inspections of water quality. Even under these circumstances, the results of their analysis would likely be of dubious value to us as a means of quantifying water quality. The problem is reflected by a simple question: Where was the sampling inspection conducted? The obvious response would be, for example, in the river. But then we would be forced to ask, where in the river? If the river runs from north to south, and the sampling inspection were conducted at point A, it would tell us a great deal about the quality of the river at that point. But if point B were south of point A, it would tell us nothing about the quality of the water at point B, or for that matter even further south at point C, point D, and so on. In short, the problem for water-quality measurement is not simply to sample the water in a river, a stream, a lake, or any other type of surface-water body, but rather to measure the quality of the water at different points along that water source. That is a much more complicated and expensive task than measuring the water at one point, which, as we noted in Chapter 2, is a highly resource-intensive activity. Given the fact that many waterways run across state boundaries, it also is a difficult political problem. Thus, the sampling of water is a complicated and expensive process. And in an age of tight fiscal resources, the second criterion may prove to be more of an impediment to the more extended use of sampling inspections than questions of feasibility.

Given the high cost of sampling the water for various sources of water pollution, what then are the alternatives? We spoke to a number of federal EPA officials about their preferred method of measuring water quality. They opposed water sampling for many of the reasons we have just suggested, predominantly on feasibility and cost grounds. Instead, they recommended that an analysis of aquatic life would provide a more feasible and cost-effective means of operationalizing water quality. As we noted earlier in this chapter, many states already employ this method, although some simply count the number of different species or visually examine the waters in which they live. This is not what the EPA officials we talked to had in mind, however. Instead, they proposed a sampling of the aquatic life in various waterways to determine the level of pollutants in the fish themselves. This, they argued, is a much more cost-effective means of determining the quality of a particular water source. It also is a method that has been opposed by some environmental groups, which prefer the water-sampling method discussed above. Thus, although EPA officials showed considerable support for sampling aquatic life in our interviews, there is no political consensus on this point as of yet.

Sampling aquatic life is more feasible and less costly than is the sampling of water quality, but it does not eliminate all of the problems of the first measure. Clearly, it is possible for part of a river or stream to be polluted, while another section is not polluted. If aquatic life does not travel across the entire river, stream, or lake, then an analysis of it might not exhibit evidence of environmental degradation present elsewhere in the water source. This problem could be overcome by examining aquatic life at different points in a river, stream, or other waterways, much as sampling inspections of water would have to be done at different points. According to the people we interviewed, this would still be less expensive than performing water-sampling tests, in that fewer samples would have to be taken with aquatic life forms. Many aquatic life forms are mobile, thus reducing both the need for taking multiple tests and the costs associated with them.

Of course, the major problem with this method, as with any method of measuring water quality, is still related to the issue of time. Even if the analysis of aquatic life were absolutely foolproof, we would still confront the problem of a lagged response to ameliorative efforts at water pollution control. Because it can take decades to clean a waterway, evidence that the cleanup has had a positive impact on the waterway could still take decades to emerge in aquatic samples.

One final issue further complicates the matter. The substantial variation in the natural level of water quality across the fifty states means that it will be difficult even to compare an untouched river in Louisiana or Pennsylvania with one in Colorado or California. In short, the conundrum of how to reliably measure water quality persists. There is in short no easy solution to it. In the end, then, no matter what system we choose to measure water quality, we will have a less than satisfactory result. That does not mean, however, that we should give up trying. With all of its limitations, EPA officials still say that the measurement of aquatic life will provide more reliable measures of water quality, and will be more cost effective, than other available means.

A Final Point

One final point needs to be addressed with regard to water quality outcomes. As Rouse and Wright demonstrated in Chapter 4, most NPDES personnel are scientists and engineers. This has important implications for the ways in which they perceive water pollution problems. In our discussions with numerous state and federal EPA enforcement personnel, it was clear to us that they simply do not see the world in the same terms as environmentalists, or for that matter academics. Whereas environmentalists often perceive issues of water quality in clear right-or-wrong terms, NPDES personnel tend to see the subtle shades of gray that often color the environmental debate. Whereas environmentalists often call for a complete cleanup of waters and zero tolerance for pollution, NPDES personnel tend to consider the costs of relative approaches to measuring water quality, as well as the benefits. The end result, of course, is that there are often conflicts between environmentalists and NPDES personnel, particularly at the state level.

This, as in many of the other issues we have presented in this volume, is a political issue for which there is no easy resolution. In practical terms, however, it means that one of the most difficult problems in agreeing on a measure, or a set of measures, of water quality will not be just the technical hurdles that must be leaped, or the time dimension we have examined in some detail, but rather the very real political differences that exist between the various political actors involved in the water pollution control issue network. There is little consensus on many important issues. This means that we are not likely to quickly agree on any method of measuring water quality. As we discuss in the next chapter, this factor, along with the difficulties in measuring water quality we have identified in this chapter, may open the door for alternatives to strict command-and-control regulation of water pollution problems. Based on the findings from this book, which have demonstrated a rejection by NPDES personnel of the strict-enforcement approach and the adoption of a pragmatic-enforcement style, we reexamine the feasibility of the various enforcement models. We also turn our attention to ongoing calls for reform of the Clean Water Act. Finally, we examine the rationale for employing an approach to water pollution control that emphasizes economic incentives rather than command-and-control techniques. As we will note, one basis for this change in emphasis is the diversity of the regulatory environment we have discussed throughout this book.

9

Conclusions and
Recommendations

Throughout this book we have provided the reader with a description of how the EPA and state NPDES personnel enforce the law, as well as an explanation for why they have adopted these enforcement strategies. In short, our theory is that the diverse nature of the regulatory environment under which surface-water pollution control enforcement occurs has promoted a pragmatic approach to enforcement problems and the employment of broad bureaucratic discretion by agency personnel. In Chapter 3 we described how this pragmatic enforcement operates in actual practice. We also argued that one by-product of the pragmatic enforcement style is the employment by EPA personnel of considerable bureaucratic discretion. In Chapter 4, Rouse and Wright used survey data to demonstrate that EPA NPDES personnel perceive themselves as exhibiting considerable discretion in their implementation of the Clean Water Act. In Chapter 5, Hunter, Waterman, and Wright then demonstrated that discretion results in considerable variation in enforcement across the EPA's ten regional offices. In Chapter 6 we then showed how similar variations in enforcement can be identified across the fifty states and began the process of explaining these variations by examining several factors related to organizational structure. Then in Chapter 7 we provided an empirical analysis that demonstrated that these variations can largely be explained with reference to the diversity of the regulatory environment itself. Finally, in Chapter 8 we showed that the diversity of the regulatory environment is related to policy outcomes as well, but not in the hypothesized direction. Our analysis of policy outcomes raised concerns about environmental justice and the adequacy of important organizational structures, as well as the need to derive better measures of water quality.

In this final chapter we use the findings from this book to make specific recommendations for reforming the NPDES enforcement process. In so doing we acknowledge that we are writing this book at a time of potentially fundamental change in the way the government addresses environmental issues. The EPA has undertaken a major internal reorganization that will change its enforcement approach from medium-specific regulation to a multimedia approach. As we write, this reorganization is ongoing and the results of it are not fully known. We will, however, try to address its probable implications for NPDES enforcement.

Likewise, with the election in 1994, a Republican majority controls both the House and Senate for the first time since the 1952 congressional elections. The House Republicans of the 104th Congress proposed fundamental changes in the way the Clean Water Act, and other environmental legislation, will be enforced. These changes include, as Bryner (1995: 2) wrote, "changes in the rulemaking process for major rules to ensure more scientific and economic analyses are performed, increase[d] opportunities for regulated industries to help shape the provisions, ensure that only relatively serious risks are regulated, require a demonstration that the benefits resulting from these regulations costs exceed the cost of compliance with them, and require a showing that the regulation proposed is the most cost-effective option." It also calls for "a regulatory moratorium on the issuance of new regulations until the regulatory reform agenda is enacted . . . changes in the way federal programs are funded, so that unfunded mandates require additional votes by Congress . . . requirements that federal agencies compensate property owners for loss in property values resulting from environmental regulation, and increased procedural protections for those subject to regulatory inspections and enforcement, such as a right to have counsel present during inspections and legal actions that can be taken against regulatory officials" (ibid.).

In May 1995 the House of Representatives, by a margin of 240–185, and voting largely along party lines, passed a revision of the Clean Water Act. Dana Wolfe (1995: 20) described the legislation:

> Most notably, the bill passed by the House completely revamps the wetlands protection program. Drawing from a proposal authored by Rep. James A. Hayes (D-LA), [Representative Bud] Shuster's [R-PA] bill establishes a wetlands classification system under which the "least valuable" wetlands would no longer be afforded any federal protection, and protection for remaining wetlands would be significantly scaled back. In addition, the bill would create new criteria for defining wetlands; to qualify as a wetland at all, land would need to meet all three criteria used to designate wetlands, and would need to meet a much more narrow definition of wetlands based on a "21 day inundation" test.

Additionally, the House bill also redefined "stormwater discharges as non-point source discharges" and established a "hierarchy" of controls affecting stormwater pollution control. These emphasize voluntary measures first, and then enforceable plans, and finally general or site-specific permitting. The bill also released "some industrial dischargers from having to pretreat waste to federally mandated levels before introducing it into a publicly owned treatment facility" (ibid.: 21). Pretreatment facilities would also be able to apply locally established standards, rather than federal standards, but would have to submit annual pretreatment reports to the EPA that demonstrate that the local standards "do not prevent it from meeting applicable water and air quality rules" (ibid.). The bill also authorized "$2.25 billion for the waste water state revolving fund in fiscal 1996, and $2.3 billion in fiscal years 1997 through 2000" (ibid.). This represented a significant reduction in funding for the wastewater fund. The bill also provided "that states' rights under the Clean Water Act to certify that federally-licensed projects are in compliance with state water quality standards," did "not extend to controlling streamflows associated with hydroelectric projects." The House also established a "dispute resolution mechanism for resolving conflicts resulting from actions taken by a state, an interstate water pollution control agency or the EPA, relating to hydroelectric projects" (ibid.).

USA Today (May 17, 1995: 6A) characterized the House version of the Clean Water Act revisions as "the first wholesale rewrite of an environmental law." It also quoted Representative John Hostettler (R.-Ind.) as saying of the legislation, "Despite all the unfounded claims by opponents of property rights and free enterprise that this bill would hurt the environment, the House stood up for the American farmer and small business today." The Clinton administration criticized the House bill, saying it would destroy the last twenty years of efforts to clean up the nation's polluted waterways (ibid.). In a public speech on May 30, 1995, President Clinton said he would veto the act, which he called the "Dirty Water Act," if it reached his desk. He also accused the Republicans of allowing lobbyists into the Capitol Building to write the offending legislation, a charge Republicans quickly denied. Throughout the summer and fall of 1995 President Clinton also said that he would veto deep Republican proposed cuts in the budget of the Environmental Protection Agency.

Although the House favored radical change in water pollution control legislation, the Senate did not. As Dana Wolfe (1995: 20) wrote,

> The fate of clean water reauthorization in the Senate is much less certain [than in the House]. Sen. John H. Chafee (R.-R.I.), chairman of the Senate

Environment and Public Works Committee, has not made reauthorization of
the Clean Water Act a priority, and has even said he does not believe such
"full-scale" reform is necessary. According to a committee staff member,
Chafee most likely will not address clean water until after reauthorization of
the Safe Drinking Water Act. Even then, clean water legislation in the Senate
may aim at much narrower reforms than those targeted in the House. Chafee
has said a bill as far-reaching as the House proposal is not necessary, but that
some reforms are needed, particularly in the areas of wetlands permitting,
funding, stormwater management and nonpoint source pollution control.

Representative Sherwood L.Boehlert (R.-N.Y.), who had favored an alternative to the House passed legislation, also noted that the House's Clean
Water Act revision would not be sufficient to survive an expected presidential veto (ibid.). For its part, the Clinton administration not only threatened
to veto the proposed revision of the Clean Water Act, but it also, in response to the earlier House regulatory reform proposal, on February 21,
1995, ordered federal agencies to "review regulations they have issued and
identify those that are 'obsolete or overly burdensome'; form grassroots
partnerships with businesses; and negotiate with regulated businesses and
local governments rather than dictate to them, and not evaluate inspectors
by how many citations they write" (Bryner 1995: 3).

On March 16, 1995, the Clinton White House then offered the following
initiatives (ibid.: 4), "give small businesses 180 days to correct violations before being fined, and waive punitive fines if the businesses agree to use the
money to correct the violation; [and] reduce by 25 percent record-keeping and
reporting requirements for businesses and local governments, and consolidate
into one form reports on air, water, and waste emissions." As of April 1996,
when this book was completed, President Clinton had signed legislation pro-
hibiting future "unfunded mandates." This legislation left open the question of
what to do with past legislation that had required such mandates. Likewise,
President Clinton criticized Republican calls for a moratorium on new regulations and several other provisions of the Republican reform agenda, specifically citing a need to protect the environment. As the Senate grappled with the
issue of regulatory reform, and the House revision of the Clean Water Act, it
was not clear whether some of the House Republican proposals would be sent
to the president. Republicans appear to be retreating on the issue, with some
House members noting the unpopularity of their environmental agenda. Republican presidential hopeful Lamar Alexander, the former governor of Tennessee, also criticized the overly zealous nature of the congressional
Republican's environmental agenda. House Speaker Newt Gingrich voiced
similar sentiments. The future of regulatory reform was thus most uncertain.

In addition to these congressional and presidential sponsored reforms, the EPA was also making changes that could have a major impact on the manner in which surface-water regulation will occur. In July 1993, EPA administrator Carol Browner announced that she would reorganize the EPA's enforcement team. The current system, created during the Reagan years by Anne Gorsuch Burford, divided enforcement into such areas as air, water, toxic substances, and so on. The Browner plan reorganized enforcement across each industry that the EPA regulates, such as transportation, agriculture, energy, and chemical companies. The reorganization also was designed to place a greater emphasis on the enforcement of multimedia sources of pollution, rather than a strict emphasis on one medium, such as air or water. In addition, enforcement was to be placed in one office, as it was before Burford's tenure. The reorganization was also designed to put more people to work on enforcement. Prior to the reorganization, between four hundred and five hundred people worked at the EPA's Washington headquarters on enforcement related tasks. The plan did not immediately specify, however, what effect it would have on the EPA's ten regional offices. Browner said the reorganization was needed to protect enforcement personnel from "pressures that can be felt" by those individuals who try to enforce the law. She also said, "strong enforcement is an absolutely essential component of how we do our job" (Beamish 1993: A8). Particularly uncertain as of April 1996 was how reorganization would affect the regional offices. Again, there was considerable uncertainty regarding the future of regulatory enforcement.

Because of the ongoing tumult created by the congressional, presidential, and agency-level reforms, the reader of this book likely will know more about the outcome of this regulatory reform process than we do. Although we cannot predict an outcome for this process, we can apply the lessons we have learned from our analysis of NPDES output and outcome data in this volume to a discussion of the current reform agenda.

In this chapter we review our findings and make recommendations for change. In so doing we note the sage advise of Duchin and Lange (1994: v–vi), who wrote,

> Probably the questions most frequently asked today about environmental pollution and the economy are as follows: How much would it cost to clean up? What would be the financial costs (and benefits) of limiting carbon dioxide emissions from human activities to specific target amounts? These appear to be sensible questions, like asking how much it would cost to buy and drive a fuel-efficient car rather than an ordinary one. . . . Before we can say how much it would cost, we need to know how to do it.

With this thought in mind, our main objective in this chapter will be to describe how to do it—that is, how state and federal NPDES enforcement personnel actually have gone about the task of enforcing the law and what can be done to improve the enforcement process.

The Strict Enforcement Approach

We begin our review by examining what our findings suggest about the debate over a strict versus a negotiated enforcement approach. In this book we have tried not to take a position as to which approach is superior. We will even admit now that entering into this project one of the coauthors favored the strict approach, whereas the other was an adherent of the negotiated alternative. Thus, we believe any personal bias we may have exhibited was ably neutralized by our contradictory a priori expectations regarding the utility of each approach. Rather than advocate an approach, our goal was to determine empirically which regulatory style EPA NPDES personnel and state environmental officials have employed in their enforcement of the clean water laws, as well as the reasons why they have adopted the approach they employ. We even labeled the implementation strategy we identified as "pragmatic enforcement," in part, to separate it from the prior literature on strict versus negotiated enforcement. In short, we have made every effort to stay out of the ideological debate regarding which approach is superior, preferring instead to describe the process as best we can.

Given this point, and our finding that bargaining (e.g., negotiation) is rampant at the EPA and among the fifty states, we thought it appropriate in the conclusion to spend some time addressing the question of whether EPA and state personnel can or should be encouraged to adopt a strict approach to enforcement. We base our answer mostly on the copious interviews we conducted with various EPA and state officials. As with the rest of this book, we want to tell you what they think, as well as what we personally prescribe.

The first answer is that a strict approach to enforcement at the EPA is unlikely to occur, for all of the reasons we have identified thus far in this book. The biggest obstacle, by far, is the incredible diversity under which water pollution regulation occurs. Although we can advise politicians to write more specific legislation (see Lowi 1979), we simply cannot legislate away the diverse nature of the regulatory environment. Water pollution will continue to occur in a number of different settings across the land. The sources of water pollution will continue to be diverse and often difficult to identify, particularly in the case of nonpoint sources of pollution. Furthermore, a variety of different actors (e.g., industry, municipalities, government facilities, farmers, miners, and so on) will continue to be involved in the enforcement process. In addition there will continue to be variations in water usage and water quantity, which, as our empirical analysis in Chapter 7 demonstrated, has a direct impact on the nature of such regulatory outputs as major and minor permit issuances. Add to this the differences in the political culture and political support across the fifty states, differences in interest-group support for the environment and economic development, and differences in organizational structures across the fifty states, and the implementation of a strict enforcement approach appears even less likely to occur.

Is it possible that the ongoing EPA shift to a multimedia approach to pollution control will increase the likelihood that a strict enforcement approach might be adopted in the future? Our answer here is somewhat speculative, but we believe it will not. The regulatory environment will continue to be diverse, perhaps even more diverse, for regulatory personnel. If a unit, for example, is dealing with transportation industries, it will now have to deal with how a particular transportation violator may pollute the air, the water, and the ground. Rather than constrain the diversity of the surface-water regulatory environment, we believe this reform will add to its diversity. As a result, a pragmatic response to environmental problems will likely be further emphasized, rather than constrained.

Given the fact that the diversity of the regulatory environment is a constant (there is little we can do to change it), what else can be done to promote a strict approach to regulatory enforcement? We believe several steps can be taken to facilitate such an approach. First, the number of EPA compliance-monitoring and enforcement personnel could be increased dramatically at both the state and federal level. This would of course mean that more money, a lot more money, would have to spent on NPDES enforcement in the future. Given the present fiscal mess in Washington, D.C., and a similar movement toward retrenchment at the state level, we do not believe this alternative is particularly realistic. In 1980, prior to the election of Ronald Reagan, and under a Democratic president, Jimmy Carter, a report of the General Accounting Office (1980b) found that staff vacancies at the state level averaged around 10 percent. In the area of water pollution control, vacancies ranged from 7 to 20 percent. In the intervening decade and a half there has been much less support for increasing the level of environmental staff at the federal and state level than there was during Carter's presidency. Consequently, rather than anticipating increases in staffing at the federal and state level, we anticipate further reductions as cost cutters look for ways to trim state and federal budgets. Sadly, the EPA and other state environmental agencies will likely have to be diligent just to keep the precious fiscal and staff resources they presently possess, particularly as Republicans in

Congress argue that a balanced budget will require cuts in a variety of programs, including the EPA's budget. With even President Bill Clinton, a Democrat, calling for cuts in water-related funding programs, the idea that increased staffing could provide an inducement to a move toward a strict-enforcement approach does not seem credible to us.

These anticipated cuts in federal and state funding are problematical to us. As Smith (1992: 121) wrote, "in water quality policy a major problem is that we have good regulations that are poorly enforced. All levels of government in the United States lack the resources necessary to monitor and test water for impurities or to build waste-water treatment plants that are necessary." With further budget cuts expected, these problems will only be exacerbated. Likewise, it is unlikely that additional funding will be found for other purposes, such as to subsidize the construction of additional wastewater-treatment plants. In the past decade the trend has been toward the elimination of such funding, partly on the basis of fiscal need, and partly on the basis of evidence suggesting that much of this money was squandered (U.S. General Accounting Office 1979, 1980c, 1982b). Consequently, there is little expectation that sufficient funding will be available for increases in staffing, to facilitate more aggressive enforcement, or for the construction of wastewater-treatment plants.

A more promising option would be to fortify the provisions of various environmental laws at both the state and federal level. For example, at the federal level the EPA cannot proceed with criminal penalties against violators, even if the actions are willful and occur repeatedly over time. As we have noted, some states do allow for criminal prosecutions. Giving the EPA the ability to prosecute violators criminally would provide agency personnel with a greater capability of enforcing the law strictly. At present, EPA NPDES employees see themselves as having little incentive to take violators to court. Changing the law could provide them with the needed incentive to apply the law more strictly. Again, however, given the present political climate in Washington, this change does not appear likely. With congressional Republicans calling for reducing litigation burdens against business, and with President Clinton calling for more negotiation with industry, there does not appear to be enough political will to make this move, at least not at present.

A second less demanding change in the law that would encourage a strict-enforcement approach would be to make more reasonable the burden of proof against violators. At present, in many states, environmental agencies have to prove that a permittee has "willfully" violated the law. Willful violation does signify certain traits, such as violating the law repeatedly over time. But clearly, the burden of proof can be changed to make it easier for the EPA and the states to pursue successful litigation against violators. If the standards for a conviction were clearer, it would provide environmental personnel with a greater incentive to take cases to court, because they would have a better chance of prevailing in court.

A third change would be to ensure that the money, or at least a substantial percentage of the money garnered in a civil penalty cases, would return to the EPA or to the various state environmental agencies. As we noted in Chapter 3, at present many state agency officials lean against litigation because even if they win a case, they seldom are adequately compensated for the court costs. By increasing the size of civil penalties against violators, and by ensuring that sufficient funds to cover costs would return to the EPA budget, agency personnel would have a clearer incentive to litigate than they do under the present circumstances. In fact, of all of our recommendations, this is probably the most likely one to bear fruit, according to our interviews with state and federal NPDES personnel.

Beyond these changes in the law, we also recommend two fiscal reforms. The first is an increase in administrative fines (e.g., the fines associated with administrative orders, and so on). Again, by putting a higher burden on permittees who violate their permits, and by providing EPA and state agencies with a higher return on violations, the incentive for stricter enforcement could be increased. Again, however, this reform is not likely at a time when President Clinton is advising that permittees be given a longer period of time to comply with the law and that they be able to apply their fines, or a portion of them, to ultimate mitigation of the existing pollution problem. Again, the political arena seems to be leaning toward working with industry and other polluters, rather than increase the regulatory burden against them.

The second fiscal reform may be more amenable to the present public mood. Lowry (1992: 73) notes that North Carolina has raised "considerable revenue" by charging permittees a fee for their NPDES permits. Because both Republicans and Democrats are recommending a greater reliance on "user fees" as a means of paying for federal programs, an increase in the cost of permits and other environmental services might provide additional revenues to prevent further cutbacks in state and EPA environmental personnel, and possibly even enough funding to pay for needed increases in compliance-monitoring and enforcement personnel. Clearly, if more money is to be raised to pay for environmental protection, we must begin devising more creative ways to pay for these programs. User fees may be one alternative (see also the discussion below).

Unless new sources of funding can be arranged, however, given the diverse nature of the regulatory environment, and the tight fiscal constraints under which the nation is now operating, we do not believe that tighter monitoring requirements or more frequent on-site visits are practicable or likely to occur. In this area EPA and state personnel will have to continue to rely on the self-reporting techniques of the DMRs. Self-monitoring will not only continue, but also, we predict, with tighter budgets EPA personnel will have to rely even more on the honesty of permittees in the future, a fact we understand will clearly prove disheartening to many people who are concerned about the environment.

Given the fiscal and staffing limitations we have identified above, then, we believe the best means toward promoting a stricter enforcement approach at the EPA is with changes in the law, at the state and federal level. Such changes could provide greater incentives for legal action. Although there are clear limitations in achieving a strict enforcement approach, these changes would put some more muscle in the EPA's regulatory punch. It would be a clear signal to permittees that they cannot repeatedly violate the law. At the same time, it would provide EPA personnel with sufficient discretion to decide on other less stringent courses of action, when they deem it acceptable. As such, by making the judicial alternative a more fruitful option, we can combine some of the better aspects of the strict and negotiated enforcement styles. Other than these modest reforms, however, we do not believe a move to a strict approach is feasible, at least not until either technological advances make it more likely, or unless this nation and the states are willing or capable of providing the necessary funding to increase the number of compliance-monitoring and enforcement personnel.

The Negotiated-Enforcement and Pragmatic-Enforcement Approaches

Our recommendations regarding the strict approach leave us with the strong expectation that the EPA and state officials will therefore continue to rely quite heavily on bargaining, compromise, and negotiation with permittees, largely, as we have argued, for pragmatic reasons. Even if the laws are changed to encourage greater litigation, negotiation with permittees will continue to exist. We understand that this is a source of considerable concern for many environmental scholars who perceive negotiation as nothing short of a sellout to the regulated industry. By presenting the enforcement perspective of EPA and state personnel throughout this book, we hope that, at a minimum, we have made the motives of surface-water enforcement personnel a bit more understandable. Clearly, there are pragmatic reasons why water personnel have adopted the negotiated enforcement approach.

We note also, admittedly not without controversy, that there are advantages to the negotiated approach. It does provide flexibility, which can allow agency personnel to choose the enforcement response they consider to be most appropriate under differing circumstances. This might lead to a concern, however, that EPA personnel would have too much discretion in enforcing the law, and therefore would be unaccountable to their elected superordinates. But as we demonstrated in Chapter 5, discretion and hierarchical political control coexist within the NPDES program. Although EPA personnel clearly perceive themselves as having discretion (see Chapter 4), the analysis in Chapters 4 and 5 demonstrates that this discretion is not unbridled. EPA personnel are still ultimately responsible to their political superiors including the president, presidential appointees, congressional oversight committees, the courts, and the state legislatures, as well as to a variety of diverse interest groups. In short, the negotiation that is typical of the pragmatic-enforcement approach does not occur without an important source of accountability from a variety of hierarchical officials.

This does not mean that there is no variation in enforcement across the EPA's ten regional offices. As we have shown, the variations are real and significant (statistically and substantively). Likewise, at the state level, EPA officials, as well as the courts, provide direct hierarchical oversight. But, as our results from Chapter 6 demonstrate, there is considerable variation in NPDES enforcement across the fifty states as well. This fact is one of our most disturbing findings. Clearly, the biggest problem with a negotiated enforcement style and with pragmatic enforcement is that they foster considerable variation in regulatory enforcement across spatial units. How can these variations be minimized?

On this point we have no easy solution. Because diversity in outputs is largely related to the diversity in the regulatory environment, variations will not be easily ameliorated. Because our analysis in Chapter 5 showed that there are fewer variations in enforcement activity across regions as we move to higher-level enforcement actions (e.g., referrals to the Justice Department for litigation), the legal reforms we have recommended would likely provide the best means of achieving more uniform enforcement across spatial units (states or EPA regions).

In addition, technological development could provide a means for enforcing the law more uniformly nationwide. Given our earlier citation from Duchin and Lange (1994) regarding their argument that one should know how to do something before one recommends how to fix it, we consider it unsatisfactory to recommend a "magic bullet" solution to environmental problems. Although technological advances may ultimately provide an important answer to the variations in enforcement, at present it is not a satisfactory recommendation.

Yet another possible means of reforming the enforcement process would be to change the focus from outputs to outcomes. As we argued in the last chapter, the focus at the EPA has been almost unidimensionally on outputs. Lost in this process has been a concern with outcomes (e.g., is the quality of the nation's waterways actually improving?). As we noted, however, there are clear operational problems with making this change of focus. First, we have to agree on a reliable means of measuring water-quality outcomes. Then, we have to deal with the problems associated with the time—lagged effect of any attempts to clean up our nation's waterways.

Another approach would be to change the focus of NPDES enforcement entirely from a command-and-control system to one that attempts to internalize the costs of environmental pollution. In recent years, a number of scholars have recommended using economic incentives as a means of ameliorating water pollution problems. Again, these recommendations have proven to be controversial, with adherents of the strict enforcement approach generally crying foul. Still, throughout this book we have demonstrated that a strict regulatory approach is not feasible within the NPDES program, though it clearly may be in other regulatory settings (e.g., nuclear-power regulation and the Nuclear Regulatory Commission). For this reason, we feel compelled to offer alternatives to the existing command-and-control approach. We do this in the next section.

Economic Approaches

Environmentalist William Ashworth (1995: 30) wrote, "Ecology and economics are often pictured as implacable foes. . . . Ultimately, if economics and ecology are both true, they cannot possibly conflict with one another." Of course, many economists would have a simple answer to Ashworth's statement: economics is right and ecology is wrong. Likewise, many environmentalists would assert that the science of ecology is correct, whereas economics is wrong. These conflictual views often permeate the debate over environmental policy, and it is clear that concerns over both economics and ecology will simply not go away. Some people will always be concerned about the state of the environment, whereas others will always be concerned about the state of the economy. Ashworth's suggestion is that we need to begin thinking about ways in which we can address these two concerns simultaneously. As a warning, he also notes that we cannot ignore the interconnection between the two sciences, even if we want to. The two are inextricably connected.

Ashworth, who we should note has also written passionately about the need to preserve and clean up our nation's waters (see Ashworth 1982), has become a critic of the standard command-and-control regulatory approach. As he wrote (Ashworth 1995: 39),

> the evidence suggests strongly that environmental laws, *even when fully enforced,* are not doing their job. Probably they cannot. Laws prescribe behavior, and prescribed behavior is necessarily inflexible and unchanging. But the essence of natural systems is change. Caught by this dichotomy, thoroughly imbued from conception with a worldview diametrically opposed to the systems it is designed to defend, our heritage of environmental law is creating failure through the offices of its own high designs.

In other words, environmental regulation has failed because it is inflexible and unchanging, precisely the types of criticisms Bardach and Kagan (1982) and other critics of the strict regulatory approach have employed. Likewise, the National Academy of Public Administration (NAPA) argued that the heterogeneous nature of the regulated industry can impede efforts at strict command-and-control regulation:

> Some environmental problems involve firms that are heterogeneous with respect to geographic dispersion, age, control options, and competitive position. Generally, these kinds of problems are not amenable to resolution using traditional command-and-control approaches. An example is the persistent problem of non-point source water run-off. Since run-off comes from both urban and agricultural sources, the cost of control varies substantially. Because the pollutants are both diverse and have multiple impacts, design standards and individual equipment performance standards fail to find cost-effective and administratively homogeneous regulatory solutions. (NAPA 1994: 8.)

To overcome these problems both Ashworth and the NAPA recommend a move toward a more flexible regulatory approach. The approach that Ashworth favors combines principles from economics and ecology. As he suggested (Ashworth 1995: 113), his approach likely will prove highly controversial:

> As you decrease the amount of pollutants spewing into a river, or an airshed, the law of diminishing returns states that the value of each additional unit of pollution will go up. At the same time, the value of each additional unit of clean water, or clean air, will come down. At some point these two curves . . . are going to cross each other. Where that crossing occurs is the point at which pollution-control efforts should stop. The goal of zero discharge is ethically attractive, but it is as impractical and illogical as the goal of zero wilderness.

This statement reflects an economic approach that many people will no doubt find unacceptable. Still, Ashworth's point that the "goal of zero discharge is ethically attractive, but . . . impractical" is one that cannot be easily ignored. Environmentalists often call for zero discharges into waterways, but that goal is simply not realistic. The question therefore becomes how best to regulate discharges. The analysis from this book has suggested that the strict enforcement, command-and-control method cannot be satisfactorily applied to surface-water pollution control efforts. Clearly, then, we need to find another answer to this question.

One of the major economic reforms to gain considerable and growing support in recent years (but not without considerable controversy) has been the idea of shifting from a command-and-control method of regulation to one that emphasizes economic incentives, instead. This idea was originally proposed two decades ago by such economists as Kneese and Schultze (1975). During the Bush administration the idea gained even more credence when a Democratic Congress and a Republican president agreed to the provisions of the Clean Air Act of 1990. That legislation provided an economic incentive–based system for ameliorating air pollution control problems—for example, the trading of permits to pollute (see Bryner 1993).

In a recent publication, the National Academy of Public Administration examined the role incentive-based systems have played in controlling pollution in such states as California. Regarding these approaches NAPA (1994: 5) wrote,

> The use of economic instruments for environmental protection is based on the concept that private managers necessarily have more complete information on their operations than regulators do. If regulators offer these managers appropriate incentives, industry can and will devise more effective and less expensive solutions to pollution problems. At a theoretical level, economic instruments offer the potential for increased regulatory flexibility, lower pollution abatement costs, and accelerated progress toward environmental goals. Because of these properties and the results of limited experiments, both regulators and private managers have expressed considerable interest in the implementation of economic instruments at the national, regional, and international levels.

Economic incentives include a variety of different approaches. For example, the NAPA report includes such approaches as monetary charges, which involve charging "a fee for each unit of pollution a firm produces"; subsidies, "which provide financial assistance that serves as an incentive to polluters to alter their behavior so as to meet the goals of the regulator"; deposit-refund systems, "which focus on minimizing waste or preventing the production or improper disposal of pollutants"; financial enforcement incentives, "which mandate compliance by requiring a deposit that is returned upon compliance or by fining a polluter that fails to comply with a standard"; and market creation, "which sets up markets within which firms can buy or sell environmental credits for actual quantities of pollution" (ibid.).

Of course the major goal of incentive-based systems is to internalize the external costs of pollution—that is, to internalize the externality. Most economists argue that this system is both more efficient, in that it provides an economic incentive for polluters to find the most cost effective means of reducing pollution, and more effective, because polluters have an actual economic incentive to reduce pollution, which, as we argued in Chapter 3, they do not now have. More pertinent to our purposes in this book, however, is NAPA's suggestion that an economic-based system would be easier to implement. On this point NAPA (1994: 9) wrote,

> Economic incentive-based regulations . . . have the great advantage of being easier for regulators to implement because regulators need not make guesstimates as to what is the right technological fix. Instead, economic incentive approaches leave the decision to affected firms and the marketplace. Given the wide diversity in both the costs of compliance and resulting environmental benefits, it has often proved more difficult to design simple and enforceable design-based regulations that meet this standard.

Furthermore, the NAPA report suggests that economic incentive approaches are more effective in regulatory fields characterized by a diverse regulatory environment, such as surface-water pollution control. They continued (ibid.), "Experience has shown that the most effective time to use direct regulatory, or command-and-control, approaches is when the pollution emitted by numerous sources is homogeneous and regulators can identify control technology that achieves the desired standards at relatively low cost." As we have demonstrated throughout this book, surface-water issues in America certainly do not fit this latter definition. Extrapolating then, surface-water pollution control would appear to be an appropriate candidate for the use of an economic-based incentive system.

In making this recommendation, we do not suggest that the present NPDES system should be dismantled. As the NAPA (1994: 15) report acknowledged, "Incentive systems may require additional monitoring and enforcement as specified by regulators." The report then noted,

> there is no evidence that monitoring and enforcement should be more difficult under incentive program. . . . But both systems [incentives and command-and-control] are predicated on permit systems that aim to capture reliable data and have enforceable discharge limits. Without a good system of permits or good monitoring systems, both systems fail. To the extent that there is a difference, however, more alternatives to assure compliance may be available

under an incentive-based system, especially if the compliance assurance technique is based on performance measures and not on design criteria.

This means, then, that there is an important, ongoing role for current NPDES personnel under an incentive system. Changes would not come in eliminating compliance-monitoring and enforcement personnel. In fact, just the opposite would be true. More people would be needed for these tasks. Given current tight budgets, where would they come from? One possibility would be to transfer personnel from rule-making and regulation-writing responsibilities to compliance-monitoring and enforcement activities. An economic-incentive approach would require fewer personnel to write rules and regulations, inasmuch as fewer rules and regulations would be in place.

Additionally, as we noted in Chapter 2, EPA personnel could make a greater use of signaling to identify violators. This would involve direct public participation in the compliance-monitoring process. For environmentalists who are skeptical of the benefits of an incentive-based approach, this would provide them not only with a direct means of participating in the process, it would also allow them to keep a watchful eye on the diligence of permittees and state and federal enforcement personnel.

There is a model for such a participatory program. Water officials in Delaware told us they could not possibly do their job were it not for the active participation of environmentalists and other members of the public, who regularly perform compliance-monitoring activities for agency personnel. In fact, there is even a training program to encourage greater and more effective participation in compliance-monitoring activities. As the Conservation Foundation (1976) reported, public participation is a vital link in the enforcement process. Clearly, more use needs to be made of these provisions of the Clean Water Act in order to improve the quality of our nation's waterways.

Another means by which more personnel could be hired for compliance-monitoring and enforcement activities would be provided by the revenues generated by the permit process. If a fee-based system were used for permits, as we discussed earlier in this chapter, then pollution control could generate money to help pay for itself. As NAPA (1994: 18) wrote, "With fee- or charge-based systems . . . initially environmental goals may provide the drive to change behavior but later may be used for such purposes as supporting regulatory agencies and promoting technology." Clearly, one of the most puzzling aspects of the current enforcement process is the manner in which states and even the federal government remove the economic incentive from agency personnel to pursue various types of enforcement actions (e.g., by ensuring that monies derived from fines or court action go to the general fund instead of to the agency). Not only should such actions be encouraged, when appropriate, but also a percentage of permit fees, fines, and court assessments should be used to help pay for the services rendered. In a time of tight governmental budgets, we need to begin thinking of new ways to generate revenues for regulatory programs. The alternative, we fear, is simply to gut their budgets, leaving the agencies incapable of performing their regulatory mandate. One way to generate revenues is through the use of a fee- or charge-based system. As NAPA (1994: 40) reported, the South Coast Air Quality Management District (SCAQMD) in Southern California gets only 16 percent of its revenues from the government. The other 84 percent of the District's revenue is generated in the following manner: emission fees account for 40 percent, "operating fees 28 percent, and permit fees 16 percent." As NAPA noted, "In the past these sources of revenue were sufficient to enable the District to carry out its mission." Because of the recession of the early 1990s and other sources of pollution (e.g., mobile sources), NAPA admitted, "It is clear the District can no longer rely on emission fees and other traditional sources to support the budget needed to carry out its mission to the degree it has in the past." Still, these fees provide a substantial source of continued funding for the SCAQMD.

This means that although such fee- or charge-based systems can generate considerable funds, they are not a panacea. Governmental funding will still be needed to pay for environmental programs. But a move to an incentive-based system with a fee-based component could provide significant fiscal relief for agencies such as the EPA, which presently face the reality of tight budgets and probable further revenue reductions.

In summary, when regulatory activity takes place in the framework of a diverse regulatory environment, command-and-control systems of regulation may not be appropriate. Under these circumstances a move to a system employing economic incentives may be more appropriate. Such systems can provide permittees with an economic incentive to obey the law, which may improve water-quality outcomes. Likewise, if the economic incentive system also includes a fee- or charge-based system of permitting, it may provide much needed funding to ensure that environmental protection will continue to be aggressive and effective. Finally, if we make greater use of citizen participatory groups, we can bring environmentalists and other motivated citizens directly into the compliance-monitoring process, thus making sure that environmental laws are properly implemented and enforced.

In recommending a shift to an economic incentive-based system, we note that many people will be skeptical. Past research (e.g., Fuchs 1988; Waterman 1989; Friedman 1995) found that economic reforms, such as cost-benefit analysis, often have been used to merely promote a less aggressive response to environmental problems and increased presidential influence over the regulatory realm. We are not encouraging a retreat from effective enforcement. Given the many problems we have identified with effective enforcement throughout this book, and the pragmatic manner in which agency personnel have adapted to these enforcement problems, we believe the time for serious changes in the way environmental laws are enforced is clearly at hand. The economic approach may offer an effective alternative in an area where command-and-control regulation simply does not appear to be working. In other areas, where a command-and-control approach is more likely to work, such as with externalities that involve a less diverse regulatory environment (e.g., nuclear power), a shift in the emphasis of regulation is probably not appropriate. In the area of surface-water pollution control, however, we believe it clearly is appropriate. Therefore we recommend this option, aware that it will not be met with approbation from all quarters. On the other hand, we hope that it will at least stimulate debate toward developing better approaches to the enforcement of surface-water regulations in America, and better ways to finance it as well.

References

Aberback, Joel D. 1990. *Keeping a Watchful Eye: The Politics of Congressional Oversight.* Washington, D.C.: Brookings Institution.

Ackerman, Bruce A., and William T. Hassler. 1981. *Clean Coal/Dirty Air: or How the Clean Air Act Became a Multibillion-Dollar Bail-Out for High-Sulfur Coal Producers and What Should be Done About It.* New Haven: Yale University Press.

Appleton, Lynn M. 1985. "Explaining Laws' Making and Their Enforcement in the American States." *Social Science Quarterly* 66: 839–53.

Arrandale, Tom. 1995a. "Small Business and the Cleanup." *Governing* March: 54.

———. 1995b. "Environmental Mandate Maze." *Governing* February: 47–52.

Ashworth, William. 1982. *Nor Any Drop To Drink: Water—the Forgotten Crisis.* New York: Summit Books.

———. 1995. *The Economy of Nature: Rethinking the Connections Between Ecology and Economics.* Boston: Houghton Mifflin.

Association of State and Interstate Water Pollution Control Administrators. 1984. *America's Clean Water: The State's Evaluation of Progress 1972–1982.* Washington, D.C.: ASIWPCA.

Ayres, Ian, and John Braithwaite. 1992. *Responsive Regulation: Transcending the Deregulation Debate.* New York: Oxford University Press.

Bardach, Eugene, and Robert A. Kagan. 1982. *Going by the Book: The Problem of Regulatory Unreasonableness.* Philadelphia: Temple University Press.

Battle, Jackson. 1986. *Environmental Law: Water Pollution and Hazardous Waste.* Cincinnati: Anderson Publishing.

Beamish, Rita. 1993. "EPA Chief Vows to Strengthen Enforcement: Centralization Will Target Industries." *Albuquerque Journal,* October 14: A8.

Bibby, John F., and Roger H. Davidson. 1972. *On Capitol Hill.* Hinsdale, Ill.: Dryden Press.

Bollier, David, and Joan Claybrook. 1986. *Freedom from Harm: Civilizing Influence of Health, Safety, and Environmental Regulation.* Washington, D.C.: Public Citizen and Democracy Project.

Bowman, Ann O'M. 1984. "Intergovernmental and Intersectoral Tensions in Environmental Policy Implementation." *Policy Studies Review* 4: 230–44.

———. 1985a. "Hazardous Waste Cleanup and Superfund Implementation in the Southeast." *Policy Studies Journal* 14: 100–10.

———. 1985b. "Hazardous Waste Management: An Emerging Policy Within an Emerging Federalism." *Publius* 15: 131–44.

Braithwaite, John. 1985. *To Punish or Persuade: Enforcement of Coal Mine Safety.* Albany: State University of New York Press.

Brickman, Ronald, Shelia Jasanoff, and Thomas Ilgen. 1985. *Controlling Chemicals:*

The Politics of Regulation in Europe and the U.S. Ithaca: Cornell University Press.

Brown, Lester R. 1995. *State of the World: A Worldwatch Institute Report on Progress Toward a Sustainable Society.* New York: W. W. Norton.

Bruce, John, John Clark, and John Kessel. 1991. "Advocacy Politics in Presidential Parties." *American Political Science Review* 85: 1089–1106.

Bryant, Bunyan, and Paul Mohai (eds.). 1992. *Race and the Incidence of Environmental Hazards.* Boulder, Colo.: Westview.

Bryner, Gary C. 1987. *Bureaucratic Discretion: Law and Policy in Federal Regulatory Agencies.* New York: Pergamon Press.

———. 1993. *Blue Skies, Green Politics: The Clean Air Act of 1990.* Washington, D.C.: Congressional Quarterly Press.

———. 1995. "Rethinking Environmental Regulation: Assessing Critiques of Environmental Regulation." Paper presented at the annual meeting of the Midwest Political Science Association, Chicago.

Bullard, Robert. 1990. *Dumping in Dixie: Race, Class and Environmental Protection.* Boulder, Colo.: Westview.

Bushwick, Nancy, Hal Hiemstra, and Sarah Brichford (eds.). 1986. *Cooperating for Clean Water.* Washington, D.C.: Farmland Project of the National Association of State Departments of Agriculture Resource Foundation.

Buttel, Frederick H. 1975. "The Environmental Movement: Consensus, Conflict, and Change." *Journal of Environmental Education* 7: 53–58.

———. 1979. "Age and Environmental Concern: A Multivariate Analysis." *Youth and Society* 10: 237–56.

Buttel, Frederick H., and William L. Flinn. 1978. "Social Class and Mass Environmental Beliefs: A Reconsideration." *Environment and Behavior* 10: 433–50.

Cable, Sherry, and Charles Cable. 1995. *Environmental Problems Grassroots Solutions: The Politics of Grassroots Environmental Conflict.* New York: St. Martin's Press.

Calvert, Randall L., Mathew D. McCubbins, and Barry R. Weingast. 1989. "A Theory of Political Control and Agency Discretion." *American Journal of Political Science* 33: 588–611.

Caron, Judi A. 1989. "Environmental Perspectives of Blacks: Acceptance of the New Environmental Paradigm." *Journal of Environmental Education* 20: 21–26.

Chesters, Gordon, and Linda-Jo Schierow. 1985. "A Primer on Nonpoint Pollution." *Journal of Soil and Water Conservation* 40: 9–13.

Chubb, John E. 1985. "The Political Economy of Federalism." *American Political Science Review* 79: 994–1015.

Claybrook, Joan. 1984. *Retreat from Safety.* New York: Pantheon Books.

Cohen, Jeffrey E. 1985. "Presidential Control of Independent Regulatory Commissions Through Appointment: The Case of the FCC." *Administration and Society* 17: 61–70.

Colquette, Kelly M., and Elizabeth H. Robertson. 1991. "Environmental Racism: The Cause, Consequences, and Commendations." *Tulane Environmental Law Journal* 5: 153–208.

Conservation Foundation. 1976. *Toward Clean Water: A Guide To Citizen Action.* Washington, D.C.: Conservation Foundation.

———. 1984. *State of the Environment: An Assessment at Mid-Decade.* Washington, D.C.: Conservation Foundation.

Cronin, Thomas E. 1980. *The State of the Presidency.* Boston: Little, Brown.

Davies, J. Clarence III. 1970. *The Politics of Pollution.* New York: Bobbs-Merrill.

Davis, Charles, and James Lester. 1989. "Federalism and Environmental Policy." In James Lester (ed.), *Environmental Politics and Policy.* Durham: Duke University Press.

Davis, Kenneth Culp. 1969a. *Discretionary Justice: A Preliminary Inquiry.* Baton Rouge: Louisiana State University Press.

———. 1969b. "A New Approach to Delegation." *University of Chicago Law Review* Summer: 713–25.

Devall, William B. 1970. "Conservation: An Upper-Middle Class Social Movement: A Replication." *Journal of Leisure Research* 2: 123–25.

Dillman, Don A. 1978. *Mail and Telephone Surveys: The Total Design Method.* New York: John Wiley and Sons.

Dodd, Lawrence C., and Richard L. Schott. 1979. *Congress and the Administrative State.* New York: John Wiley and Sons.

Downing, Paul B. 1983. "Bargaining in Pollution Control." *Policy Studies Journal* 11: 577–86.

Downing, Paul B., and Kenneth Hanf (eds.). 1983. *International Comparisons of Pollution Enforcement.* Boston: Kluwer-Nijhoff Publishing.

Downing, Paul B., and James Kimball. 1982. "Enforcing Pollution Control Laws in the U.S." *Policy Studies Journal* 11: 55–65.

Downs, Anthony. 1967. *Inside Bureaucracy.* Boston: Little, Brown.

Duchin, Faye, and Glenn-Marie Lange. 1994. *The Future of the Environment: Ecological Economics & Technological Change.* New York: Oxford University Press.

Dunlap, Riley E. 1989. "Public Opinion and Environmental Policy." In James Lester (ed.), *Environmental Politics and Policy,* 87–134. Durham: Duke University Press.

Dunlap, Riley E., and Robert James Jones. 1987. "Is Environmental Quality Really a 'White Thing'?: Levels of Environmental Concern among Whites, Blacks, and Hispanics." Paper presented at the annual meeting of the American Sociological Association, Chicago.

Durant, Robert F., Michael R. Fitzgerald, and Larry W. Thomas. 1983. "When Government Regulates Itself: The EPA/TVA Air Pollution Control Experience." *Public Administration Review* 43: 209–19.

Dye, Thomas. 1966. *Politics, Economics, and the Public: Policy Outcomes in the American States.* Chicago: Rand McNally.

Elliott, Euel, James L. Regens, and Barry J. Seldon. 1995. "Exploring Variation in Public Support for Environmental Protection." *Social Science Quarterly* 76: 41–52.

EPA Administrator. 1991. *Environmental Investments: The Costs of a Clean Environment.* Covelo, Calif.: Island Press.

Erskine, Hazel. 1972. "The Polls: Pollution and Its Costs." *Public Opinion Quarterly* 36: 120–35.

Federal Water Pollution Control Act (Clean Water Act) 1986. *Environmental Statutes.* Rockville, Md.: Government Institutes, Inc.

Fenno, Richard F. Jr. 1959. *The President's Cabinet.* New York: Vintage Books.

———. 1966. *The Power of the Purse: Appropriations Politics in Congress.* Boston: Little, Brown.

Freeman, A. Myrick, and Robert Haveman. 1972. "Clean Rhetoric and Dirty Water." *The Public Interest* 28: 51–65.

Friedman, Barry D. 1995. *Regulation in the Reagan-Bush Era: The Eruption of Presidential Influence.* Pittsburgh: University of Pittsburgh Press.

Fuchs, Edward Paul. 1988. *Presidents, Management, and Regulation.* Englewood Cliffs, N.J.: Prentice-Hall.

Fund for Renewable Energy and the Environment. 1988. *The State of the States: 1988.* Washington, D.C.: FREE.

Galloway, George B. 1946. *Congress at the Crossroads.* New York: Crowell.

———. 1951. "The Operation of the Legislative Reorganization Act of 1946." *American Political Science Review* 45: 41–68.

Godschalk, David, and Bruce Stiftel. 1981. "Making Waves: Public Participation in State Water Planning." *Journal of Applied Behavioral Science* 17: 597–614.

Godsil, Rachel. 1991. "Remedying Environmental Racism." *Michigan Law Review* 90: 394–427.

Gormley, William T. Jr. 1987. "Intergovernmental Conflict on Environmental Policy: The Attitudinal Connection." *Western Political Quarterly* 40: 285–303.

———. 1989. *Taming the Bureaucracy: Muscles, Prayers, and Other Strategies.* Princeton: Princeton University Press.

Greve, Michael. 1989. "Environmentalism and Bounty Hunting." *The Public Interest* 97: 15–32.

Gurwitt, Rob. 1994. "Something in the Water." *Governing,* September: 32–38.

Guth, James L., John C. Green, Lyman A. Kellstedt, and Corwin E. Smidt. 1995. "Faith and the Environment: Religious Beliefs and Attitudes on Environmental Policy." *American Journal of Political Science* 39: 364–82.

Handler, Joel. 1986. *The Conditions of Discretion: Autonomy, Community, Bureaucracy.* New York: Russell Sage Foundation.

Hansen, Wendy L. 1990. "The International Trade Commission and the Politics of Protectionism." *American Political Science Review* 84: 21–43.

Harris, Joseph P. 1965. *Congressional Control of Administration.* Washington, D.C.: Brookings Institution.

Harris, Rhonda, Paulette Johnsey, Brent Larsen, and Monica Berrel. 1993. "Promoting Stormwater Education." *Water Environment and Technology* June: 40–46.

Harris, Richard A., and Sydney M. Milkis. 1989. *The Politics of Regulatory Change: A Tale of Two Agencies.* New York: Oxford University Press.

Harry, Joseph, Richard Gale, and John Hendee. 1969. "Conservation: An Upper-Middle Class Social Movement." *Journal of Leisure Research* 1: 246–54.

Hawkins, Keith. 1984. *Environment and Enforcement: Regulation and the Social Definition of Pollution.* Oxford: Clarendon Press.

Hayes, Michael T. 1992. *Incrementalism and Public Policy.* New York: Longman.

Heberlein, Thomas. 1976. "Some Observations on Alternative Mechanisms for Public Involvement: The Hearing, Public Opinion Poll, the Workshop and the Quasi-Experiment." *Natural Resources Journal* 1: 27–32.

Heclo, Hugh. 1977. *A Government of Strangers: Executive Politics in Washington.* Washington, D.C.: Brookings Institution.

Hedge, David, and Saba Jallow. 1990. "The Federal Context of Regulation: The Spatial Allocation of Federal Enforcement." *Social Science Quarterly* 70: 285–99.

Hedge, David, Donald Menzel, and George Williams. 1988. "Regulatory Attitudes and Behavior: The Case of Surface Mining Regulation." *Western Political Quarterly* 41: 323–40.

Honnold, Julie A. 1984. "Age and Environmental Concern: Some Specification of Effects." *Journal of Environmental Education* 16: 4–9.

Huff, Warren. 1993. "Biological Indices Define Water Quality Standards." *Water Environment and Technology,* September: 20–21.

Hunter, Susan, and Richard W. Waterman. 1992. "Determining an Agency's Regulatory Style: How Does the EPA Water Office Enforce the Law?" *Western Political Quarterly* 45: 403–17.

Huntington, Samuel P. 1952. "The Marasmus of the ICC: The Commission, the Railroads, and the Public Interest." *Yale Law Journal* 61: 467–509.

Hutter, Bridget. 1989. "Variations in Regulatory Enforcement Styles." *Law and Policy* 11: 153–74.

Ingram, Helen. 1977. "Policy Implementation through Bargaining: The Case of Federal Grants-in-Aid." *Public Policy* 4: 499–526.

———. 1990. *Water Politics: Continuity and Change.* Albuquerque: University of New Mexico Press.

Ingram, Helen, and Dean Mann. 1984. "Preserving the Clean Water Act: The Appearance of Environmental Victory." In Norman Vig and Michael Kraft (eds.), *Environmental Policy in the 1980s,* 251–71. Washington, D.C.: Congressional Quarterly Press.

Jennings, Aaron, and N. Earl Spangenberg (eds.). 1991. *Surface and Ground Water Quality: Pollution Prevention, Remediation, and the Great Lakes.* Symposium proceedings, American Water Resources Institute.

John, DeWitt. 1994. *Civic Environmentalism: Alternatives to Regulation in States and Communities.* Washington, D.C.: Congressional Quarterly Press.

Jones, Charles O. 1975. *Clean Air: The Policies and Politics of Pollution Control.* Pittsburgh: University of Pittsburgh Press.

Jones, Robert Emmet, and Lewis F. Carter. 1994. "Concern for the Environment Among Black Americans: An Assessment of Common Assumptions." *Social Science Quarterly* 75: 560–79.

Jones, Robert Emmet, and Riley Dunlap. 1992. "The Social Bases of Environmental Concern: Have They Changed Over Time?" *Rural Sociology* 57: 28–47.

Kagan, Robert A. 1980. *Regulatory Justice: Implementing a Wage Price Freeze.* New York: Russell Sage Foundation.

———. 1989. "Editor's Introduction: Understanding Regulatory Enforcement." *Law and Policy* 11: 89.

Kanagy, Conrad L., Craig R. Humphrey, and Glenn Firebaugh. 1994. "Surging Environmentalism: Changing Public Opinion or Changing Publics." *Social Science Quarterly* 75: 804–19.

Katzman, Robert A. 1980a. "The Federal Trade Commission." In James Q. Wilson (ed.), *The Politics of Regulation,* New York: Basic Books.

———. 1980b. *Regulatory Bureaucracy: The Federal Trade Commission and Antitrust Policy.* Cambridge: MIT Press.

Kaufman, Herbert. 1991. *The Administrative Behavior of Federal Bureau Chiefs.* Washington, D.C.: Brookings Institution.

Keiser, K. Robert. 1980. "The New Regulation of Health and Safety." *Political Science Quarterly* 95: 479–91.

Knesse, Allen V., and Charles L. Schultze. 1975. *Pollution, Prices, and Public Policy.* Washington, D. C.: Brookings Institution.

Koenig, Louis. 1975. *The Chief Executive.* New York: Harcourt, Brace, Jovanovich.

Kohlmeier, Louis M. Jr. 1969. *The Regulators: Watchdog Agencies and the Public Interest.* New York: Harper and Row.

Kolko, Gabriel. 1963. *The Triumph of Conservatism: A Reinterpretation of American History 1900–1916.* New York: Macmillan.

———. 1965. *Railroads and Regulation, 1877–1916.* Princeton: Princeton University Press.

Ladd, Everett C. 1982. "Clearing the Air: Public Opinion and Public Policy on the Environment." *Public Opinion* 5: 16–20.

Landy, Mark K., Marc J. Roberts, and Stephen R. Thomas. 1994. *The Environmental Protection Agency: Asking the Wrong Questions from Nixon to Clinton.* New York: Oxford University Press.

Lave, Lester B. 1981. *The Strategy of Social Regulation: Decision Frameworks for Policy.* Washington, D.C.: Brookings Institution.

Lester, James. 1990. "A New Federalism: Environmental Policy in the States." In Norman J. Vig and Michael E. Kraft (eds.), *Environmental Policy in the 1990s,* Washington, D.C.: Congressional Quarterly Press.

Lipsky, Michael. 1971. "Street-Level Bureaucracy and the Analysis of Urban Reform." *Urban Affairs Quarterly* 6: 391–409.

———. 1980. *Street-Level Bureaucracy.* New York: Russell Sage Foundation.

Lowi, Theodore J. 1979. *The End of Liberalism.* New York: W. W. Norton.

Lowry, William R. 1992. *The Dimensions of Federalism: State Governments and Pollution Control Policies.* Durham: Duke University Press.

Lundqvist, Lennart. 1980. *The Hare and the Tortoise: Clean Air Policies in the United States and Sweden.* Ann Arbor: University of Michigan Press.

Magat, Wesley, and W. Kip Viscusi. 1990. "Effectiveness of the EPA's Regulatory Enforcement: The Case of Industrial Effluent Standards." *Journal of Law and Economics* 33: 331–60.

Marcus, Alfred. 1980. "Environmental Protection Agency." In James Q. Wilson (ed.), *The Politics of Regulation,* 267–303. New York: Basic Books.

McCann, Bill. 1993. "River and Water Quality Assessed." *Water and Environment Technology,* August: 29–33.

McConnell, Grant. 1966. *Private Power and American Democracy.* New York: Knopf.

McEwen, Malcolm, et al. 1993. "Watching Out for Water Quality." *Water Environment and Technology,* June: 40–46.

Meier, Kenneth J. 1979. *Politics and the Bureaucracy: Policymaking in the Fourth Branch of Government.* Pacific Grove: Brooks/Cole.

Meier, Kenneth J., Joseph Stewart, and Robert E. England. 1991. "The Politics of Bureaucratic Discretion: Education Access as an Urban Service." *American Journal of Political Science* 35: 155–77.

Melnick, R. Shep. 1983. *Regulation and the Courts: The Case of the Clean Air Act.* Washington, D.C.: Brookings Institution.

Mendeloff, John. 1979. *Regulating Safety: An Economic and Political Analysis of Occupational Safety and Health Policy.* Cambridge: MIT Press.

Mitchell, Robert Cameron. 1984. "Public Opinion and Environmental Politics in the 1970s and 1980s." In Michael Kraft and Norman Vig (eds.), *Environmental Policy in the 1980s: Reagan's New Agenda,* 51–74. Washington, D.C.: Congressional Quarterly Press.

Mitchell, Robert Cameron, Angela G. Mertig, and Riley E. Dunlap. 1992. "Twenty Years of Environmental Mobilization: Trends among National Organizations." In Riley E. Dunlap and Angela G. Mertig (eds.), *American Environmentalism: The U.S. Environmental Movement 1970–1990,* 11–26. Philadelphia: Taylor and Francis.

Moe, Terry M. 1982. "Regulatory Performance and Presidential Administrations." *American Journal of Political Science* 26: 197–224.

———. 1985. "Control and Feedback in Economic Regulation: The Case of the NLRB." *American Political Science Review* 79: 1094–1116.

Mohai, Paul, 1990. "Black Environmentalism." *Social Science Quarterly* 71: 744–65.

Mohai, Paul, and Ben W. Twight. 1987. "Age and Environmentalism: An Elaboration of the Buttel Model Using National Survey Evidence." *Social Science Quarterly* 68: 798–815.

Munro, John F. 1993. "California Water Politics: Explaining Policy Change in a Cognitively Polarized Subsystem." In Paul A. Sabatier and Hank Jenkins-Smith (eds.), *Policy Change and Learning: An Advocacy Coalition Approach.* Boulder, Colo.: Westview Press.

Nathan, Richard P. 1983. *The Administrative Presidency.* New York: John Wiley & Sons.

National Academy of Public Administration. 1994. *The Environment Goes to Market: The Implementation of Economic Incentives for Pollution Control.* Washington, D.C.: NAPA.

Nichols, Alan B. 1992. "Citizens Monitor Water Quality." *Water Environment and Technology,* March: 55–59.

———. 1993. "Bureau of Reclamation Tends Its Western Garden." *Water Environment and Technology,* February.

Noll, Roger G. 1971. *Reforming Regulation.* Washington, D.C.: Brookings Institution.

Ogul, Morris. 1976. *Congress Oversees the Bureaucracy.* Pittsburgh: University of Pittsburgh Press.

———. "Congressional Oversight: Structures and Incentives." In Lawrence C. Dodd and Bruce I. Oppenheimer (eds.), *Congress Reconsidered,* 317–31. Washington, D.C.: Congressional Quarterly Press.

Olivier, Cecilio, Mustafa Emir, and Steven R. McComas. 1994. "Local Surface Water Quality Management: A Practical Approach to Water Quality Enhancement." In Gary Pedersen (ed.), *Proceedings of the American Water Resources Association,* Norcross: American Water Resources Association.

Ostrom, Elinor. 1990. *Governing the Commons: The Evolution of Institutions for Collective Action.* New York: Cambridge University Press.

Paehlke, Robert, and Pauline V. Rosenau. 1993. "Environmental Equity: Tensions in North American Politics." *Policy Studies Journal* 21: 672–86.

Pollock, Philip H., and M. Elliot Vittas. 1995. "Who Bears the Burdens of Environmental Pollution? Race, Ethnicity, and Environmental Equity in Florida." *Social Science Quarterly* 76: 294–310.

Randall, Ronald. 1979. "Presidential Power versus Bureaucratic Intransigence." *American Political Science Review* 74: 795–810.

Redford, Emmette S. 1969. *Democracy in the Administrative State.* New York: Oxford University Press.

Regens, James L. 1991. "Measuring Environmental Benefits with Contingent Markets." *Public Administration Review* 51: 345–52.

Regens, James L., and Margaret A. Reams. 1988. "State Strategies for Regulating Groundwater Quality." *Social Science Quarterly* 69: 53–69.

Reichichar, Stephen J., and Michael R. Fitzgerald. 1983. *The Consequences of Administrative Decision: TVA's Economic Development Mission and Intragovernmental Regulation.* Knoxville: Bureau of Public Administration, University of Tennessee.

Ringquist, Evan J. 1993. *Environmental Protection at the State Level: Politics and Progress in Controlling Pollution.* Armonk, N.Y.: M.E. Sharpe.

———. 1995a. "Political Control and Policy Impact in EPA's Office of Water Quality." *American Journal of Political Science* 39: 336–63.

———. 1995b. "Is 'Effective Regulation' Always Oxymoronic?: The States and Ambient Air Quality." *Social Science Quarterly* 76: 69–87.

———. 1995c. "Environmental Protection Regulation." In Kenneth J. Meier and E. Thomas Garman (eds.), *Regulation and Consumer Protection,* Houston: Dame Publications.

Ripley, Randall B., and Grace A. Franklin. 1986. *Policy Implementation and Bureaucracy.* Chicago: Dorsey Press.

Rogers, Peter. 1993. *America's Water: Federal Roles and Responsibilities.* Cambridge: MIT Press.

Rosenbaum, Walter A. 1991/1985. *Environmental Politics and Policy.* Washington, D.C.: Congressional Quarterly Press.

Rosener, Judy. 1982. "Making Bureaucrats Responsive: A Study of the Impact of Citizen Participation and Staff Recommendations on Regulatory Decision Making." *Public Administration Review* 42: 339–45.

Rossiter, Clinton. 1956. *The American Presidency.* New York: Harcourt, Brace, and Javanovich.

Sapat, Alka. 1995. "Environmental Policy Innovation: A Comparative State Analysis of Groundwater Protection Legislation." Paper presented at the annual meeting of the Midwest Political Science Association, Chicago.

Scher, Seymour. 1960. "Congressional Committee Members as Independent Agency Overseers: A Case Study." *American Political Science Review* 54: 911–20.

Scholz, John T., and Wayne Gray. 1995. "Can Regulation Enhance Social Cooperation: A Signaling Model of OHSA Enforcement." Paper presented at the annual meeting of the Midwest Political Science Association, Chicago.

Scholz, John T., and Feng Heng Wei. 1986. "Regulatory Enforcement in a Federalist System." *American Political Science Review* 80: 1249–70.

Shaiko, Ronald G. 1987. "Religion, Politics, and Environmental Concern: A Powerful Mix of Passions." *Social Science Quarterly* 68: 241–62.

Sharfman, I. L. 1931–37. *The Interstate Commerce Commission: A Study in Administrative Law and Procedure.* Four volumes. New York: Commonwealth Fund.

Shover, Neal, Donald A. Clelland, and John Lynxwiler. 1986. *Enforcement or Negotiation: Constructing a Regulatory Bureaucracy.* Albany: State University of New York Press.

Stewart, Doug. 1993. "Will This Lake Stay Superior?" *National Wildlife,* August–September: 4–10.

Stewart, Joseph Jr., and Jane S. Cromartie. 1982. "Partisan Presidential Change and Regulatory Policy: The Case of the FTC and Deceptive Practices Cases." *Presidential Studies Quarterly* 12: 568–73.

Stimson, James. 1985. "Regression Models in Space and Time: A Statistical Essay." *American Journal of Political Science* 29: 914–47.

Stone, Alan. 1977. *Economic Regulation and the Public Interest: The Federal Trade Commission in Theory and Practice.* Ithaca: Cornell University Press.

Sundquist, James L. 1981. *The Decline and Resurgence of Congress.* Washington, D.C.: Brookings Institution.

Szasa, Andrew. 1994. *Ecopopulism: Toxic Waste and the Movement for Environmental Justice.* Minneapolis: University of Minnesota Press.

Taylor, Dorceta E. 1989. "Blacks and the Environment: Toward an Explanation of the Concern Gap between Blacks and Whites." *Environment and Behavior* 21: 175–205.

Tchobanoglous, George, and Edward D. Schroeder. 1985. *Water Quality.* Reading, Mass.: Addison-Wesley.

Thomas, Norman, Joseph Pika, and Thomas Watson. 1994. *The Politics of the Presidency.* Washington, D.C.: Congressional Quarterly Press.

Truman, David B. 1951. *The Governmental Process: Political Interests and Public Opinion.* New York: Knopf.

Twenty-fifth Environmental Quality Index. 1993. National Wildlife Federation. February/March.

U.S. Council on Environmental Quality. 1993. *23rd Annual Report of the Council on Environmental Quality together with the President's Message to Congress.* Washington, D.C.: U.S. Government Printing Office.

U.S. Environmental Protection Agency. 1986. *Enforcement Management System for the National Pollutant Discharge Elimination System.* Washington, D.C.: Government Printing Office.

U.S. Government. 1993. "The NAFTA Report on Environmental Issues." Washington, D.C.: Government Printing Office.

U.S. Government Accounting Office. 1977. "National Water Quality Goals Cannot Be Attained without More Attention to Pollution from Diffused or Nonpoint Sources." Report No. CED–78–6 (December 20). Washington, D.C.: U.S. Government Printing Office.

―――. 1979. "Large Construction Projects to Correct Combined Sewer Overflows Too Costly." Report No. CED–80–40 (December 28). Washington, D.C.: U.S. Government Printing Office.

―――. 1980a. "Ground Water Overdrafting Must Be Controlled." Report No. CED–8–96 (September 12). Washington, D.C.: Government Printing Office.

―――. 1980b. "Federal-State Environmental Programs—The State Perspective." Report No. CED–80–106 (August). Washington, D.C.: U. S. Government Printing Office.

―――. 1980c. "Costly Wastewater Treatment Plants Fail to Perform as Expected." Report No. CED–81–9 (November 14). Washington, D.C.: U. S. Government Printing Office.

―――. 1982a. "State Compliance Lacking in Meeting Safe Drinking Water Regulations." Report No. CED–82–43 (March 3). Washington, D.C.: U.S. Government Printing Office.

―――. 1982b. "Better Planning Can Reduce Size of Wastewater Treatment Facilities; Saving Millions in Construction Costs." Report No. CED–82–82 (July 8). Washington, D.C.: U.S. Government Printing Office.

U.S. Nuclear Regulatory Agency. 1986. *Rules of Practice for Domestic Licensing Proceedings*. Washington, D.C.: U.S. Government Printing Office.

Valente, Christina M., and William D. Valente. 1995. *Introduction to Environmental Law and Policy: Protecting the Environment through Law*. New York: West Publishing.

Van Liere, Kent D., and Riley E. Dunlap. 1980. "The Social Bases of Environmental Concern: A Review of Hypotheses, Explanations, and Empirical Evidence." *Public Opinion Quarterly* 44: 181–97.

Viscusi, W. Kip, and Richard J. Zeckhauser. 1979. "Optimal Standards with Incomplete Enforcement." *Public Policy* 27: 437–56.

Vogel, David. 1986. *National Styles of Regulation: Environmental Policy in Great Britain and the U.S.* Ithaca: Cornell University Press.

Waterman, Richard W. 1989. *Presidential Influence and the Administrative State*. Knoxville: University of Tennessee Press.

Waterman, Richard W., and Kenneth Meier. 1995. "Principal-Agent Models: A Theoretical Culdesac." Paper presented at the annual meeting of the Midwest Political Science Association, Chicago.

Waterman, Richard W., and B. Dan Wood. 1992. "What Do We Do With Applied Research?" *PS: Political Science and Politics* September: 59–64.

―――. 1993. "Policy Monitoring and Policy Analysis." *Journal of Policy Analysis and Management* 12: 685–89.

Waterman, Richard W., Amelia Rouse, and Robert Wright. 1994. "The Other Side of Political Control of the Bureaucracy: Agents' Perceptions of Influence and Control." Paper presented at the annual meeting of the American Political Science Association, New York.

Weaver, Paul H. 1978. "Regulation, Social Policy, and Class Conflict." *The Public Interest* 50: 45–63.

Weingast, Barry R. 1981. "Regulation, Reregulation, and Deregulation: The Political Foundations of Agency Clientele Relationships." *Law and Contemporary Problems* 44: 149–77.

————. 1984. "The Congressional-Bureaucratic System: A Principal Agent Perspective (with Applications to the SEC)." *Public Choice* 44: 147–91.

Weingast, Barry R., and Mark J. Moran. 1983. "Bureaucratic Discretion or Congressional Control: Regulatory Policymaking by the Federal Trade Commission." *Journal of Political Economy* 91: 756–800.

Wernette, D. R., and L. A. Nieves. 1992. "Breathing Polluted Air: Minorities Are Disproportionately Exposed." *EPA Journal* 18: 16–17.

Whitaker, James B. 1993. "Launching the Great Lakes Initiative." *Water Environment and Technology,* June: 40–46.

Wildavsky, Aaron. 1964. *The Politics of the Budgetary Process.* Boston: Little, Brown.

Wilson, James Q. 1989. *Bureaucracy: What Government Agencies Do and Why They Do It.* New York: Basic Books.

Wolfe, Dana. 1995. "Senate Gets Clean Water Bill." *Environmental and Energy Study Institute Weekly Report,* May 22, 1995.

Wood, B. Dan. 1988. "Principal, Bureaucrats, and Responsiveness in Clean Air Enforcements." *American Political Science Review* 82: 213–34.

————. 1990. "Does Politics Make A Difference at the EEOC?" *American Journal of Political Science* 34: 503–30.

————. 1991. "Federalism and Policy Responsiveness: The Clean Case." *Journal of Politics* 53: 851–59.

————. 1992. "Modeling Federal Implementation as a System." *American Journal of Political Science* 36: 40–67.

————. 1993. "Presidential Control of Intergovernmental Bureaucracies." In Richard W. Waterman (ed.), *The Presidency Reconsidered,* 93–113. Itasca: F. E. Peacock Press.

Wood, B. Dan, and James Anderson. 1993. "The Politics of U.S. Antitrust Regulation." *American Journal of Political Science* 37: 1–39.

Wood, B. Dan, and Richard W. Waterman. 1991. "The Dynamics of Political Control of the Bureaucracy." *American Political Science Review* 85: 801–28.

————. 1993. "The Dynamics of Bureaucratic Adaptation." *American Journal of Political Science* 37: 497–528.

————. 1994. *Bureaucratic Dynamics: The Role of a Bureaucracy in a Democracy.* Boulder: Westview Press.

Wool, Peter. 1963. *American Bureaucracy.* New York: W. W. Norton.

Woolley, John T. 1993. "Conflict Among Regulators and the Hypothesis of Congressional Dominance." *Journal of Politics* 55: 92–114.

Worden, Robert E. 1984. "Patrol Officers' Attitudes and the Distribution of Police Services: A Preliminary Study." In *Understanding Police Agency Performance,* 42–54. Washington, D.C.: Department of Justice, National Institute of Justice.

World Resource Institute. 1994. *The 1994 Information Please Environmental Almanac.* Boston: Houghton Mifflin.

Yandle, Bruce. 1989. *The Political Limits of Environmental Regulation.* Westport: Quorum.

Yanket, Thom, and Kenneth D. Gartrell. 1988. "Political Climate and Corporate Mergers: When Politics Effects Economics." *Western Political Quarterly* 41: 309–22.

Yin, Robert K., and Douglas Yates. 1975. *Street-Level Governments: Assessing Decentralization and Urban Services.* Lexington: Lexington Books.

Index

About the Authors
and Contributors

Susan Hunter is an associate professor of political science at West Virginia University, where she teaches courses in environmental politics, contemporary theory, and evaluation. She has published articles in the *Western Political Quarterly, Policy Studies Journal,* and other professional journals.

Richard W. Waterman is an associate professor of political science at the University of New Mexico, where he teaches courses in public policy and the presidency. He has published articles in the *American Political Science Review,* the *American Journal of Political Science,* the *Journal of Politics,* and other academic journals.

Amelia Rouse and **Robert Wright** are Ph.D. candidates at the University of New Mexico. Both are working on a project on bureaucratic discretion at the EPA.